'A must-read for anyone interested in the institutional design of courts! Cristóbal Caviedes has produced a superb, deep and surprising piece of scholarship that invites the readers to rethink conventional wisdom by providing strong reasons for replacing majority rule with supermajority rules in constitutional review.'

Yaniv Roznai, *Reichman University, Israel*

'In this insightful book, Cristóbal Caviedes fills a major gap in scholarship on institutional design and constitutional review. Identifying the importance and neglect of judicial decision procedures, he presents a rigorously argued case for supermajority voting rules on constitutional courts. A tour de force.'

Stephen Gardbaum, *UCLA School of Law, California, USA*

'An indispensable book for anyone concerned with the politization of courts and the legitimacy of their decisions.'

Francisco J Urbina, *University of Notre Dame, Indiana, USA*

Supermajority Voting in Constitutional Courts

This book challenges the wide use of majority rule in many constitutional courts for declaring statutes unconstitutional and argues that these courts should rather perform constitutional review by using supermajority rules. Considering that constitutional courts often tackle hard moral issues, it is questionable whether a bare majority of judges should suffice for settling them, especially considering these courts' counter-majoritarian nature. Further, the wide use of majority rule for checking the constitutionality of legislation may increasingly risk their reputation. Such a concern is developing in the United States following a series of Supreme Court decisions. This book argues that majority rule is unjustified in constitutional review. This means that, in constitutional review, considering majority rule's traits, there are no decisive reasons for using this voting rule over other voting rules. Additionally, the book argues that, when checking the constitutionality of legislation, constitutional courts should replace majority rule with supermajority rules. Thus, for declaring statutes unconstitutional, it is argued that more than 50% of the judges present plus one judge present should be needed. This book will be of interest to academics, researchers, and policy-makers working in the areas of Constitutional Law and Politics.

Cristóbal Caviedes is Assistant Professor of Law, Universidad Católica del Norte, Chile.

Comparative Constitutional Change

Comparative Constitutional Change has developed into a distinct field of constitutional law. It encompasses the study of constitutions through the way they change and covers a wide scope of topics and methodologies. Books in this series include work on developments in the functions of the constitution, the organization of powers and the protection of rights, as well as research that focuses on formal amendment rules and the relation between constituent and constituted power. The series includes comparative approaches along with books that focus on single jurisdictions, and brings together research monographs and edited collections which allow the expression of different schools of thought. While the focus is primarily on law, where relevant the series may also include political science, historical, philosophical and empirical approaches that explore constitutional change.

Series editors:
Xenophon Contiades is Professor of Public Law, Panteion University, Athens, Greece and Managing Director, Centre for European Constitutional Law, Athens, Greece.
Thomas Fleiner is Emeritus Professor of Law at the University of Fribourg, Switzerland.
Alkmene Fotiadou is Research Associate at the Centre for European Constitutional Law, Athens, Greece.
Richard Albert is the William Stamps Farish Professor in Law and Professor of Government at the University of Texas at Austin, USA.

Also in the series:

Constitutionality of Law without a Constitutional Court
A View from Europe
Edited by Mirosław Granat

The Constitutional Law and Politics of Ethnic Accommodation
Institutional Design in Afghanistan
Bashir Mobasher

EU Law and National Constitutions
The Constitutional Dynamics of Multi-Level Governance
Edited by Alberto Nicòtina, Patricia Popelier and Peter Bursens

Supermajority Voting in Constitutional Courts
The Problem of Majority Rule for Democracy and Legislation
Cristóbal Caviedes

For more information about this series, please visit: www.routledge.com/Comparative-Constitutional-Change/book-series/COMPCONST

Supermajority Voting in Constitutional Courts

The Problem of Majority Rule for Democracy and Legislation

Cristóbal Caviedes

Routledge
Taylor & Francis Group
LONDON AND NEW YORK

First published 2025
by Routledge
4 Park Square, Milton Park, Abingdon, Oxon OX14 4RN

and by Routledge
605 Third Avenue, New York, NY 10158

Routledge is an imprint of the Taylor & Francis Group, an informa business

British Library Cataloguing-in-Publication Data
A catalogue record for this book is available from the British Library

Library of Congress Cataloging-in-Publication Data
Names: Caviedes, Cristóbal, author.
Title: Supermajority voting in constitutional courts: the problem of majority rule for democracy and legislation / Cristóbal Caviedes.
Description: Abingdon, Oxon [UK]; New York, NY: Routledge, 2024. |
Series: Comparative constitutional change |
Includes bibliographical references and index. |
Identifiers: LCCN 2024012842 (print) | LCCN 2024012843 (ebook) |
ISBN 9781032723945 (hardback) | ISBN 9781032723976 (paperback) |
ISBN 9781032723952 (ebook)
Subjects: LCSH: United States. Supreme Court–Decision making. |
Judicial review–United States. | Constitutional courts–United States. |
Constitutional law–United States. | Majorities–United States. |
Voting–United States. | Legislation–United States. |
Representative government and representation–United States.
Classification: LCC KF8748 .C35 2024 (print) | LCC KF8748 (ebook) |
DDC 347/.035–dc23/eng/20240325
LC record available at https://lccn.loc.gov/2024012842
LC ebook record available at https://lccn.loc.gov/2024012843

ISBN: 978-1-032-72394-5 (hbk)
ISBN: 978-1-032-72397-6 (pbk)
ISBN: 978-1-032-72395-2 (ebk)

DOI: 10.4324/9781032723952

Typeset in Galliard
by Deanta Global Publishing Services, Chennai, India

To my parents, Iván and Francisca, and to my brothers, Julián, Diego, and Joaquín.

Contents

Preface

Why I Wrote This Book

Before addressing the point of this book, it's helpful to tell readers what inspired me to write it. As in most cases, this book originates in my personal experience and intellectual journey.

As the reader can easily discover, I'm Chilean. I was born in the early 80s, grew up in the 90s, and reached adulthood in the 2000s. This made me a privileged witness of the massive cultural, economic, and social changes that Chile endured—changes that globalisation has replicated in other parts of the globe. Since my early adulthood, I was deeply interested in what's likely one of the main questions that, in many countries, intellectuals, social researchers, state authorities, and ordinary citizens regularly make: how do we turn *our* country (in my case, Chile) into a 'developed' one? How do we make our country richer, more democratic, and more egalitarian than it currently is?

Considering this background, as my education progressed, I became increasingly perplexed by the way in which most current legal and political studies seemed to dodge institutional design as an object of analysis. Though I admired lawyers' and philosophers' skills at building arguments and at questioning assumptions, I realised that most modern legal and philosophical works were saying relatively little about how to build and maintain 'good' (or at least 'good enough') democratic institutions.[1] Most public law works I read focused extensively on how judges must reason when adjudicating constitutional disputes.[2] Yet they seldom mentioned the institutional conditions that judges require to act accordingly.[3] And unlike what I found when engaging with classical works,[4] most political philosophy works I found focused on

1 For akin critiques, see Waldron 2016: ch 1.
2 Eg, see Kumm 2007; Tsakyrakis 2009; Webber 2009; Barak 2012; Möller 2012; Urbina 2017.
3 For exceptions, see Elhauge 1991; Komesar 1994; Vermeule 2006; Hübner Mendes 2015; Yowell 2018.
4 Eg, see Montesquieu [1748] 2020: 1689-755; Bentham [1843] 1999; Hamilton [1788] 2015.

the specific demands of ideas such as equality[5] or justice.[6] But without saying much about the institutions needed to realise them. Needless to say, I found this omission rather puzzling.

Further, during this period, a key constitutional debate started in Chile—a debate that resulted in our recent constitutional processes. A big part of this debate tackled the role of the so-called 'counter-majoritarian devices' of the Chilean Constitution, including our Constitutional Court. For its defenders, though Chile's Constitution was imposed by Pinochet, its counter-majoritarian devices were the cornerstone of the country's modernisation; particularly by ensuring stability and by being a bulwark against any serious threat to private property and free-market values. For its critics—and along with the problems posed by its non-democratic origin—the Chilean Constitution's counter-majoritarian devices have choked citizens' voice; especially by preventing the adoption of more socialist, welfare-state policies that most of them allegedly support.[7]

Still, when addressing the Constitutional Court, I found few reflections on whether its decision procedures were the most appropriate for performing its tasks.[8] When addressing this court, the debate mainly focused on probing its decisions,[9] challenging its power to review bills,[10] or questioning whether we should have constitutional adjudication altogether;[11] all key issues for building or reforming constitutional courts. But I also found the omission regarding judicial decision procedures rather puzzling.

Finally, I realised that, in many constitutional courts, whether a statute ended up being voided ultimately depended on counting heads: it depended on how many judges claimed that a statute was void. And I realised that many constitutional courts seemed to decide this issue by majority rule. But unlike what happens with representative assemblies and referenda[12]—and barring some notable exceptions[13]—I found no deep body of ideas justifying why a bare majority of unelected judges sufficed to override an elected legislature's majority decision. Yet again, I found this omission rather puzzling.

This is what grounded my interest in voting rules in constitutional courts, thus inspiring this book. If anything, I hope these reflections contribute

5 Eg, see Sen 1995; Arneson 1997; Anderson 1999.

6 Eg, see Rawls 1999; Sandel 2007; Nozick 2013.

7 See generally Atria 1993; Fuentes 2010; Atria 2013; Fuentes & Joignant 2015; Alvarado 2016; Zapata Larraín 2020.

8 For exceptions focusing on the publicity of judicial debates and of dissents, see Verdugo Ramírez 2011; Busch Venthur 2018; Orellana 2019; Busch Venthur & Szmulewicz Ramírez 2020.

9 Eg, see Gómez Bernales 2013; Fermandois Vöhringer & Echeverría Lavín 2020; Figueroa García-Huidobro 2020.

10 Bordalí Salamanca 2005; Verdugo Ramírez 2010.

11 Atria 1993; Zapata Larraín 2008: ch 1; Verdugo Ramírez 2013; Silva 2020: ch 3-4.

12 Eg, see Gutmann 1980; Beitz 1989; Dahl 1989: 139-41; Christiano 2008; Dworkin 2013: ch 18.

13 Waldron 2016: ch 10; Krishnamurthi 2020.

something to the debates on how to improve constitutional democracy, particularly when facing its mid-21st century crisis. Constitutional democracy's current global troubles—and Chile's constituent processes—remind me of MTV's famous show ***Pimp My Ride***. In it, the owner of a scruffy, run-down, barely functioning car would ask an MTV-sponsored garage to repair it and improve it: to 'pimp their ride,' in street jargon. Nowadays, many countries face a similar situation. They have 19th century institutions overhauled in the 20th century that seem to be in dire need of 'pimping.'

We are using technology that may be obsolete. Yet unlike the MTV show, in our case, nobody ***really*** knows how to currently 'pimp' a democracy. We mainly have theories, correlational studies, and historical experience to turn to—theories, data, and experience that, considering the changes generated by globalisation (particularly on culture, politics, economics, and communications), may not be well-suited to our present conditions. Nowadays, it seems that we can only argue for an improvement, gradually tinker with our institutions, see if the tinkering works, amend whatever part of the tinkering doesn't seem to be working, try again, do our best to avert our institutions from blowing up, and wish for good luck.

Considering our lack of information when 'pimping' our constitutional courts, this book tries to fill the theoretical void; the experiential void will have to be gradually filled in the future. In this book, I claim that majority rule is an inadequate technology to declare statutes unconstitutional, and that therefore we should replace it with supermajority rules. Due to its theoretical nature, many of this book's factual claims haven't been falsified: they remain speculative, though some of that speculation follows the axiomatic logic of mathematics. Still, as Nassim Taleb argues, '[m]athematics is to knowledge what an artificial hand is to the real one, some amputate to replace.'[14] Reality can—and usually does—behave unlike the small-world of mathematics, in which every variable is considered and controlled for.[15] Therefore, my factual claims may not hold. Indeed, I encourage future researchers to empirically try to bring them down so we can know for sure.

In such case, I will readily bite the bullet, admit that I was wrong, and bear the associated reputational costs. But even if my factual claims are refuted, they'll still be valuable insofar as they show us what *not* to do when improving a constitutional review system. Thus, in the worst-case scenario, this book will work as a sort of 'don't enter' sign for reforming our constitutional courts. In this sense, considering our current knowledge on how to improve our democratic institutions—and considering that knowledge usually operates by subtraction rather than addition[16]—this book may still contribute to strengthen them.

14 2015: 40.
15 Hayek 1989; Kay & King 2020.
16 Peirce [1878] 1992; Popper 2002.

References

Alvarado C, *La ilusión constitucional: sentido y límites del proceso constituyente [The Constitutional Illusion: Meaning and Limits of the Constituent Process] (IES 2016*)

Anderson ES, 'What is the Point of Equality?' (1999) 109(2) *Ethics* 287 https://doi.org/10.1086/233897

Arneson R, 'Equality and Equality of Opportunity for Welfare' in Pojman L and Westmoreland R (eds*), Equality: Selected Readings* (Oxford University Press 1997)

Atria F, 'El Tribunal Constitucional y la objeción democrática' ['The Constitutional Court and the Democratic Objection'] (1993) 20(2-3) *Revista Chilena de Derecho* 367 https://repositorio.uc.cl/handle/11534/14557

——— *La Constitución tramposa* [The Cheat Constitution] (LOM Ediciones 2013)

Barak A, Proportionality: Constitutional Rights and their Limitations (Cambridge University Press 2012) https://doi.org/10.1017/CBO9781139035293

Beitz CR, *Political Equality: An Essay in Democratic Theory* (Princeton University Press 1989) https://doi.org/10.1515/9780691221410

Bentham J, *Political Tactics (first published 1843*, James M, Blamires C and Please-Watkin C edn, Oxford University Press 1999) https://doi.org/10.1093/actrade/9780198207726.book.1

Bordalí Salamanca A, 'Análisis crítico del control preventivo y represivo de constitucionalidad de las normas jurídicas por los Tribunales Constitucionales' ['A Critical Analysis of Preemptive and Represive Controls of the Constitutionality of Legal Norms by Constitutional Courts'] in Nogueira Alcalá H (ed), *Jurisdicción Constitucional en Chile y América Latina: presente y prospectiva [Constitutional Jurisdiction in Chile and Latin America: present and future]* (LexisNexis 2005)

Busch Venthur T, *El control del juez constitucional [The Control of the Constitutional Judge]* (DPhil thesis, Pontifical Catholic University of Chile 2018) https://repositorio.uc.cl/handle/11534/22156

——— & Szmulewicz Ramírez E, 'Deliberación, legitimidad y organización interna de los tribunales constitucionales. Una mirada desde Latinoamérica' ['Deliberation, Legitimacy, and Internal Organization of Constitutional Courts. Perspectives from Latin America] (2020) 54 *Revista de Derecho de la Pontificia Universidad Católica de Valparaíso* 127 http://dx.doi.org/10.4067/S0718-68512020005000102

Christiano T, *The Constitution of Equality: Democratic Authority and its Limits* (Oxford University Press 2008) https://doi.org/10.1093/acprof:oso/9780198297475.001.0001

Dahl RA, *Democracy and its Critics* (Yale University Press 1989)

Dworkin R, *Justice for Hedgehogs* (Harvard University Press 2013)

Elhauge E, 'Does Interest Group Theory Justify More Intrusive Judicial Review?' (1991) 101 *Yale Law Journal* 31 https://doi.org/10.2307/796935

Fermandois Vöhringer A & Echeverría Lavín J (eds), *Sentencias Destacadas 2019: Una mirada desde la perspectiva de las políticas públicas* [Prominent Judgments 2019: A View from a Public Policy Perspective] (Ediciones LyD 2020)

Figueroa García-Huidobro R (ed), *Anuario de Derecho Público 2019 [Public Law Yearbook 2019]* (Ediciones UDP 2020)

Fuentes C (ed), *En el nombre del pueblo: debate sobre el cambio constitucional en Chile [In the Name of the People: the Debate on Constitutional Change in Chile] (*ICSO Universidad Diego Portales and Heinrich Böll Stiftung Cono Sur 2010) https://cl.boell.org/sites/default/files/en_el_nombre_del_pueblo_1.pdf

——— & Joignant A (eds), *La solución constitucional: plebiscitos, asambleas, congresos, sorteos y mecanismos híbridos [The Constitutional Solution: Plebiscites, Assemblies, Congresses, Sortition, and Hybrid Mechanisms]* (Catalonia 2015)

Gómez Bernales G, *Las sentencias del Tribunal Constitucional y sus efectos sobre la jurisdicción común [The Constitutional Court's Judgments and its Effects on Ordinary Courts]* (Ediciones UDP 2013)

Gutmann A, *Liberal Equality* (Cambridge University Press 1980)

Hamilton A, 'Federalist No 78. The Judiciary Department' in *The US Constitution and Other Key American Writings (first published 1788,* Canterbury Classics 2015)

Hayek FA, 'The Pretence of Knowledge' (1989) 79(6) *American Economic Review* 3 https://www.jstor.org/stable/1914347

Hübner Mendes C, *Constitutional Courts and Deliberative Democracy* (Oxford University Press 2015) https://doi.org/10.1093/acprof:oso/9780199670451.001.0001

Kay J & King M, *Radical Uncertainty: Decision-Making Beyond the Numbers* (WW Norton 2020)

Komesar NK, *Imperfect Alternatives: Choosing Institutions in Law, Economics, and Public Policy* (University of Chicago Press 1994)

Krishnamurthi G, 'For Judicial Majoritarianism' (2020) 22 *University of Pennsylvania Journal of Constitutional Law 1201* https://scholarship.law.upenn.edu/jcl/vol22/iss5/2

Kumm M, 'Institutionalising Socratic Contestation: The Rationalist Human Rights Paradigm, Legitimate Authority, and the Point of Judicial Review' (2007) 1(2) *European Journal of Legal Studies* 153 http://hdl.handle.net/1814/7708

Möller K, *The Global Model of Constitutional Rights* (Oxford University Press 2012) https://doi.org/10.1093/acprof:oso/9780199664603.001.0001

Montesquieu, *The Spirit of the Laws (first published 1748,* Anne M Coller, Basia Carolyn Miller and Harold Samuel Stone eds, Cambridge University Press 2020)

Nozick R, *Anarchy, State, and Utopia* (Basic Books 2013)

Orellana E, 'Publicidad de votos, concurrencias y disidencias en las sentencias del Tribunal Constitucional chileno: un análisis crítico' ['Publicity of Votes and Dissenting and Concurring Opinions in the Chilean Constitutional Court: A critical review'] (2019) *90 Revista de Derecho Público 61 https://doi.org/10.5354/0719-5249.2019.53995*

Peirce CS, 'Deduction, Induction, and Hypothesis' in Houser K and Kloessel C (eds), *The Essential Peirce: Selected Philosophical Writings,* vol 1 (first published 1878, Indiana University Press 1992)

Popper K, *The Logic of Scientific Discovery (first published 1935,* Routledge 2002)

Rawls J, *A Theory of Justice* (Revised edn, Harvard University Press 1999)

Sandel MJ (ed), *Justice: A Reader* (Oxford University Press 2007)

Sen AK, *Inequality Reexamined* (Harvard University Press 1995)

Silva LA, *La Garantía Política de la Constitución [The Political Guarantee of the Constitution]* (Tirant lo Blanch 2020)

Taleb NN, *The Bed of Procrustes: Philosophical and Practical Aphorisms* (2019 Box Set edn, Random House 2015)

Tsakyrakis S, 'Proportionality: An Assault on Human Rights?' (2009) 7(3) *International Journal of Constitutional Law* 468 https://doi.org/10.1093/icon/mop011

Urbina FJ, *A Critique of Proportionality and Balancing* (Cambridge University Press 2017) https://doi.org/10.1017/9781316796276

Verdugo Ramírez S, 'Control Preventivo Obligatorio: Auge y Caída de la Toma de Razón al Legislador' ['Compulsory Ex Ante Control: Raise and Fall of the Control Over the Legislator'] (2010) 8(1) *Estudios Constitucionales* 201 http://dx.doi.org/10.4067/S0718-52002010000100008

——— 'Aportes del modelo de disidencias judiciales al sistema político' ['Contribution of the Judicial Dissent Model to the Political System. Judicial Pluralism and Democratic Debate'] (2011) 18(2) *Revista de Derecho Universidad Católica del Norte 217* http://dx.doi.org/10.4067/S0718-97532011000200009

——— 'La discusión democrática sobre la revisión judicial de las leyes de diseño institucional y modelos constitucionales' ['Democratic Objection Against Judicial Review of Legislation. Institutional Design Alternatives and Constitutional Theories'] (2013) 40(1) *Revista Chilena de Derecho* 181 http://dx.doi.org/10.4067/S0718-34372013000100008

Vermeule A, *Judging Under Uncertainty: An Institutional Theory of Legal Interpretation* (Harvard University Press 2006)

Waldron J, *Political Political Theory: Essays on Institutions* (Harvard University Press 2016) https://doi.org/10.4159/9780674970342

Webber GCN, *The Negotiable Constitution* (Cambridge University Press 2009)

Yowell P, *Constitutional Rights and Constitutional Design: Moral and Empirical Reasoning in Judicial Review* (Hart Publishing 2018) https://doi.org/10.5040/9781509913626

Zapata Larraín P, *Justicia constitucional: teoría y práctica en el derecho chileno y comparado [Constitutional Justice: Theory and Practice in Chilean and Comparative Law]* (Editorial Jurídica de Chile 2008)

——— *La casa de todos y todas.* La Nueva Constitución que Chile merece y necesita [A House for All: The New Constitution that Chile Deserves and Needs] (Ediciones UC 2020)

Acknowledgements

Through the writing of this book, I've gotten massive help from several people and institutions, most of which I won't be able to do justice here. Many of the ideas developed in this book started while researching and drafting my PhD thesis—called 'Bare Majorities: On Voting in Constitutional Adjudication (http://hdl.handle.net/1974/27555)—at Queen's University at Kingston Faculty of Law. So, I owe a huge debt of gratitude to my supervisors, Jean Thomas and Grégoire Webber. I wouldn't have been able to do this research without their generous and invaluable encouragement. Alongside the fact that their expertise and detailed comments were essential for sharpening my research, Jean and Grégoire enthusiastically endorsed it and gave advice when most needed. Thanks are also due to the members of my thesis defence committee, Andrew Lister, Benjamin Ewing, David Dyzenhaus, and Jacob Weinrib for their insightful comments.

The claims developed in Chapter 5 were previously shown in the article 'Is Majority Rule Justified in Constitutional Adjudication,' published in (2021) 41(2) *Oxford Journal of Legal Studies* 376 https://doi.org/10.1093/ojls/gqaa055. And Chapter 6 expands on the ideas shown in the article 'A Core Case for Supermajority Rules in Constitutional Adjudication,' published in (2022) 20(3) *International Journal of Constitutional Law* 1162 https://doi.org/10.1093/icon/moac072. I'm thankful to these journals, and to Oxford University Press, for allowing me to use these resources here. Likewise, among other scholars, I'm grateful to Gabrielle Appleby, Virgílio Afonso da Silva, Tania Busch Venthur, Jon Elster, Pablo Grez, Tom Hickey, Rodrigo Kaufmann, Mathias Kumm, Piotr Mikuli, Margaret Moore, Jairo Néia Lima, Mauro Rivera León, Pasquale Pasquino, Yaniv Roznai, Yung-Djong Shaw, Melissa Schwartzberg, Nina Varsava, Sergio Verdugo, Francisco Urbina, Paul Yowell, and the anonymous reviewers of this book (and of the forenamed articles) for their interest in this research and their constructive feedback.

Many scholars introduced me to comparative literature without which this book's quality would have been severely hindered. I'm grateful to: (i) Nurina Ally, Akongburo Raymond Atuguba, John Baloro, Sebastian Kanunda, Heinz Klug, Charles Manga Fombad, Maame Mensa-Bonsu, Theunis Roux, and Francois Venter for sharing data on the Botswanan, Ghanaian, and

Namibian supreme courts, and on the South African Constitutional Court; (ii) Bill Flanagan, Eduardo Esteva, Diego Gamarra, María Paula Garat, Roberto Gargarella, Walter Guerra, and Martín Risso for sharing data on the Argentinian, Canadian, and Uruguayan supreme courts; (iii) Hyo-Won Lee for sharing data on the South Korean Constitutional Court; (iv) João Carlos Loureiro for sharing data on the Portuguese Constitutional Court; (v) Olli Mäenpää, Janne Salminen, and Akritas Kaidatzis for sharing data on the Finnish supreme courts, and on the Greek 'Special Highest Court;' (vi) Jens Elo Rytter, Pétur Dam Leifsson, and Trausti Fannar Valsson for sharing data on the Danish and Icelandic supreme courts; and (vii) Penny Miller for sharing data on the North Dakotan supreme court.

I wouldn't have been able to do this research without the excellent environments provided by Queen's University at Kingston Faculty of Law, the Max Planck Institute for Comparative Public Law and International Law, and Universidad Católica del Norte Faculty of Law. Further, I'm deeply thankful to Chile's *Agencia Nacional de Investigación y Desarrollo* [National Research and Development Agency]; the Government of Ontario, Canada; Queen's University at Kingston; and the Max Planck Institute for Comparative Public Law and International Law for their funding via the FONDECYT de Iniciación en Investigación grant number 11220386; the Becas Chile programme; the Queen's Funding, Awards, and Scholarships programme; and the Max Planck Institute for Comparative Public Law and International Law's Visiting Researchers programme. I also owe a debt of gratitude to Richard Albert, Alison Kirk, Anna Gallagher, and Routledge's editorial team for assessing my book proposal, and for their indispensable commitment and professionalism in ensuring that it's now published.

Last but not least, though I have the terrible tendency of taking them for granted, I can't be grateful enough to my parents—Iván and Francisca—and to my brothers—Julián, Diego, and Joaquín—for their unconditional love and support. This book is dedicated to them.

Constitutions and Statutes Cited

Argentina

— Ley No 27 Organización de la Justicia Nacional [Law on the Organisation of the National Judiciary], Registro Nacional, IV, 496 https://www.argentina.gob.ar/normativa/nacional/ley-27-116333

Botswana

— Constitution of Botswana https://www.parliament.gov.bw/images/constitution.pdf
— Court of Appeal Act, 1972 https://botswanalaws.com/alphabetical-list-of-statutes/court-of-appeal-1

Catholic Church

— Apostolic Constitution Universi Dominici Gregis on the Vacancy of the Holy See and the Election of the Roman Pontiff https://www.vatican.va/content/john-paul-ii/en/apost_constitutions/documents/hf_jp-ii_apc_22021996_universi-dominici-gregis.html
— Code of Canon Law (Canadian Conference of Catholic Bishops 1983)

Canada

— Canadian Charter of Rights and Freedoms, Part I of the Constitution Act, 1982, being Schedule B to the Canada Act 1982 (UK), 1982 https://canlii.ca/t/8q7l
— Constitution Act, 1867 (UK) 30 and 31 Vict., c. 3 https://canlii.ca/t/8q7k
— Supreme Court Act, RSC 1985, c S-26 https://canlii.ca/t/7vlk

Ghana

— Constitution of the Republic of Ghana https://www.constituteproject.org/constitutions?lang=en

Chile

— Código Orgánico de Tribunales [Organic Code of Courts] http://bcn.cl/2im2j
— Constitución Política de la República de Chile [Political Constitution of the Republic of Chile] http://bcn.cl/2f6sk
— Ley N° 17.997 Orgánica Constitucional del Tribunal Constitucional [Organic Law of the Constitutional Court] http://bcn.cl/2f894

Costa Rica

— Constitución Política de la República de Costa Rica [Political Constitution of the Republic of Costa Rica] (1949) https://www.constituteproject.org/constitutions?lang=en
— Ley de la Jurisdicción Constitucional n° 7135 del 11 de octubre [Law of the Constitutional Jurisdiction] (1989) https://www.pgrweb.go.cr/scij/Busqueda/Normativa/Normas/nrm_texto_completo.aspx?param1=NRTCandnValor1=1andnValor2=38533andnValor3=127124andparam2=1andstrTipM=TCandlResultado=3andstrSim=simp

Czech Republic

— Ústavni zákon České republiky [Constitution of the Czech Republic]. Abbreviation: Ústavy ČR [Constitution] https://www.constituteproject.org/constitutions?lang=en
— Zákon o Ústavním soudu [Constitutional Court Act] https://www.usoud.cz/en/legal-basis

Denmark

— Danmarks Riges Grundlov [The Constitutional Act of Denmark] https://www.constituteproject.org/constitutions?lang=en
— Retsplejeloven [Administration of Justice Act]

Estonia

— Constitution of the Republic of Estonia https://www.constituteproject.org/constitutions?lang=en
— Constitutional Review Court Procedure Act https://www.riigiteataja.ee/en/eli/528122016013/consolide

Finland

— Laki Korkeimmasta hallinto-oikeudesta [Supreme Administrative Court Act] https://finlex.fi/en/laki/kaannokset/2006/en20061265
— Laki Korkeimmasta oikeudesta [Supreme Court Act] https://finlex.fi/en/laki/kaannokset/1918/en19180074
— Laki oikeudenkäynnistä rikosasioissa [Criminal Procedure Act] https://finlex.fi/en/laki/kaannokset/1997/en19970689
— Oikeudenkäymiskaari [Code of Judicial Procedure] https://finlex.fi/en/laki/kaannokset/1734/en17340004
— Suomen perustuslaki [Constitution of Finland] https://www.constituteproject.org/constitutions?lang=en

Germany

— Bundesverfassungsgerichtsgesetz [Act on the Federal Constitutional Court] v 11.08.1993. BGBI. I 1993, p 1473. https://www.bundesverfassungsgericht.de/EN/Verfahren/Rechtsquellen/rechtsquellen_node.html
— Grundgesetz der Bundesrepublik Deutschland [Basic Law for the Federal Republic of Germany] https://www.constituteproject.org/constitutions?lang=en

Greece

— Syntagma tis Elladas [Constitution of Greece] https://www.constituteproject.org/constitutions?lang=en
— Nomos 345/1976 [Law 345/1976]

Iceland

— Lög um meðferð einkamála nr. 91/1991 [Statute on Civil Procedure no. 91/1991]

Japan

— Nihonkoku Kenpo (1946) [Constitution of Japan (1946)] https://www.constituteproject.org/constitutions?lang=en
— Saibanshohō [Judiciary Act], Law n° 59 of 1947, as last amended by Law n° 67 of 2017 https://www.cas.go.jp/jp/seisaku/hourei/data/CACT.pdf

Latvia

— Constitution of the Republic of Latvia https://www.constituteproject.org/constitutions?lang=en

— Law on the Constitutional Court of Latvia https://www.satv.tiesa.gov.lv/en/category/regulations/

Lithuania

— Constitution of the Republic of Lithuania https://www.constituteproject.org/constitutions?lang=en
— Law on the Constitutional Court, published in alstybės žinios (Official Gazette) 1993, n° 6-120 https://www.lrkt.lt/en/about-the-court/legal-information/the-law-on-the-constitutional-court/1475

Mexico

— Constitución Política de los Estados Unidos Mexicanos [Political Constitution of the United Mexican States] https://www.constituteproject.org/constitutions?lang=en
— Ley Orgánica del Poder Judicial de la Federación [Organic Law of the Judicial Branch of the Federation] http://www.diputados.gob.mx/LeyesBiblio/pdf/LOPJF_070621.pdf

Mongolia

— Constitution of Mongolia https://www.constituteproject.org/constitutions?lang=en
— Law on Constitutional Court Procedure https://constitutionalcourt.mn/?page_id=851andlang=en

Namibia

— Constitution of Namibia https://www.constituteproject.org/constitutions?lang=en
— Supreme Court Act 15, of 1990 https://ejustice.moj.na/Supreme%20Court/LegislationAndDirectives/Pages/default.aspx

Nebraska

— Constitution of the State of Nebraska https://law.justia.com/constitution/nebraska/

Norway

— Domstolloven [Courts of Justice Act] https://www.domstol.no/en/norwegian-courts-administration/publications/
— Grunnloven [Constitution of the Kingdom of Norway] https://www.constituteproject.org/constitutions?lang=en

— Tvisteloven [The Dispute Act] 17 juni 2005 nr 90 https://lovdata.no/dokument/NLE/lov/2005-06-17-90

North Dakota

— Constitution of the State of North Dakota https://www.legis.nd.gov/constitution

Panama

— Código Judicial [Judicial Code] https://www.organojudicial.gob.pa/cendoj/files/codigo-judicial
— Constitución Política de la República de Panamá [Political Constitution of the Republic of Panama]. Abbreviation: Constitución Panameña [Panamanian Constitution] https://www.constituteproject.org/constitutions?lang=en

Peru

— Ley Orgánica del Tribunal Constitucional [Organic Law of the Constitutional Court] https://www.tc.gob.pe/institucional/normatividad/

Portugal

— Constitution of the Portuguese Republic Seventh Revision [2005]. Portuguese Constitution https://www.constituteproject.org/constitutions?lang=en
— Law of the Constitutional Court, Law n° 28/82, of 15 November https://www.tribunalconstitucional.pt/tc/en/tclaw.html

Slovakia

— Constitution of the Slovak Republic. https://www.constituteproject.org/constitutions?lang=en
— Law of 24 October 2018 on the Constitutional Court of the Slovak Republic, amending and supplementing other laws https://www.ustavnysud.sk/en/o-ustavnom-sude-slovenskej-republiky

Slovenia

— Constitution, Official Gazette of the Republic of Slovenia n° 33/91-I 33/91-I, 42/97, 66/2000, 24/03, 69/04, 68/06, and 47/13 https://www.constituteproject.org/constitutions?lang=en
— Rules of Procedure, Official Gazette of the Republic of Slovenia, n° 86/07, 54/10 and 56/11 https://www.us-rs.si/legal-basis/the-rules-of-procedure/?lang=en

— The Constitutional Court Act (ZUstS), Official Gazette of the Republic of Slovenia, n° 64/07—official consolidated text https://www.us-rs.si/legal-basis/statutes/?lang=en

South Africa

— Constitution of the Republic of South Africa https://www.constituteproject.org/constitutions?lang=en

South Korea

— Daehanminguk Hyonbop [Constitution of the Republic of Korea]. Hyonbop [Constitution] https://www.constituteproject.org/constitutions?lang=en
— Constitutional Court Act (Law No 4017, 1988) https://english.ccourt.go.kr/site/eng/main.do

Spain

— Constitución Española [Spanish Constitution] https://www.constituteproject.org/constitutions?lang=en
— Ley Orgánica del Poder Judicial [Organic Law of the Judicial Branch] https://www.boe.es/eli/es/lo/1985/07/01/6/con
— Ley Orgánica del Tribunal Constitucional [Organic Law of the Constitutional Court] https://www.boe.es/eli/es/lo/1979/10/03/2/con

Sweden

— Regeringsformen RF (SFS) [The Instrument of Government] https://www.constituteproject.org/constitutions?lang=en
— SFS 1942:740 Den svenska rättegångsbalken [Code of Judicial Procedure (1942:740)] https://www.government.se/government-policy/judicial-system/the-swedish-code-of-judicial-procedure/
— SFS 1971:291 Förvaltningsprocesslag [The Administrative Court Procedure Act] https://www.government.se/government-policy/judicial-system/the-administrative-court-procedure-act/

Switzerland

— Bundesverfassung der Schweizerischen Eidgenossenschaft [Federal Constitution of the Swiss Confederation] https://www.constituteproject.org/constitutions?lang=en

Taiwan

— Chung Hua Min Guo Hsien Fa, Min Guo 36 nien, December 25 [Republic of China Constitution, 25 December 1947]. Hsien Fa [Constitution] https://www.constituteproject.org/constitutions?lang=en
— Constitutional Court Procedure Act https://legal.judicial.gov.tw/LAWENG//FLAW/dat02.aspx?lsid=FL000849
— Constitutional Interpretation Procedure Act https://cons.judicial.gov.tw/jcc/en-us/relatelaw/y19yzwxhdgvfcnvszq%3d%3d

The Netherlands

— Grondwet voor het Koninkrijk der Nederlanden [Constitution of the Kingdom of the Netherlands] https://www.constituteproject.org/constitutions?lang=en

Uruguay

— Constitución de la República Oriental del Uruguay [Constitution of the Oriental Republic of Uruguay], Diario Oficial 02 Febrero 1967 https://www.constituteproject.org/constitutions?lang=en
— Ley nº 15982 Código General del Proceso [General Code of Judicial Procedure], Diario Oficial 18 Octubre 1988 https://www.impo.com.uy/bases/codigo-general-proceso/15982-1988
— Ley nº 15750 orgánica de la judicatura y de la organización de los tribunales [Organic Law of the Judiciary and Court Organisation], Diario Oficial 08 Julio 1985 https://www.impo.com.uy/bases/leyes/15750-1985

United States

— United States Code https://www.govinfo.gov/help/uscode
— Constitution of the United States of America https://www.constituteproject.org/constitutions?lang=en

Cases Cited

Constitutional Tribunal of Poland

— K 47/15 of 9 March 2016 of the Constitutional Tribunal

Supreme Court of Canada

— Chaoulli v Quebec, [2005] 1 SCR 791 https://canlii.ca/t/1kxrh
— Sauvé v Canada (Chief Electoral Officer), [2002] 3 SCR 519 https://canlii.ca/t/50cw

Supreme Court of the United States

— Borden's Farms Prods Co v Baldwin, 293 US 194, 209 (1934) https://supreme.justia.com/cases/federal/us/293/194/
— Brown v Board of Education of Topeka, 347 US 483 (1954) https://supreme.justia.com/cases/federal/us/347/483/
— Burnett v Coronado Oil and Gas Co 285 US 393, 406–7 (1932) https://supreme.justia.com/cases/federal/us/285/393/
— Citizens United v Federal Elections Commission, 558 US 310 (2010) https://supreme.justia.com/cases/federal/us/558/310/
— Marbury v Madison, 5 US 137 (1805) https://supreme.justia.com/cases/federal/us/5/137/
— Obergefell v Hodges, 576 US __ (2015) https://supreme.justia.com/cases/federal/us/576/14-556/
— Seminole Tribe v Florida, 517 US 44, 63 (1996) https://supreme.justia.com/cases/federal/us/517/44/

Abbreviations

BVerfG Act	Bundesverfassungsgerichtsgesetz [Act on the Federal Constitutional Court] (Germany)
Swi Const	Bundesverfassung der Schweizerischen Eidgenossenschaft [Federal Constitution of the Swiss Confederation] (Switzerland)
Dan Const	Danmarks Riges Grundlov [The Constitutional Act of Denmark]
Nor Jud Act	Domstolloven [Courts of Justice Act] (Norway)
Can Cht	Canadian Charter of Rights and Freedoms, 1982, Part I of the Constitution Act, 1982, being Schedule B to the Canada Act 1982 (UK), 1982, c 11 (Canada)
Twn Const	Chung Hua Min Guo Hsien Fa, Min Guo 36 nien, December 25 [Republic of China Constitution, 25 December 1947]
Pan Jud Code	Código Judicial [Judicial Code] (Panama)
Ch Courts Code	Código Orgánico de Tribunales [Organic Code of Courts] (Chile)
Uru Const	Constitución de la República Oriental del Uruguay [Constitution of the Oriental Republic of Uruguay], Diario Oficial 02 Febrero 1967
Spn Const	Constitución Española [Spanish Constitution]
Ch Const	Constitución Política de la República de Chile [Political Constitution of the Republic of Chile]
CR Const	Constitución Política de la República de Costa Rica [Political Constitution of the Republic of Costa Rica]
Pan Const	Constitución Política de la República de Panamá [Political Constitution of the Republic of Panama]
Mex Const	Constitución Política de los Estados Unidos Mexicanos [Political Constitution of the United Mexican States]

Can Const	Constitution Act, 1867 (UK), 30 and 31 Vic, c 3 (Canada)
Slv Const	Constitution, Official Gazette of the Republic of Slovenia n° 33/91-I 33/91-I, 42/97, 66/2000, 24/03, 69/04, 68/06, and 47/13
Bots Const	Constitution of Botswana
Gk Const	Constitution of Greece [Syntagma tis Elladas]
Mong Const	Constitution of Mongolia
Nam Const	Constitution of Namibia
Port Const	Constitution of the Portuguese Republic Seventh Revision [2005]
Est Const	Constitution of the Republic of Estonia
Gh Const	Constitution of the Republic of Ghana
Lat Const	Constitution of the Republic of Latvia
Lit Const	Constitution of the Republic of Lithuania
SA Const	Constitution of the Republic of South Africa
Slk Const	Constitution of the Slovak Republic
Neb Const	Constitution of the State of Nebraska
ND Const	Constitution of the State of North Dakota
US Const	Constitution of the United States
SK CC Act	Constitutional Court Act (Law No 4017, 1988) (South Korea)
Slv CC Act	Constitutional Court Act (ZUstS), Official Gazette of the Republic of Slovenia, n° 64/07—official consolidated text
Twn CC Proc Act	Constitutional Court Procedure Act (Taiwan)
Est CC Proc Act	Constitutional Review Court Procedure Act (Estonia)
Twn C Int Proc Act	Constitutional Interpretation Procedure Act (Taiwan)
Bots CA Act	Court of Appeal Act, 1972 (Botswana)
SK Const	Daehanminguk Hyonbop [Constitution of the Republic of Korea] (South Korea)
Ned Const	Grondwet voor het Koninkrijk der Nederlanden [Constitution of the Kingdom of the Netherlands]
Ger Const	Grundgesetz der Bundesrepublik Deutschland [Basic Law for the Federal Republic of Germany]
Nor Const	Grunnloven [Constitution of the Kingdom of Norway]
Fin SAC Act	Laki korkeimmasta hallinto-oikeudesta [Supreme Administrative Court Act] (Finland)
Fin SC Act	Laki Korkeimmasta oikeudesta [Supreme Court Act] (Finland)
Fin Crim Proc Act	Laki oikeudenkäynnistä rikosasioissa [Criminal Procedure Act] (Finland)

Mong CC Proc Law	Law on Constitutional Court Procedure (Mongolia)
Slk CC Law	Law of 24 October 2018 on the Constitutional Court of the Slovak Republic, amending and supplementing other laws
Port CC Law	Law of the Constitutional Court, Law n° 28/82, of 15 November (Portugal)
Lit CC Law	Law on the Constitutional Court, published in alstybės žinios (Official Gazette) 1993, n° 6-120 (Lithuania)
Mong CC Proc Law	Law on Constitutional Court Procedure (Mongolia)
Lat CC Law	Law on the Constitutional Court of Latvia
Uru Proc Code	Ley n° 15982 Código General del Proceso [General Code of Judicial Procedure] (Uruguay)
Uru Jud Law	Ley n° 15750 orgánica de la judicatura y de la organización de los tribunales [Organic Law of the Judiciary and Court Organisation] (Uruguay)
Arg Jud Law	Ley No 27 Organización de la Justicia Nacional [Law on the Organisation of the National Judiciary], Registro Nacional, IV, 496 (Argentina)
Ch CC Law	Ley N° 17.997 Orgánica Constitucional del Tribunal Constitucional [Organic Law of the Constitutional Court] (Chile)
CR Jud Law	Ley de la Jurisdicción Constitucional n° 7135 del 11 de octubre [Law of the Constitutional Jurisdiction] (1989) (Costa Rica)
Spn Jud Law	Ley Orgánica del Poder Judicial [Organic Law of the Judicial Branch] (Spain)
Mex Jud Law	Ley Orgánica del Poder Judicial de la Federación [Organic Law of the Judicial Branch of the Federation] (Mexico)
Per CC Law	Ley Orgánica del Tribunal Constitucional [Organic Law of the Constitutional Court] (Peru)
Spn CC Law	Ley Orgánica del Tribunal Constitucional [Organic Law of the Constitutional Court] (Spain)
Ice Proc Law	Lög um meðferð einkamála nr. 91/1991 [Statute on Civil Procedure no. 91/1991] (Iceland)
Jpn Const	Nihonkoku Kenpo (1946) [Constitution of Japan (1946)]
Gk CC Law	Nomos 345/1976 [Law 345/1976] (Greece)
Fin Proc Code	Oikeudenkäymiskaari [Code of Judicial Procedure] (Finland)
Swe Const	Regeringsformen RF (SFS) [The Instrument of Government] (Sweden)
Dan Jud Act	Retsplejeloven [Administration of Justice Act]

	(Denmark)
Slv Proc Rules	Rules of Procedure, Official Gazette of the Republic of Slovenia, n° 86/07, 54/10 and 56/11 (Slovenia)
Jpn Jud Act	Saibanshohō [Judiciary Act], Law n° 59 of 1947 (Japan)
Swe Proc Code	SFS 1942.740 Den svenska rättegångsbalken [Code of Judicial Procedure (1942:740] (Sweden)
Swe AC Proc Act	SFS 1971:291 Förvaltningsprocesslag [The Administrative Court Procedure Act] (Sweden)
Fin Const	Suomen perustuslaki [Constitution of Finland]
Nam SC Act	Supreme Court Act 15, of 1990 (Namibia)
Can SC Act	Supreme Court Act, RSC 1985, c S-26 (Canada)
Nor Disp Act	Tvisteloven [The Dispute Act] 17 juni 2005 nr 90 (Norway)
USC	United States Code
CzR Const	Ústavni zákon České republiky [Constitution of the Czech Republic]
CzR CC Act	Zákon o Ústavním soudu [Constitutional Court Act] (Czech Republic)

1 Introduction

One of the most under-studied issues in legal and political theory is the voting rules by which, in many democracies, courts[1] decide on the constitutionality of legislation.[2] That is, the voting rules by which courts decide on the validity of laws or statutes enacted by legislatures.[3] There's been scant attention paid to the fact that many courts can declare statutes unconstitutional by majority rule:[4] they can declare statutes unconstitutional by aggregating or counting the opinions of just 50% of their judges present plus one judge present.[5] This contrasts starkly with the scholarly awareness of other democratic institutions[6] and practices, such as legislatures and referenda[7]—an awareness that has translated into deep, dense, fully-fledged bodies of thought justifying why citizens and elected representatives must generally decide by majority rule.[8]

1 With the word 'courts,' I'm referring to institutions that can solve disputes according to legal norms and whose decisions are usually not subject to more legal recourses.
2 With the word 'statutes,' I'm referring to full statutes, sets of statutory provisions, or a single statutory provision.
3 Following Yowell, with the word 'legislatures' I'm referring to 'group[s] of officials responsible for formulating, proposing, and enacting legislation, at whatever place they occupy in [a State's] political structure.' (2018: 97). I consider unicameral and bicameral legislatures. I assume that *most* or *all* legislators are elected.
4 For exceptions, see Waldron 2016; Krishnamurthi 2020.
5 This concept is indeterminate when applied to groups with odd numbers. When odd numbers are split into two, the result is always a decimal number with five tenths that must be rounded up or down to get a natural number (eg, in a nine-member group, 50% of group members present is 4.5, therefore, this number must be rounded to four or five). I round these numbers down since this suffices to get a majority when adding the number one.
6 I only use the word 'institutions' to refer to 'state institutions'. Consequently, I'm not using the word 'institutions' broadly, as used by political scientists and economists. For this broader use of the word 'institutions,' see North 1990.
7 With the word 'referenda,' I'm referring to what Altman (2011: ch 1) calls 'mechanisms of direct democracy,' whether they are initiated by citizens or by state authorities. For overviews of these mechanisms, see also Morel & Qvortrup 2018.
8 Eg, see Gutmann 1980; Beitz 1989; Dahl 1989: 139–41; Rawls 1999; Christiano 2008: ch 3; Dworkin 2013: ch 18.

DOI: 10.4324/9781032723952-1

This situation is challenging since discussions on whether democracies should have courts that assess, scrutinise, or check the constitutionality of legislation—the so-called 'legitimacy of judicial review debate'[9]—are joined with discussions of issues regarding these courts' design.[10] When constitutional courts[11] solve a case, a mere majority of unelected judges may annul, void, or strike down laws passed by a majority of citizens' elected representatives. And these laws may tackle hard moral issues on which people deeply disagree, such as the regulation of abortion; what kinds of speech should be allowed in the public sphere (and under what conditions); the bounds of the separation between Church and State; the financing of electoral campaigns, health services, or pensions; whether one may buy, sell, or grow certain drugs; or whether one may kill oneself with the help of others without them being penalised for giving such help.

Further, if one considers research undertaken in other disciplines—especially history and social choice theory—one may argue that different voting rules have contrasting features, properties, or traits[12] that may boost or hinder the odds[13] that constitutional courts realise their goals, as proposed by these institutions' main defenders (eg, guarding political participation,[14] promoting public reason,[15] upholding principles,[16] ensuring 'Socratic contestation,'[17] etc.). Thus, considering such goals from the viewpoint of voting rules' traits, it's worth assessing whether majority rule is the best voting rule at judges' disposal, or whether other voting rules—particularly, supermajority rules—may work better to realise them.

Finally, constitutional courts' use of majority rule to declare statutes unconstitutional may hinder their reputation. Considering that these courts regularly review hard—and thus controversial—moral issues, these courts' split or highly divided decisions, such as the US Supreme Court's 'five-to-four decisions,'

9 For pro-constitutional review literature, see Ely 1980; Ackerman 1993; Dworkin 1996; Rawls 2005); Cross 1999; Kumm 2007; Fallon 2008; Harel & Kahana 2010. For opposite views, see Tomkins 2005; Bellamy 2007; Waldron 2016: ch 9.

10 Yowell 2018.

11 I use the word 'constitutional courts' broadly. Thus, I include 'Kelsenian' and 'supreme' courts. In federal polities, I mainly focus on constitutional review of federal legislation made by a Kelsenian constitutional court—or by the supreme court at the apex of the federal legal system. On the distinction between 'Kelsenian' and 'supreme' courts, see Cappelletti 1971; Brewer-Carías 1989; Stone Sweet 2012.

12 List & Pettit 2011; Landemore 2013: ch 6–7; Schwartzberg 2013: ch 3–5; Lagerspetz 2016.

13 I use the word 'odds' as a synonyms of 'probabilities.' And I understand probabilities as mainly referring to *degrees of belief* in the truth or falsity of propositions rather than just referring to the *frequencies* in which facts occur. These degrees of beliefs may be represented cardinally or ordinally. On probabilities generally, see Peirce [1878a] 1992; Keynes 2007; Binmore 2011; Kay & King 2020.

14 Ely 1980.

15 Rawls 2005.

16 Dworkin 1996.

17 Kumm 2007.

may hurt their reputation as competent, reliable, and impartial institutions, especially among citizens that oppose such decisions. Actually, though this may sound exaggerated, if highly divided decisions become the norm in a constitutional court, the cumulative damage to that court's reputation may one day become severe enough to erode citizens' sense of obligation towards its decisions.

Ordinary citizens may have the hunch that unanimous (or highly agreed upon) judicial decisions are quite different than highly divided judicial decisions. This hunch is supported by some empirical research,[18] and it influences debates on whether judges should be able to publish concurring and dissenting opinions.[19] In the first scenario, constitutional courts' decisions may look as principled compromises made after sincere, strenuous debates between judges trying to solve hard cases as best they can. This may partly explain why some constitutional courts—including the US[20] and German courts[21]—tend to render unanimous (or seemingly unanimous) decisions during their early years. Conversely, in the second scenario, constitutional courts' decisions may look like situations in which some judges 'steamroll' their peers to entrench their contestable values into law.[22] Or worse, as situations in which judges decide almost by flipping a coin. Therefore, it's worth assessing voting rules' effects in producing highly divided or highly agreed upon judicial decisions, since different levels of judicial agreement may affect constitutional courts' reputation; hence affecting their perceived authority[23] over citizens and other officials.

Research on constitutional courts' voting rules is fragmentary, yet many constitutional courts use majority rule to declare statutes unconstitutional. This happens in most constitutional courts in the Americas and Europe. In Africa, this happens in the Botswanan, Ghanaian, Namibian, and South African courts. And, in Asia, this happens in the Japanese court.[24] Conversely, few constitutional courts use supermajority rules to declare statutes unconstitutional: these courts use a gamut, range, or spectrum of voting rules whose threshold is higher than majority rule (that is, higher than 50% of the judges present plus one judge present), but lower than unanimity rule (that is, lower than 100% of the judges present). In North America, this happens in Mexico,

18 Zink et al 2009. For similar results among the members of other small groups, see Tjosvold & Field 1983. For opposite results regarding citizens' perception of judicial decisions, see Salamonte 2014.

19 For overviews of this debate, see European Parliament 2012: 9–16; Kelemen 2019:ch 5.

20 Corley et al 2013: ch 1.

21 Ferejohn & Pasquino 2004; Kelemen 2019: ch 3–4.

22 Arguably, the archetype seems to be the US Supreme Court. On the amount of split decisions in this court, see Epstein et al 2001; Henderson 2007; Corley et al 2013 ch 1. For statistics on the US Supreme Court, see Epstein et al 2021.

23 I use the word 'authority' to refer to an agent's moral power to impose obligations. Raz 2009. This is akin to what philosophers such as Estlund (2008: 2, 41–2) and Brennan (2016: 149–51) call 'legitimacy.'

24 See the Appendix.

Nebraska and North Dakota. In South America, this happens in Chile and Peru. In Europe, this happens in the Czech Republic. In Asia, this happens in Mongolia and South Korea.[25] And some literature suggests replacing the US Supreme Court's majority rule with a supermajority rule.[26]

To partially address the lack of attention given to voting rules for declaring statutes unconstitutional, I propose two main arguments in this book. First, once we consider majority rule's traits, it's not possible to decisively argue for its use in constitutional review; meaning, there aren't strong enough reasons to claim that judges should check the constitutionality of legislation by majority rule rather than by other voting rules (particularly, supermajority rules). Second, constitutional courts should use supermajority rules in constitutional review. Thus, to declare statutes unconstitutional, more than 50% of the judges present plus one judge present should be required.

Including this introductory chapter, I divide this book into seven chapters plus an appendix for building my claims. In Chapter 2, I present this book's methodology. This chapter gives the factual and normative framework for the rest of the book. In this book, I develop qualified claims: I develop claims that mainly work under certain assumptions—assumptions that, though reasonable, are contestable. Consequently, I can't immediately treat these assumptions as given, but must explicitly show and justify them to the reader. This is the aim of Chapter 2.

In Chapters 3 and 4, I present a broad picture of voting rules' main traits, especially majority rule's and supermajority rules' traits. In Chapter 3, I identify some of unanimity rule's, majority rule's, and supermajority rules' traits by examining how these voting rules have been used in Western history—from Ancient Greece to the Italian city-states—and by analysing the reflections on these rules made by some of the Enlightenment's pre-eminent philosophers; particularly Condorcet and Pufendorf. Next, in Chapter 4, I show the full picture of majority rule's and supermajority rules' traits by considering the insights given by social choice and political philosophy scholars. In these chapters, I hold that unanimity rule shouldn't be considered as an option for replacing majority rule in constitutional review since this voting rule has a strong potential to coerce dissenters.

After introducing majority rule's traits, in Chapter 5, I analyse these traits separately and jointly, and hold that they don't give decisive reasons for using majority rule in constitutional review. Put differently, once one considers majority rule's traits, there are no sufficient reasons for using majority rule

25 See the Appendix. For the Mexican court, see Ferrer Mac-Gregor & Herrera 2009: 335; Mex Jud Law, art 7 inc 1°. For the Peruvian court, see Carpio Marcos & Grandez Castro 2009: 446–7; Per CC Law, art 5°.

26 Shugerman 2002; Carminker 1999; Gersen & Vermeule 2007; Epps & Sitaraman 2019; Doerfler & Moyn 2021. For critiques, see Entin 2001: 441; Zellmer & Miller 2015; Krishnamurthi 2020.

over other voting rules to check the constitutionality of legislation. Thus, in Chapter 5, I claim that there's enough normative room to hold that, when declaring statutes unconstitutional, constitutional courts should use supermajority rules rather than majority rule.

In Chapter 6, I present the reasons for replacing majority rule with supermajority rules in constitutional review. In short, in Chapter 6, I claim that constitutional courts should use supermajority rules to check the constitutionality of legislation since: (i) supermajority rules boost judges' accuracy more than majority rule; (ii) supermajority rules likely boost constitutional courts' reputation more than majority rule; and (iii) supermajority rules reflect the presumption of constitutionality of legislation. In this chapter, I also answer some of the main possible objections that may be raised against these claims.

In Chapter 7, I tackle some practical challenges that arise when applying supermajority rules in constitutional review. Specifically, in this chapter, I make three claims. First, when specifying the supermajority rule, one should choose the voting rule that's closest to majority rule. Second, when applying a supermajority rule—and provided a formal distinction between debating and voting—judges shouldn't see how their peers vote *at the time of voting*, but they should see how they did so *at the time of counting the votes.* Lastly, when mixing deliberation and voting, judges should only vote after discussing the case, and after it's clear that a unanimous agreement on its decision can't be reached.

I finish by presenting this book's general conclusion and an appendix. The appendix has two goals: first, it gives examples of current constitutional courts to which my claims likely apply; and second, it is a small database of these courts' decision procedures, hence serving as a starting point for more research. Specifically, the appendix addresses: (i) whether the respective court is a 'Kelsenian' court or a 'supreme' court; (ii) the number of judges in these courts; (iii) whether the judges generally decide constitutional cases in plenary sessions or by panels; (iv) the number of judges needed to get a quorum; (v) the voting rule for declaring statutes unconstitutional; and (vi) whether the judges are simply allowed to publish separate opinions, or whether they are obligated to do so if they have them. The appendix only considers constitutional courts of polities ranked as 'free' or as 'consolidated democracies' by Freedom House.

References

Ackerman BA, *We the People, vol 1: Foundations* (Harvard University Press 1993)

Altman D, *Direct Democracy Worldwide* (Cambridge University Press 2011) https://doi.org/10.1017/CBO9780511933950

Beitz CR, *Political Equality: An Essay in Democratic Theory* (Princeton University Press 1989) https://doi.org/10.1515/9780691221410

Bellamy R, *Political Constitutionalism: A Republican Defence of the Constitutionality of Democracy* (Cambridge University Press 2007) https://doi.org/10.1017/CBO9780511490187

Brewer-Carías AR, *Judicial Review in Comparative Law* (Cambridge University Press 1989)

Brennan J, *Against Democracy* (Princeton University Press 2016) https://doi.org/10.1515/9781400882939

Binmore K, *Rational Decisions* (Princeton University Press 2011) https://doi.org/10.1515/9781400833092

Cappelletti M, *Judicial Review in the Contemporary World* (Bobbs-Merrill 1971)

Carminker EH, 'Sincere and Strategic Voting Norms on Multimember Courts' (1999) 97 *Michigan Law Review* 2297 https://doi.org/10.2307/1290189

Carpio Marcos E & Grandez Castro P, 'Tribunal Constitucional (Perú)' ['Constitutional Court (Peru)'] in Ferrer Mac-Gregor E (coord) *Crónica de Tribunales Constitucionales en Iberoamerica [Chronicle of Constitutional Courts in Iberian America]* (UNAM Marcial Pons 2009)

Christiano T, *The Constitution of Equality: Democratic Authority and its Limits* (Oxford University Press 2008) https://doi.org/10.1093/acprof:oso/9780198297475.001.0001

Corley PC, Steigerwalt A & Ward A, *The Puzzle of Unanimity: Consensus on the United States Supreme Court* (Stanford Law Books 2013) https://doi.org/10.1515/9780804786324

Cross FB, 'Institutions and Enforcement of the Bill of Rights' (1999) 85 *Cornell Law Review 1529 http://scholarship.law.cornell.edu/clr/vol85/iss6/1*

Dahl RA, *Democracy and its Critics* (Yale University Press 1989)

Dworkin R, *Freedom's Law: The Moral Reading of the American Constitution* (Harvard University Press 1996)

——— *Justice for Hedgehogs* (Harvard University Press 2013)

Doerfler RD & Moyn SM, 'Democratizing the Supreme Court' (2021) 109 *California Law Review* 1703 https://www.californialawreview.org/print/democratizing-the-supreme-court

Ely JH, *Democracy and Distrust: A Theory of Judicial Review* (Harvard University Press 1980)

Entin J, 'Judicial Supermajorities and the Validity of Statutes: How Mapp Became a Fourth Amendment Landmark Instead of a First Amendment Footnote' (2001) 52(2) *Case Western Reserve Law Review 441 https://scholarlycommons.law.case.edu/caselrev/vol52/iss2/7*

Epstein L, Segal JA & Spaeth HJ, 'The Norm of Consensus in the US Supreme Court' (2001) 45 *American Journal of Political Science* 362 https://doi.org/10.2307/2669346

——— Segal JA, Spaeth HJ, & Walker TG, *The Supreme Court Compendium: Two Centuries of Data, Decisions, and Developments* (7th edn, CQ Press 2021)

Epps D & Sitaraman G, 'How to Save the Supreme Court' (2019) 129(1) *Yale Law Journal* 148 https://www.yalelawjournal.org/feature/how-to-save-the-supreme-court

Estlund DM, *Democratic Authority: A Philosophical Framework* (Princeton University Press 2008)

European Parliament, 'Dissenting Opinions in the Supreme Courts of the Member States' (PE 462.470, Directorate-General for Internal Policies. Policy Department C, Citizens' Rights and Constitutional Affairs, November 2012) <http://www.europarl.europa.eu/studies> accessed 30 September 2021

Fallon RH, 'The Core of an Uneasy Case for Judicial Review' (2008) 121 *Harvard Law Review* 1694 https://harvardlawreview.org/2008/05/the-core-of-an-uneasy-case-for-judicial-review/

Ferejohn J & Pasquino P, 'Constitutional Adjudication: Lessons from Europe' (2004) 82 *Texas Law Review 1671* https://heinonline.org/HOL/P?h=hein.journals/tlr82andi=1687

Ferrer Mac-Gregor E & Herrera García A. (2009), 'Suprema Corte de Justicia de la Nación (México)' ['Supreme Court of the Nation (Mexico)'] in Ferrer Mac-Gregor E (coord), *Crónica de Tribunales Constitucionales en Iberoamerica [Chronicle of Constitutional Courts in Iberian America] (*UNAM Marcial Pons 2009)

Gersen J & Vermeule A, 'Chevron as a Voting Rule' (2007) 116 *Yale Law Journal* 676 https://doi.org/10.2307/20455738

Gutmann A, *Liberal Equality* (Cambridge University Press 1980)

Harel A and Kahana T, 'The Easy Core Case for Judicial Review' (2010) 2 *Journal of Legal Analysis* 227 https://doi.org/10.1093/jla/2.1.227

Henderson MT, 'From Seriatim to Consensus and Back Again: A Theory of Dissent' (2007) 7 *Supreme Court Review* 283

Kay J & King M, *Radical Uncertainty: Decision-Making Beyond the Numbers* (WW Norton 2020)

Kelemen K, *Judicial Dissent in European Constitutional Courts: A Comparative and Legal Perspective* (Routledge 2019) https://doi.org/10.4324/9781315590769

Keynes JM, *A Treatise on Probability (first published 1920*, Cosimo 2007)

Krishnamurthi G, 'For Judicial Majoritarianism' (2020) 22 *University of Pennsylvania Journal of Constitutional Law 1201* https://scholarship.law.upenn.edu/jcl/vol22/iss5/2

Kumm M, 'Institutionalising Socratic Contestation: The Rationalist Human Rights Paradigm, Legitimate Authority, and the Point of Judicial Review' (2007) 1(2) *European Journal of Legal Studies* 153 http://hdl.handle.net/1814/7708

Lagerspetz E, *Social Choice and Democratic Values* (Springer 2016) https://doi.org/10.1007/978-3-319-23261-4

Landemore H, *Democratic Reason: Politics, Collective Intelligence and the Rule of the Many* (Princeton University Press 2013)

List C & Pettit P, *Group Agency: The Possibility, Design, and Status of Corporate Agents* (Cambridge University Press 2011) https://doi.org./10.1093/acprof:oso/9780199591565.001.0001

Morel L & Qvortrup M (eds), *The Routledge Handbook to Referendums and Direct Democracy* (Routledge 2018) https://doi.org/10.4324/9780203713181

North DC, *Institutions, Institutional Change and Economic Performance* (Cambridge University Press 1990) https://doi.org/10.1017/CBO9780511808678

Peirce CS, 'The Doctrine of Chances' in Houser K and Kloessel C (eds), *The Essential Peirce: Selected Philosophical Writings,* vol 1 (first published 1878a, Indiana University Press 1992)

Rawls J, *A Theory of Justice* (Revised edn, Harvard University Press 1999)

——— *Political Liberalism* (Expanded edn, Columbia University Press)

Raz J, *The Authority of Law: Essays on Law and Morality* (2nd edn, Oxford University Press 2009 https://doi.org/10.1093/acprof:oso/9780198253457.001.0001

Salamonte MF, 'Judicial Consensus and Public Opinion: Conditional Response to Supreme Court Majority Size' (2014) 67(2) *Political Research Quarterly* 320 https://doi.org/10.1177/1065912913497840

Schwartzberg M, *Counting the Many. The Origins and Limits of Supermajority Rule* (Cambridge University Press 2013) https://doi.org/10.1017/CBO9781139013970

Shugerman JH, 'A Six-Three Rule: Reviving Consensus and Deference on the Supreme Court' (2002) 37 *Georgia Law Review 893 https://heinonline.org/HOL/P?h=hein.journals/geolr37andi=915*

Stone Sweet A, 'Constitutional Courts' in Rosenfeld M and Sajó A (eds), *The Oxford Handbook of Comparative Constitutional Law* (Oxford University Press 2012) https://doi.org/10.1093/oxfordhb/9780199578610.013.0040

——— Tjosvold D & Field RHG, 'Effects of Social Context on Consensus and Majority Vote Decision Making' (1983) 26(3) *The Academy of Management Journal* 500 https://www.jstor.org/stable/256261

Tomkins A, *Our Republican Constitution* (Hart Publishing 2005) https://doi.org/10.5040/9781472559678

Waldron J, *Political Political Theory: Essays on Institutions* (Harvard University Press 2016) https://doi.org/10.4159/9780674970342

Yowell P, *Constitutional Rights and Constitutional Design: Moral and Empirical Reasoning in Judicial Review* (Hart Publishing 2018) https://doi.org/10.5040/9781509913626

Zellmer SB & Miller K, 'The Fallacy of Supermajority Clauses in State Constitutions' (2015) 47 *University of Toledo Law Review* 73 https://scholarship.law.umt.edu/faculty_lawreviews/163

Zink JR, Spriggs II JF & Scott JT, 'The Influence of Decision Attributes on Individuals' Views of Court Opinions' (2009) 71(3) *Journal of Politics* 909 https://doi.org/10.1017/s0022381609090793

2 Methodology

In this book, I build two arguments—also called 'central cases' or 'core cases'[1]—against and for some voting rules in constitutional review, respectively. The first core case is *against* majority rule in constitutional review, while the second core case is *for* supermajority rules in this practice. Thus, the point of this book is to present reasons that, given some assumptions: (i) justify eliminating majority rule to declare statutes unconstitutional; and (ii) justify replacing majority rule with supermajority rules to declare statutes unconstitutional. Put differently, in this book, I hold that, given some assumptions, there isn't enough normative support for majority rule over other voting rules to check the constitutionality of legislation; and that there's a stronger normative support for supermajority rules rather than for majority rule to perform this task.

My core cases are akin to those built for or against some forms of constitutional review by Waldron,[2] Fallon,[3] Harel & Kahana,[4] Dixon,[5] and Hickey,[6] among others. As in many of these cases, my core cases are restrictive. My core cases are *conditioned* arguments: they are arguments that mainly apply when their assumptions hold, but not necessarily otherwise. The idea isn't to deny the existence of 'non-core cases.' That is, cases in which these assumptions don't hold. Instead, the idea is to 'give explanatory priority in philosophical argument to cases that are fully responsive to the reasons'[7] against and for majority rule and supermajority rules in constitutional review, respectively—the idea is to mainly analyse cases in which *it makes the most sense* to eliminate majority rule (and use supermajority rules instead) to check the constitutionality of legislation. After all, it's only by analysing core cases that one may detect what non-core cases lack.

1 On the core case method, see Webber et al 2018; Webber & Yowell 2020. For a critique, see Roux 2018.
2 Waldron 2016: ch 9.
3 Fallon 2008.
4 Harel & Kahana 2010.
5 Dixon 2017.
6 Hickey 2019.
7 Webber et al 2018: 3.

DOI: 10.4324/9781032723952-2

Hence, this book is mainly normative—not empirical. It isn't mainly about how constitutional courts' voting rules *are,* but about how they *should be.* I don't focus on refuting factual claims made about constitutional review. Rather, I focus on presenting arguments that I try to defend. Still, though this book is mainly normative, I consider empirical and mathematical research when building my claims. Thus, I proceed inductively. I consider historical research on voting rules in Western civilisation,[8] social choice research,[9] and empirical research in group decision making.[10] Additionally, I consider philosophical research on majority rule's justifications,[11] and comparative constitutional law[12] and political science research;[13] especially to identify the kinds of constitutional courts—and the kinds of polities[14]—to which my claims apply.

Now, although I consider empirical research, my claims on supermajority rules' effects in constitutional review are mainly *hypotheses*: they are guesses, conjectures, hunches, or inferences on what may happen if we replace majority rule with supermajority rules to declare statutes unconstitutional.[15] True, my claims are educated, research-based guesses. But they are still just guesses. Thus, they may be empirically refuted.[16] In this sense—and just as economists[17] and mathematicians[18] do—my claims build a *model:* they build a picture of what may happen if we apply supermajority rules in constitutional review. Yet, whether that model holds true remains to be seen. More research, or small-scale, context-sensitive experimentation, is needed.

I work this way for three reasons. First, there's too little empirical research on judicial decision making outside the US,[19] and most of it doesn't tackle courts deciding by supermajority rules.[20] Second, this research is mainly correlational (hence not being very informative about causation), and it doesn't tackle voting rules' effects, but links courts' decisions with variables such as

8 Eg, see Staveley 1972; Gaudemet et al 1979; Manin 1997; Lagerspetz 2010; Colomer & McLean 1998; Schwartzberg 2013.

9 For overviews of this research, see List & Pettit 2011; Landemore 2013: ch 6-7; Lagerspetz 2016.

10 For overviews of this research, see Saks 1997; Sunstein 2006; Vidmar & Hans 2007; Devine 2012; Barry 2021.

11 Eg, see Dahl 1989: ch 7; Rawls 1999: 194-200; Christiano 2008: ch 3; Dworkin 2013: ch 18.

12 Eg, see Cappelletti 1971; Brewer-Carías 1989; Stone Sweet 2012.

13 Eg, see Linz & Stepan 1996; Levitsky & Ziblatt 2018; Mounk 2018; Ginsburg & Huq 2019.

14 I use the word 'polities' rather than 'countries' due to Taiwan's international situation.

15 Peirce [1878] 1992; Popper 2002: ch 4.

16 Popper 2002: ch 4.

17 Rodrik 2016.

18 Binmore 2011; Kay & King 2020.

19 Barry 2021: 1–4.

20 For exceptions, see Carroll & Tiede 2011; Couso & Hilbink 2011; Sánchez et al 2011; Garoupa et al 2013; Cortés Salinas 2014; Tiede & Ponce 2014; Garoupa & Grembi 2015; Seok Hong 2019.

judges' alleged political views.[21] Lastly, though the results of jury decision making research may apply to constitutional courts,[22] juries usually decide by unanimity rule and have other key institutional differences against courts—eg, having lay members, not having to justify their decisions, etc.—that question whether the results of this research can be safely transplanted to judicial contexts. The same can be argued about the results of experiments made by deliberative democracy scholars involving mini publics, such as citizens' juries and deliberative polls.[23]

Now that I've addressed the point of this book, let's present the assumptions underlying it.

Assumptions

I work under eight assumptions. I assume that: (i) there are substantive standards under which judges may be 'accurate' as a group; (ii) due to reasonable disagreement, statutes must be presumed constitutional; (iii) my claims mainly apply to 'well-functioning democracies;' (iv) my claims mainly apply to some 'strong-form' constitutional review systems; (v) my claims mainly apply to legislative actions—not legislative omissions; (vi) judges vote on conclusions; (vii) judicial deliberation is cognitively or epistemically sound; and (viii) institutional variables other than voting rules stay constant.

Let's develop these assumptions.

Substantive Standards

First, I assume that there are 'substantive' (or 'procedure-independent') standards, yardsticks, or criteria in constitutional review: I assume that there are some 'truths' for answering constitutional questions 'rightly' or 'correctly,' and that these truths don't depend on constitutional review as a procedure, but are found outside it. Following Rawls, I assume that constitutional review isn't a case of 'pure procedural justice,' but a case of 'imperfect procedural justice.'[24] I don't consider constitutional review as a practice in which decisions' rightness only depends on fulfilling certain procedures, but as a practice in which there are substantive standards for assessing decisions as 'right' or 'wrong,' 'good' or 'bad,' 'true' or 'false,' etc. Simply put, statutes aren't constitutional or unconstitutional just because some judges say so following

21 Eg, see Epstein & Knight 1998; Segal & Spaeth 2002; Sunstein et al 2006; Corley et al 2013: ch 1; Epstein et al 2013; Songer et al 2014).

22 Saks 1997; Vidmar & Hans 2007; Devine 2012.

23 Among other differences, mini publics differ from courts in that their members are laypeople that are usually chosen by random selection methods, and that if they vote, they do so secretly. For overviews of research on mini publics, see Fishkin 2009; Mendelberg 2002; Delli Carpini et al 2004; Ryfe 2005; Steiner 2012; Neblo 2015; Fishkin 2018; Smith & Setälä 2018.

24 Rawls 1999: 74–9. See also Kornhauser & Sager 1986: 82, 85–6; Landemore 2013: ch 8.

some procedures, but because—in a way—statutes *really* are constitutional or unconstitutional.

Once one accepts substantive standards, just as an individual may be more or less 'accurate'—in the sense of being able to make right decisions according to a substantive standard (or, put differently, in the sense of being able to 'track the truth,' of making right decisions according to the truth)—groups may also be more or less accurate. So, I use the concept 'group accuracy'[25] to refer to a group's skill at making right decisions according to a substantive standard. This concept applies to constitutional courts since these institutions are made of groups of judges that collectively resolve cases. (For stylistic purposes, whenever I refer to 'judges' accuracy,' I am referring to their accuracy *as a group*.)

Assuming substantive standards doesn't necessarily imply endorsing 'moral objectivity;' meaning, it doesn't necessarily imply accepting that these standards stem from universally valid basic values. One can endorse substantive standards even if one is a 'moral relativist.' That is, even if one considers these standards as based on agreements that are in turn based on purely contingent facts, such as the cultural, economic, historical, and political forces that shape a legal system.[26] Thus, though one *can* be a moral objectivist when endorsing substantive standards, one doesn't *have to* be a moral objectivist to do so. Between the objective and the subjective lies the inter-subjective.[27] As it occurs with other social phenomena—such as states, money, or companies (phenomena that the historian Yuval Noah Harari aptly calls 'imagined orders')[28]—in law, one can hold that substantive standards exist since they are based on 'the communication network linking the subjective consciousness of many individuals.'[29] Put differently, one may claim that the constitutionality of legislation hinges on substantive standards just because many people believe in such standards.

Understood this way, substantive standards aren't only compatible with value-laden theories of legal interpretation (eg, Dworkin's);[30] they are also compatible with more 'rhetorical' theories of legal interpretation, such as those of Phillip Bobbitt[31] and Theodor Viehweg.[32] Indeed, Bobbitt's 'constitutional

25 I take this concept from Kornhauser & Sager 1986. With the word 'group,' I indicate that it isn't an individual, but a collective that must decide rightly. For akin concepts, see List & Pettit 2011: 82; Landemore 2013: 17–23.
26 Kornhauser & Sager 1986: 85–6; Landemore 2013: 217–9.
27 Harari 2014: 116–8; Harari 2016: 143–9.
28 Harari 2014: 116–8; Harari 2016: 143–9.
29 Harari 2014: 117.
30 1986.
31 1984: 6–8, 230–4.
32 2016: ch 3.

arguments'[33] and Viehweg's 'topics'[34] can only convince others if arguers and listeners share somewhat common views of what are 'good' arguments or topics. Hence, I assume substantive standards though I'm agnostic as to their basis.

Further, to assume substantive standards doesn't necessarily mean one must fully distill, refine, or 'unpack' the contents of these standards to make deductive inferences. Rather, one may work inductively: one may hold that, due to their features, properties, or traits, different policies or institutions likely produce good results under different substantive standards, broadly understood. One can see this approach in David Estlund's[35] and Hélène Landemore's[36] claims that democracies likely outperform other political systems; and in Charles Lindblom's's[37] claim that, when facing moral disagreement, the 'litmus test' of good policies is whether people holding different moral views agree on them. In these cases, substantive standards are recognised without further ado. Instead, these authors suggest that, due to the traits of a policy or institution, people endorsing different moral views may agree that such policy or institution likely realises their values. So, rather than developing fully-fledged views of substantive standards, one may try to produce 'overlapping consensus'[38] or 'incompletely theorised agreements'[39] on policies or institutions according to different substantive standards.

I follow this approach. Thus, though I assume substantive standards in constitutional review, I don't 'wed,' wholeheartedly agree, or get fully on board with any theory specifying their content (eg, Ely's,[40] Dworkin's,[41] Ackerman's,[42] etc.). Instead, I try to be ecumenical. I take these theories' basic premise—substantive standards—and claim that, considering majority rule's and supermajority rules' traits, there are strong reasons to prefer the latter rules over the former rule to realise these standards.

Some may object that substantive standards in constitutional review are doubtful since, in hard cases, people strongly disagree on constitutional courts' decisions. This claim has merit. Yet the claim isn't exactly that there are no right constitutional review decisions; the claim is that such assessment is *uncertain*:[43] that it's very hard to identify constitutional courts' decisions as

33 Bobbitt 1984: 6–8, 230–4.
34 Viehweg 2016: ch 3.
35 2008.
36 2013.
37 1959: 81, 83–4.
38 Rawls 2005.
39 Sunstein 2006: ch 2.
40 1980.
41 1996.
42 1993.
43 Unlike many economists, I don't fully distinguish between 'risk' and 'uncertainty.' Rather—following Taleb—I treat these concepts as synonyms and assume that there are different

right, and thus that it's very hard to gauge the odds that such decisions are right. But this only means that constitutional review is tricky—not that it can't be done rightly.[44] True, there may not be any substantive standards in constitutional review, yet to claim that this practice is tricky isn't enough to prove so. Additionally, there are methods for deciding under uncertainty. These methods assume substantive standards even when it's very hard to identify (and thus gauge the odds of) right decisions. Some of these methods support supermajority rules in constitutional review. I tackle these methods in Chapter 6.

Presumption of Constitutionality of Legislation

Second, I assume that, many times, citizens reasonably disagree on moral issues, and that these disagreements ground a presumption of constitutionality of legislation. Following Rawls,[45] I call these disagreements 'reasonable' to note that: (i) these disagreements ***don't*** stem from citizens acting wrongly or in bad faith; (ii) citizens' opposing opinions during these disagreements can be grounded in the constitution; and (iii) the reasons supporting citizens' opinions during these disagreements are—or at least, seem—equally strong. Obviously, reasonable disagreements mainly show themselves in hard constitutional cases.

Reasonable disagreement is a key claim against constitutional review.[46] If there's something at the core of constitutional review's 'counter-majoritarian difficulty,'[47] that something is reasonable disagreement; so much so that no serious defence of this practice can ignore it. In its most *Jacobin* versions (eg, Bellamy's[48] and Waldron's),[49] reasonable disagreement is a decisive reason for eliminating constitutional review, or at least eliminating its application to open-ended constitutional provisions.[50] In turn, in its most *Girondin* versions (eg, Thayer's),[51] reasonable disagreement is a strong factor for binding judges' interpretive powers; particularly through 'deferential' or 'restrictive' adjudicative methods.[52]

I work on *Girondin* grounds. So, despite reasonable disagreement, I assume that constitutional review is justified. I'm not convinced by 'disagreement-all-the-way-down' claims; meaning, I don't consider the claims made by

degrees of risk (2019: 127-9). On the distinction between risk and uncertainty, see Knight 2018.

44 Dworkin 2013: 90–6, 178–9.

45 2005.

46 Tomkins 2005; Bellamy 2007; Waldron 2016: ch 9.

47 Bickel 1962.

48 2007.

49 2016: ch 9.

50 Hans Kelsen argues similarly, though he doesn't use the term 'reasonable disagreement' (2015).

51 1893.

52 For an overview of this literature in English, see King 2008.

Bellamy[53] and Waldron,[54] among others, as strong enough to eliminate constitutional review. I share the worry that, when unchecked by constitutional courts, elected officials may gravely violate people's rights, especially if the affected belong to vulnerable minorities. And, due to the claims developed by authors such as Ely,[55] Rawls,[56] and Dworkin,[57] there's a strong case for constitutional review.

Still, reasonable disagreement is a key factor for shaping constitutional review. Specifically, reasonable disagreement justifies a presumption of constitutionality of legislation.[58] Given reasonable disagreement, statutes should be presumed constitutional unless there are sound reasons to declare them unconstitutional. When there's reasonable disagreement, citizens hold views that seem (or are) supported by equally strong constitutionally permissible reasons, but that are generally incompatible.[59] As Waldron claims, 'the fact that people disagree about [the constitution] does not mean that there must be one party that does not take [it] seriously.'[60] Instead, what may happen is that citizens hold sound moral views that fall within the scope of the constitution, but that also go against each other.

One may argue for reasonable disagreement even after assuming substantive standards. Though substantive standards imply right answers to constitutional questions, these standards don't necessarily imply *single* right answers to them. As it's been claimed in morality, in constitutional interpretation, once the bad is avoided, the good may be plural.[61] Thus, in morality and in constitutional review, beyond banning some bad actions (eg, torture, arresting someone without prior judicial warrants, depriving someone of legal recourses against criminal charges, etc.), substantive standards may support more than one incompatible right decisions. For example, even if a standard states that we shouldn't usually kill animals for food, that standard may not indicate whether one should become a vegetarian, a vegan, or an omnivore that only eats cultured meat. All of these lifestyles may be right under the same standard. Likewise, even if a constitutional standard requires the State to regulate, operate, and finance a health care system, that standard may not determine if only the State should provide some medical treatments—or whether these treatments may also be provided by private agents under certain conditions. Both practices may be constitutionally permissible under that same standard.

53 2007.
54 2016: ch 9.
55 Ely 1980.
56 Rawls 2005: 158–63, 227–8.
57 Dworkin 1996: 8, 16–7, 23–6.
58 The US Supreme Court reasoned similarly in *Borden's Farms Prods Co v Baldwin* 293 US 194, 209 (1934).
59 Rawls 2005: 54–6, 240–6; Waldron 2016: 210.
60 Waldron 2016: 210.
61 For authors that take this view, see Berlin 2002; Raz 2009.

When we reasonably disagree, Rawls' 'burdens of judgment'[62] may apply; meaning, the respective issues may be so hard that, considering our bounds (of time, resources, knowledge, skills, etc.) we can't find a single right answer. And it may happen that, even if one overcomes these limits, the values at stake may be immensurable[63] or on a par;[64] hence being no strong enough reasons to prefer any reasonable views against opposing ones. (Actually, even Dworkin accepted this possibility.)[65] Therefore, in many cases, even after assuming that the constitution may be rightly interpreted, it's seldom possible to find '*a* best' moral view compatible with it. Conversely, there may be more than one 'good enough' view—'good enough' as in 'being supported by reasons that seem (or are) as strong as the reasons supporting the contrary view'—that, while fitting with the constitution, don't fit well with each other.

If people are political equals, when facing reasonable disagreement, the issues behind constitutional disputes should mainly be resolved by citizens themselves (through referenda) or by their elected representatives. Thus, though constitutional review is justifiable, judges should consider reasonable disagreement when checking statutes; hence not declaring them unconstitutional when there are strong indications that such disagreements occur.

True, even when acting in good faith, citizens may disagree about the constitution since they are wrong, for they may not have the right data about its factual and normative grounds. Or they may not have the time, resources, inclination, or skill to search and understand that data.[66] And citizens may act badly when arguing about hard issues.[67] People may oppose criminalising 'hate-speech' not since they value freedom of expression, but since they want to impunely spread their racism. Likewise, people may want to limit immigration not to guard public safety, but to ease their cultural anxieties. Something similar may happen in other controversies, in which citizens may pay lip service to the constitution, its core values, or the idea of rights.

Yet, as Rawls held, it's 'unrealistic ... to suppose that all our differences are rooted solely in ignorance and perversity, or else in rivalries for power, status

62 2005: 54–6, 240–46.

63 I understand 'immensurability' (also called 'incommensurability') as a synonym of 'incomparabiliy.' Thus, immensurabilty is the impossibility of ranking two or more things using common ordinal or cardinal scales. Put differently, immensurability means that it isn't possible to claim that one thing is 'better,' 'worse,' or 'as good as' others according to such scales. On immensurability generally, see De Sousa 1974; Sinnott-Armstrong 1985; Griffin 1988: ch 5; Chang 1997; Berlin 2002; Raz 2009: ch 13.

64 According to Ruth Chang, in most cases of alleged immensurability, it's still possible to compare things. For Chang, this is due to a comparative relation between things called 'parity' or 'on a par' (2014). See also Caviedes 2017.

65 2013: 90–6, 178–9.

66 These are also manifestations of Rawls' burdens of judgment (2005: 54–6, 240–6).

67 On how social commitments to democracy and basic rights have deteriorated in many countries, see Levitsky & Ziblatt 2018: ch 4; Mounk 2018: ch 3; Ginsburg & Huq 2019; Sadurski 2019.

or economic gain.'[68] As cliché as it sounds, life is complicated. Our common human life—including our common *moral* life—is just far too complex to pretend that it can be fully captured by our ideas. Reducing all conflict to error or bad faith is too simplistic. As hard as it is—and let's not fool ourselves, this is very hard to do, particularly since our self-righteousness may have evolutionary roots[69]—one should recognise a space for reasonable disagreement. Thus, one may claim that constitutional courts should account for reasonable disagreement when assessing the constitutionality of legislation; especially considering political equality's relevance as one of democracy's key tenets.

Well-Functioning Democracies

Third, I focus on 'well-functioning democracies.' This concept is based on Linz and Stepan's idea of 'consolidated democracies,'[70] and on Waldron's assumptions for his core case against constitutional review.[71] Moreover, this concept overlaps with Ginsburg and Huq's idea of 'liberal constitutional democracy.'[72] At a more practical level, this concept likely applies to at least some of the polities indicated in the appendix. That is, polities ranked as 'free' according to Freedom House's 'Freedom in the World Report 2023,'[73] and polities ranked as 'consolidated democracies' according to Freedom House' 'Nations in Transit Report 2023.'[74]

Well-functioning democracies are polities that possess three main properties. First, in these polities, most citizens must believe that 'democratic procedures and institutions are the most appropriate way [of governing] collective life,'[75] hence behaving accordingly. Thus, in well-functioning democracies, there mustn't be any main political actors trying to create a non-democratic regime, or violently secede from the State. And most citizens must generally reject pursuing political ends through violent means.[76]

68 Rawls 2005: 58.

69 According to some of the latest psychological research, reason didn't evolve as a tool for thinking accurately about issues, but as a tool for promoting long-term cooperation. This partly explains why we build key parts of our identities around some beliefs, and it partly explains why it's hard to discard such beliefs when presented with new data. Haidt 2012; Mercier & Sperber 2017.

70 1996

71 2016: 202–12.

72 Ginsburg & Huq's concept is more limited than mine since it only includes: (i) a 'democratic electoral system'; (ii) the 'liberal rights to speech and association that are closely linked to democracy in practice'; and (iii) the 'rule of law' (2019: 9–15).

73 2023a.

74 2023b.

75 Linz & Stepan 1996: 16.

76 Id 15–6.

Second, in well-functioning democracies, representative assemblies and courts must be in 'reasonably good working order' (as described by Waldron).[77] On representative assemblies—such as legislatures, municipal councils, etc.—this implies that representatives must be elected by 'universal adult suffrage … on a fair and regular basis.'[78] And that they must argue and decide on state policies under 'elaborate and responsible'[79] procedures that 'incorporate various safeguards and multiple levels of consultation, debate, and voting.'[80] On courts, a reasonably good working order implies that: (i) judges must generally be appointed instead of elected, and their role shouldn't be understood as that of representing citizens; (ii) along with resolving private disputes, judges must be able to check the constitutionality (or legality) of administrative acts; (iii) judges must act as third parties in disputes. Thus, they mustn't usually act ex officio, but adjudicate when required to do so by others; and (iv) the judicial office must be organised in ways that guard judicial independence, especially against other officials and citizens at large.[81]

Finally, in well-functioning democracies, most citizens must support the idea of rights, though they may have deep, good faith moral disagreements about their content. Thus, in well-functioning democracies, most citizens must 'accept that individuals have certain interests … that should not be denied simply because it would be more convenient for most people to deny them'[82]. Yet, though most citizens must endorse rights, they need not endorse a specific conception of these rights. So, in these polities, 'the consensus about rights is not exempt from the incidence of general disagreement about all major [moral] issues which we find in modern … societies.'[83] For example, in well-functioning democracies, when interpreting the right to life, citizens may reasonably disagree on how to regulate abortion; when interpreting free-speech, citizens may reasonably disagree on whether to ban lobbying, or bind campaign spending; when interpreting the right to health, citizens may reasonably disagree on how to organise and finance a health care system; etc.[84]

Another way of identifying well-functioning democracies is *via negativa* or by exclusion; meaning, by indicating which polities *aren't* so. Thus, my claims neither apply to polities usually ranked as 'not free' or 'partially free' by Freedom House,[85] nor to polities in which democracy has acutely backslid,

77 2016: 203.
78 Id 204.
79 Id.
80 Id.
81 Id 203–5.
82 Id 207.
83 Id 209.
84 Id 207–12.
85 Freedom House 2023a.

eroded, or de-consolidated.[86] So, following Mounk,[87] my claims don't apply to polities in which most citizens are no longer committed to democracy as a political system. This includes not rejecting authoritarian options—or even being overtly open to military rule. Further, my claims don't apply to polities in which rulers no longer respect basic legal and social norms necessary for a democracy's proper functioning. Put differently, my claims don't apply to polities in which officials regularly play 'constitutional hardball,'[88] pushing their legal boundaries to the limit, and behaving as if 'winning … important election[s] and passing … urgent law[s] [are more] important than preserving the system.'[89]

In sum, my claims don't apply to polities in which officials—among other things—regularly

> re-write electoral rules months before an election to maximize [their] chance[s] of winning, … glorify authoritarian rulers of the past, threaten to lock up their opponents, or set out to violate the rights of ethnic and religious minorities, … [limit] the scope of an office to which and adversary has been elected in their last days on the job, … or [does not confirm] a competent judge whose ideology [they] dislike rather than leaving a seat of the highest court in the land vacant.[90]

To be even more precise, my claims don't apply to polities such as Hungary, Poland, Turkey, and Venezuela.

Yet, to neutralise Poland's Constitutional Tribunal, the Polish Government tried to apply a 2/3 rule for voiding statutes.[91] Hence, governments may try to erode a democracy by implementing a supermajority rule to check the constitutionality of legislation in their courts. This means I should refer to the Polish case though my claims don't apply to it. For now, I bracket the Polish case. But I tackle this case in detail in Chapter 6.

Strong-Form Systems

Fourth, among well-functioning democracies, I mainly focus on constitutional review systems that share certain traits. Specifically, I focus on 'strong-form'[92]

86 This includes the polities in Central Europe and Central Asia which aren't 'consolidated democracies' according to Freedom House's 'Nations in Transit 2023' report. Freedom House 2023b. On democratic erosion generally, see Levitsky & Ziblatt 2018: ch 4; Mounk 2018: ch 3; Ginsburg & Huq 2019: ch 4.

87 2018: ch 3.

88 Tushnet 2004. See also Levitsky & Ziblatt 2018: 106–11.

89 Mounk 2018: 113.

90 Id.

91 Levitsky & Ziblatt 2018: 80; Ginsburg & Huq 2019: 98–101; Sadurski 2019.

92 Tushnet 2003.

systems with odd numbers of judges, and in which judges debate secretly, but in which they may publish separate opinions. Let's analyse these traits in more detail.

In this book, I mainly analyse strong-form constitutional review systems. These are systems in which: (i) there's a written constitution with a bill of rights;[93] (ii) generally speaking, this constitution may only be amended by legislative supermajority rules, though it may have unamendable provisions; (iii) constitutional provisions (including rights provisions) may be directly applied by constitutional courts to check the constitutionality of legislation; and (iv) after such review, these courts may annul, invalidate, or strike down statutes—that is, they may void statutes with general effects[94]—or they may dis-apply statutes in specific cases, but this remedy is joined by a doctrine of precedent (or procedural rules)[95] allowing them to keep a jurisprudential line.[96] Thus, in the US, my claims extend to 'facial' and 'as-applied' challenges to legislation;[97] while in other polities, my claims extend to 'abstract' and 'concrete' challenges to legislation.[98] Put differently, my claims involve cases in which a statute itself is declared unconstitutional, and cases in which the way in which such a statute is applied in particular cases is declared unconstitutional. I focus on strong-form systems since they are the most common (and the most questioned) worldwide. So, I don't focus on constitutional review systems such as those of New Zealand and the UK.[99]

Due to this focus, I assume that, once a statute is declared unconstitutional, the default remedy is annulment or dis-application. Many constitutional courts try to harmonise statutes with the constitution via interpretation. And many times, after declaring a statute unconstitutional, courts avoid voiding or dis-applying it by changing its prima facie meaning—or even by adding new norms.[100] Lastly, many times, constitutional courts avoid voiding or dis-applying statutes, or delay the effects of annulments or dis-applications, to prevent normative gaps.[101] Still, it's reasonable to suppose that annulment or dis-application are default remedies. Strong-form systems are designed assuming that

93 I don't include Israel among the analysed polities since it's heavily discussed whether Israel has a constitution in the sense presented in this book. For an overview of this debate, see Weill 2012.

94 Kelsen 1942: 44–7.

95 Eg, see Uru Proc Code, art 519.

96 Cappelletti 1971: 85–8.

97 On this distinction—and some of its challenges—see Dorf 1994; Kreit 2010.

98 Stone Sweet 2012: 822–4.

99 Gardbaum 2013. Canada is a borderline case. Though the Canadian court's decisions declaring statutes unconstitutional produce legal effects, Parliament and provincial legislatures can immunise statutes by applying section 33 of Canada's Charter of Rights and Freedoms. But this section has been used sparingly, and its use has carried heavy political costs. Thus, I consider the Canadian system as a strong-form system. See Kahana 2001; Weinrib 2016: 163–4.

100 Ferreres Comella 2009: 112–6; Brewer-Carías 2011: 73–94.

101 Brewer-Carías 2011: 95–102; Yowell 2018: 159–62.

judges shouldn't generally behave as positive legislators: they are designed assuming that judges shouldn't generally enact new statutes, either directly or via interpretation. Thus, absent strong reasons against it, once a statute is declared unconstitutional, that statute should be voided or dis-applied since there's an incompatibility between a 'lower law' (a statute) and a 'higher law' (the constitution).[102] Hence, even if judges may use other remedies, to assume that—analytically speaking—annulment or dis-application are default remedies is sensible.

Further, among strong-form systems, I focus on courts with odd numbers of judges. I focus on these courts since, in courts with even numbers of judges, when ties occur, supermajority rules' benefits may be achieved by eliminating the presiding judge's casting vote, as happens in the German court.[103] My core case for supermajority rules in constitutional review heavily depends on their non-neutrality. That is, it depends on supermajority rules' capacity to guard a worthy status quo (in this case, the presumption of constitutionality of legislation). But in even-judges courts, absent a casting vote—and given that statutes are presumed constitutional—majority rule becomes non-neutral, hence sharing supermajority rules' traits. After all, without a casting vote, when ties happen in these courts, defied statutes stay constitutional.[104] Thus, in even-judges courts, my core case should be interpreted as supporting the elimination of casting votes.

Finally, I focus on courts in which judges debate secretly, but in which they may publish separate (that is, concurring or dissenting) opinions. So, I don't focus on courts in which judges' inner debates are broadcast to the public (most notably, Brazil's[105] and Mexico's)[106]—nor do I focus on courts in which the publication of separate opinions is banned, such as Belgium's, France's, or Italy's.[107]

I only focus on courts in which judges debate secretly—but in which they may publish separate opinions—since, as Ferejohn and Pasquino,[108] da Silva,[109] do Vale,[110] Pou Giménez,[111] and others have claimed, what the judges may disclose to the public can heavily affect whether they deliberate among themselves and the manner of such deliberations.[112] Using the Brazilian court as

102 Hamilton [1878] 2015: 91–4; *Marbury v Madison,* 5 US 137 (1805); Kelsen 2015: 65.
103 Kelemen 2019: 30–5.
104 Lagerspetz 2016: 36–8.
105 da Silva 2013; do Vale 2017.
106 Ferrer Mac-Gregor & Herrera 2009: 33–4.
107 European Parliament 2012: 17–9; Kelemen 2019: ch 4.
108 Ferejohn & Pasquino 2004: 1692–700. See also Pasquino 2015: 201–8.
109 da Silva 2013.
110 do Vale 2017.
111 Pou Giménez 2017: 213-18.
112 On the tensions between secrecy and publicity of debates in all kinds of groups, see Shapiro 2002; Chambers 2004. For an overview of empirical research tackling how publicity influences deliberation in groups other than courts—including the US Federal Reserve—see

an example, da Silva[113] holds that publishing judges' inner debates hinders their willingness to change their minds out of fear that this will damage their reputation. As da Silva argues, 'the bigger the audience, the higher the risk of "losing face" when one has to admit that [one's] arguments are untenable.'[114] Therefore, in da Silva's view, publishing judges' inner debates curbs deliberation among themselves, since one of deliberation's core values is one's willingness to change one's opinion when presented with sound reasons to do so.

Moreover, and arguing along da Silva's lines, Ferejohn and Pasquino[115] distinguish between 'internal deliberation'—that is, deliberation among the judges—and 'external deliberation.' That is, deliberation that extends beyond the judges to include other agents, such as other officials, journalists, and citizens generally. For these authors, there's a tension between internal and external deliberation. If everything happening inside a constitutional court is secret, there's little accountability. But if everything happening inside a constitutional court is public, there are strong incentives for judges to develop and protect a coherent public image instead of rationally engaging with their peers. In Ferejohn and Pasquino's view,[116] in some European courts—particularly those of France, Italy, Germany, and Spain—judges have developed a collaborative culture. Thus, in these courts, judges try to reach unanimous decisions whenever possible. For Ferejohn and Pasquino,[117] this means that, in these courts, judges tend to deliberate among themselves more than in the US Supreme Court. And in the case of the Italian and French courts, this collaborative culture is linked to the fact that judges can't publish separate opinions.[118]

So, since different publicity levels may heavily boost or hinder deliberation among judges, I can't seriously claim that supermajority rules may have the same effects on judicial deliberation if the examined courts vary on what they can publish. Thus, in this book, I neither include courts in which judges' inner debates are public, nor do I include courts in which judges are banned from publicly concurring or dissenting with their peers.

Steiner 2012: 127–30. Much of this research questions whether publicity aids deliberation among group members.

113 da Silva 2013: 579–83.

114 Id 583.

115 Ferejohn & Pasquino 2004: 1692–700.

116 Id. See also Baum 2019: 116–9; Kelemen 2019: ch 4.

117 Id.

118 In the case of the German court, this culture has developed even though judges may publish separate opinions. Indeed, in the German court decisions are usually issued per curiam; meaning, they are issued as decisions 'of the court as a whole.' So, the only opinion that is usually published is that of most judges, which in turn is unsigned. Ferejohn & Pasquino 2004: 1692-700; Kelemen 2019: 86–9.

Legislative Actions

Fifth, I focus on legislative actions—not legislative omissions. My claims tackle constitutional courts' voting rules when declaring *enacted statutes* unconstitutional—not when declaring the *lack of statutes* unconstitutional. Specifically, my core case for supermajority rules in constitutional review doesn't apply to situations in which legislatures haven't enacted legislation that they are constitutionally bound to enact, and the respective court declares such omission unconstitutional.[119] (Some legislation that usually falls into this category is that regulating electoral systems; power distributions between institutions; administrative, legislative, or judicial procedures; etc.) To be more precise, my core case for supermajority rules in constitutional review doesn't apply to situations in which—though obligated to do so—legislatures haven't legislated on some issues at all.[120]

As we'll see in more detail in Chapter 6, my core case for supermajority rules in constitutional review highly depends on error asymmetry; meaning, it highly depends on the idea that mistakenly declaring statutes unconstitutional (what I call 'false positives') is worse than mistakenly not doing so (what I call 'false negatives'). In turn, error asymmetry is based on two claims: first, false positives are intrinsically worse than false negatives since they infringe majority government[121] and void constitutionally acceptable decisions; and second, false positives are worse than false negatives since they are harder to rectify than false negatives. But these claims don't necessarily apply to legislative omissions. It's doubtful to hold that mistakenly declaring legislative omissions unconstitutional is worse than mistakenly not doing so. This is because it's doubtful to hold that mistakenly declaring legislative omissions unconstitutional infringes majority government.

Broadly speaking, the idea of majority government seems to imply that legislatures at least have discretion on: (i) whether to regulate an issue; and (ii) once it's decided that an issue should be regulated, how to regulate it. Yet in legislative omissions, legislatures' discretion is limited. In these cases, legislatures are bound to enact some statutes: legislatures can only make discretionary decisions on (ii), they can't make discretionary decisions on (i). Put differently, legislatures can't choose whether to regulate an issue, they can

119 Verdugo Ramírez 2009; Brewer-Carías 2011: ch 4; Al-Dulaimi 2018: ch 4–5.

120 Conversely, this core case applies to cases in which legislatures have legislated on such issues, but the respective constitutional court finds that legislation incomplete or discriminatory. Brewer-Carías 2011: ch 4. After all, these latter cases happen when courts check the constitutionality of enacted legislation.

121 I understand 'majority government' as government by the majority of citizens—or by the majority of citizens' elected representatives. I return to this concept in Chapter 6. I use the word 'majority government' rather than 'democracy,' 'majority democracy,' or 'majoritarian democracy' due to the highly contested nature of what democracy stands for, and thus on what it really demands.

only choose how to regulate it. Thus, in legislative omissions, a key aspect of majority government is challenged.

Moreover, in legislative omissions, legislatures may rectify all potential errors that constitutional courts may make through normal legislative procedures: they may rectify these errors by enacting new statutes. Thus, in legislative omissions, it's also doubtful to claim that some errors are harder to rectify than others. Therefore, my argument for using supermajority rules to check the constitutionality of legislation doesn't seem to justify these voting rules to check legislative omissions. Hence, I leave these omissions from the analysis.

Conclusion-Voting

Sixth, I assume that judges regularly decide by counting their conclusions on the constitutionality of legislation—not by counting their premises for supporting such conclusions. Thus, I focus on voting rules that count judges' claims that a statute is or isn't unconstitutional—not on voting rules that count the reasons behind these claims.

In judicial settings, voting is a decision procedure that counts *judgments* or *opinions*.[122] This means that, when voting, judges aren't counting mere preferences: they aren't counting claims that lack a rational basis and that speak only to the claimant's values or advantage. Instead, when voting, judges count 'truths'—they count claims that other people may endorse due to their supporting reasons.[123] Thus, unlike preferences, judgments are inter-subjective and reason-based. Due to their inter-subjective and reason-based nature, judgments are usually made of different propositions. Some of these propositions are premises, while others are conclusions.

According to Hecksher,[124] Vacca,[125] Kornhauser & Sager,[126] and List & Pettit,[127] group decisions can vary widely depending on whether groups' voting rules count premises or conclusions. Kornhauser & Sager call this phenomenon 'the doctrinal paradox,'[128] while List & Pettit call it 'the discursive dilemma.'[129] To show the paradox, suppose that Weirdland's[130] constitutional court must decide whether a statute compelling parents to vaccinate their children is unconstitutional on free-speech and religious freedom grounds. And

122 Though the word 'opinion' has a broader meaning than the word 'judgment,' in this book, I consider these words as synonyms for stylistic aims.
123 Kornhauser & Sager 1986: 85; Pasquino 2015: 198-9. See also Brennan & Pettit 1990.
124 Cited in Lagerspetz 2016.
125 2013.
126 1993.
127 2011.
128 1993.
129 2011: 43–7.
130 I invented the word Weirdland from the acronym 'WEIRD,' which means 'western,' 'educated,' 'industrialised,' and 'rich' countries. I took the word WEIRD from Haidt 2012: 112–5.

suppose that the court only has three judges (call them 'Margarita,' 'Sakura,' and 'Azalée'). Judge Margarita thinks the statute is constitutional on religious freedom and free-speech grounds; judge Sakura thinks the statute is constitutional on religious freedom grounds, but not on free-speech grounds; and judge Azalée thinks it's constitutional on free-speech grounds, but not on religious freedom grounds. Lastly, suppose that the voting rule for counting premises or conclusions is majority rule.

As we can see in Figure 2.1, whether the defied statute is declared unconstitutional depends on whether the court's voting rule counts premises or conclusions. In the first case, the statute stays constitutional since: (i) when defied on religious freedom grounds, judges Margarita and Sakura consider it constitutional while only judge Azalée considers it unconstitutional; and (ii) when defied on free-speech grounds, judges Margarita and Azalée consider it constitutional while only judge Sakura considers it unconstitutional. Conversely, in the second scenario, the statute is declared unconstitutional since judges Sakura and Azalée conclude so, while only judge Margarita considers it constitutional.

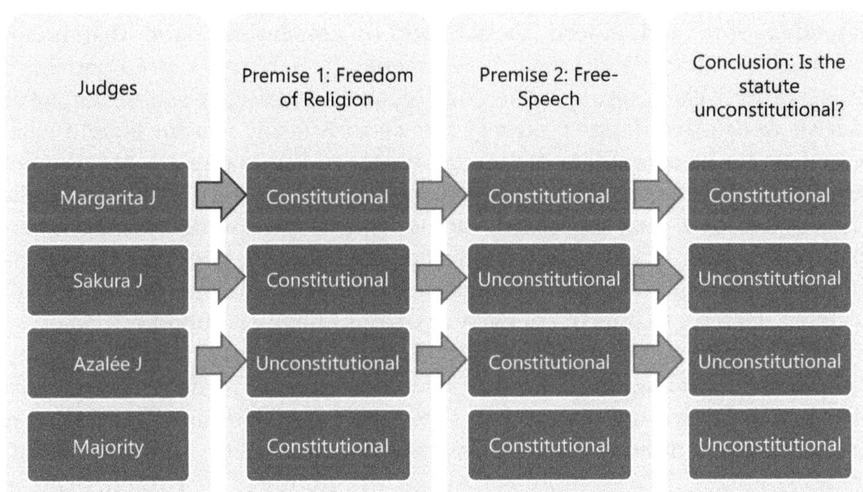

Figure 2.1 The 'doctrinal paradox' or 'discursive dilemma'

There's a strong debate on whether groups should count premises or conclusions to decide. Voting on premises may produce more rationally coherent decisions, in the sense of decisions that are more consistent with the premises that most group members support. But voting on conclusions may produce more adaptable decisions, in the sense of decisions that are better suited to different circumstances.[131]

131 Kornhauser & Sager 1993: 21–30; List & Pettit 2011: 47-58; Lagerspetz 2016: 177–9, 323–6. See also Pettit 2001; List & Pettit 2002; Kornhauser & Sager 2004; List & Pettit 2004; Kornhauser 2008; Ottonelli 2010; Vermeule 2014; Neblo 2015: 98–102.

Currently, the philosopher Phillip Pettit[132] is the main defender of premise-voting inside the State. For Pettit, in collective institutions, voting rules should count premises rather than conclusions since—in order not to be arbitrarily dominated by the State—one should always be able to dispute the reasons behind its decisions. In Pettit's view, if the State doesn't offer coherent reasons for its decisions, citizens would be largely hindered in their capacity to dispute them, and thus would likely be subject to arbitrary power. So, for Pettit, coherence is a key part of making the State responsive to citizens; especially when the State's past decisions influence its new decisions, and when its collective institutions '[stay] over time despite changes in its membership.'[133] Moreover, in judicial contexts, there's a link between coherence and legal certainty. Those bound to apply judicial decisions—or those wanting to forecast them—'will do better if they are given a theory that is coherent at the group level than if they are not.'[134] After all, requiring claims made by groups to have the same level of coherence than claims made by individuals greatly simplifies the task of analysing them.[135]

But despite these arguments for premise-based voting, in this book, I assume that judges vote (and, indeed, should vote) on conclusions rather than premises. As Kornhauser,[136] Ottonelli,[137] Vermeule,[138] Neblo,[139] and Lagespetz,[140] among others, claim, group coherence seems too taxing. Groups that agree on *what to do* often disagree on *why they do it.* And the reasons behind what to do may not be contradictory, but just different. For example, a government may decide to stop subsidising sugar cane plantations since its economically inclined members want to balance the budget, its environmentalist members want to curb large-scale industrial farming, and its health-concerned members want to tackle child obesity. No single coherent rationale may be available to ground a decision that most (or even all) group members support.

This situation seems applicable in collegiate courts since judicial decisions may pursue opposing ends. Judicial decisions may be made to ensure that other courts follow similar rationales when resolving akin cases. Yet they may also be made to indicate how the law should be applied. And in these latter cases, judges may be more certain on the rightness of a result than on the rightness of the logical structure behind it. As Kornhauser argues, judicial

132 Pettit 2001: 280–7.
133 Id 285.
134 Vermeule 2014: 341.
135 Kornhauser 2008: 10.
136 Id 15–6.
137 2010 679–83.
138 2014: 341–2.
139 2015: 98–102.
140 2016: 330–4.

decisions' potentially conflicting requirements may 'bar the achievement of [group coherence] in judgment.'[141]

Moreover, as Ottonelli[142] holds, if a single set of premises is required for deciding, since group members may disagree on such premises, a decision may not be made even if everyone initially agrees on it. In our example, if the government tries to justify its decision on fiscal responsibility grounds, its environmentalist and health-concerned members may change their minds and oppose it since they don't want to establish a precedent for further budget cuts but want to increase state spending on environmental protection and health-prevention. So, focusing on premises 'can lead to deep disagreement where a compromise would otherwise be possible.'[143]

Finally, according to Vermeule,[144] the link between legal certainty and coherence is often contingent. Many times, certainty stems from conclusions on how to apply legal norms—not from 'the theoretical depth of [their] premises.'[145] When courts vote on conclusions, their decisions may be very predictable due to the wide scope of such conclusions. Contrariwise, when courts vote on premises, their coherent views may apply quite narrowly, hence leaving many relevant issues unanswered. Therefore, in this book, I assume that judges generally vote on conclusions rather than premises. Still, in Chapter 4, I refer again to the doctrinal paradox, but only to show that this paradox allows judges to misrepresent their opinions on premises or conclusions to influence a voting process' result.

Judicial Deliberation Is Cognitively Sound

Seventh, I assume that judicial deliberation[146] is a *cognitively* or *epistemically sound* practice. Thus, I assume that, when deciding, judges must deliberate among themselves since, at best, deliberation boosts their group accuracy, while at worst, it shows each judge's position.[147] In turn, following authors such as Habermas,[148] Kornhauser & Sager,[149] Hübner Mendes,[150] and Landemore,[151] deliberation is at best collectively accurate since: (i) it widens the set of arguments at judges' disposal; (ii) it filters good arguments from bad arguments; and (iii) it leads to 'sincere agreements' on decisions; meaning, it leads to

141 2008: 23.
142 2010: 679–83.
143 Id 682.
144 Vermeule 2014: 341–3.
145 Id 342.
146 On deliberation generally, see Bächtinger et al 2018.
147 For other benefits attributed to deliberation, see Hübner Mendes 2013: 22–36.
148 Habermas 1987.
149 Kornhauser & Sager 1986: 101.
150 Hübner Mendes 2015: 23–5.
151 Landemore 2013: 97–103.

agreements[152] on decisions based on shared rational convictions rather than on coercion, or on judges' mere self-interest. Put differently, at best, deliberation leads to agreements on decisions based on the 'unforced force of the better argument.'[153] Deliberation implies trying to change people's opinions by using arguments based on impartial reasons. That is, arguments appealing to values and not just to the speaker's self-interest.[154] Usually, deliberation is positively compared to bargaining,[155] a practice that also implies trying to change other people's opinions, but this time by making credible threats or promises rather than by arguing.[156]

Assuming that judicial deliberation is cognitively sound may seem obvious. Many scholars have emphasised the links between deliberation and adjudication. Alongside Lon Fuller's[157] account of adjudication—an account that's akin to that of deliberation since a key tenet of both practices is making reason-based arguments—it's been claimed that constitutional review is a core instrument for guarding society-wide deliberation (as in Habermas' theory);[158] or that constitutional courts are salient examples of deliberative institutions. (Dworkin's and Rawls' remarks that the US Supreme Court is 'the forum of principle'[159] and 'the exemplar of public reason,'[160] respectively, immediately come to mind.) Thus, according to many scholars, and in Ferejohn & Pasquino's words, 'constitutional courts everywhere are "deliberative institutions," whose base of legitimacy has to be established in reasons.'[161]

Moreover, law is a deliberative discipline. A core aspect of law is '[the] vigorous exchange of arguments that try to come up with the best solutions to both easy and hard cases.'[162] If there's a trait that most views of law share, that trait is likely the idea that law is a kind of rational discourse, and hence a discipline that—by nature—demands its users to deliberate in order to decide. True, many times, legal scholars disagree on the kinds of claims acceptable in

152 I use the word 'agreement' rather than 'consensus' to remark that I don't understand deliberation as requiring unanimity. Though unanimity is *desirable,* I don't see it as *necessary* for a decision process to be deliberative. On the debate on whether deliberation demands unanimity, see Bächtinger et al 2018: 7–8.
153 Habermas 1987.
154 Elster 2013: 30–6, 45.
155 I use the 'classical' idea of deliberation endorsed by most deliberative democracy scholars—not the version analysed by Mansbridge et al 2010, in which this practice is compatible with bargaining. I do this for two reasons: first, judges aren't supposed to base their decisions on threats or promises; and second—following Landemore (2013: 94)—the 'classical' version of deliberation allows us to assess its cognitive traits without mixing it with other decision procedures.
156 Elster 2013: 30–6, 45. See also Manin 1997: 198–202.
157 Fuller 1978.
158 Habermas 1996: ch 5, 7.
159 Dworkin 1985: ch 2.
160 Rawls 2005: 215–6, 231–40.
161 Ferejohn & Pasquino 2004: 1692–700.
162 Hübner Mendes 2015: 58.

legal discourse.[163] Still, most legal scholars agree that law requires rationally grounded argumentation, thus requiring deliberation. So, when linking law and deliberation, most legal scholars are on the same page.

Yet it's relevant to indicate that, in constitutional review, deliberation is cognitively sound for two reasons: first, due to the tensions between different kinds of deliberation, it's not clear that judges must deliberate among themselves; and second, the evidence on deliberation's capacity to boost group accuracy is sketchy,[164] thus questioning this practice's cognitive soundness. Even if law is a deliberative discipline, it isn't clear that judges must deliberate among themselves considering the tensions between judicial deliberation and deliberation that includes other actors. One can think of constitutional review systems in which the judges listen to the parties' claims—hence deliberating only at this stage—and then vote without inter-personally communicating. (Some examples of similar forms of adjudication are criminal juries in Ancient Greece and Brazil.)[165]

The remark that judges must justify their decisions wouldn't defeat this objection. And it wouldn't defeat it since one can conceive constitutional review systems in which, after the judges decide, each judge publishes their opinion in an 'autistic-seriatim' way; meaning, without interacting with their peers and without trying to agree with them. (As previously seen, da Silva claims that this happens in the Supreme Federal Court of Brazil.[166] And there are debates in Australia[167] the US,[168] and the UK[169] as to whether judges *have* behaved—and on whether they *should* behave—this way.) Hence, even assuming that law is a rational discourse, this isn't enough to claim that judges should deliberate among themselves: one needs further reasons to claim so.

163 For an overview of these debates, see Id 54–61.

164 As Elster claims, deliberation experiments are usually 'fraught with a basic methodological dilemma. If debates are recorded for posterity or are conducted before a public, one can never be certain whether the participants are partly or wholly speaking to one of these two audiences rather than to each other. If they are not recorded or conducted behind closed doors, they may not leave behind any material for empirical analysis' (2013: 42, 100–1). And as Devine holds, even when debates are recorded, '[c]oding [them] is a time-consuming, labor-intensive activity that first requires figuring out what will be coded, as well as what will count as an instance of each code. Transcripts can run up to hundreds of pages in length, and all of those statements must be classified' (2012: 163).

165 Elster 2013: 120–1.

166 da Silva 2013: 579–83.

167 In Australia, the debate on how much judges should consult with their peers was sparked by a speech given by former High Court of Australia Justice Dyson Heydon. On this debate, see Appleby & Roberts 2016: 351–4. See also Heerey 2013; Heydon 2013; Mason 2013; Gageler 2014: 190–2; Kiefel 2014. I'm grateful to Gabrielle Appleby for sharing this literature with me.

168 Epstein et al 2001; Corley et al 2013: ch 1; Ferejohn & Pasquino 2004: 1692–700; Baum 2019: 116-9.

169 Patterson 2013: 84–90.

Still, what tips the scales for judicial deliberation is the need to interpret the constitution in relatively uniform ways to realise two values of the rule of law: impartiality and predictability. Here, judicial deliberation plays a key role since—by seeking to generate sincere agreements among judges—deliberation boost the odds that they make relatively uniform decisions. Following Hübner Mendes, insofar as judges deliberate among themselves, a judge 'may well defer to a majority position in the name of a more cohesive legal decision'[170] if they '[do] not have a firm position about a subject matter.'[171] So, in constitutional review, judicial deliberation is cognitively sound insofar as it boosts the odds that judges make relatively uniform decisions, hence boosting impartiality and predictability, and thus the rule of law.

Further, there's a strong debate on whether deliberation really helps groups at deciding rightly—a debate aided by the fact that the evidence is sketchy.[172] Authors such as Mendelberg,[173] Sunstein,[174] and Brennan[175] suggest that, when deciding, deliberation often influences people for the worse, especially due to our cognitive biases.[176] Specifically, deliberating groups often decide poorly due to: (i) 'group polarisation,' meaning, our tendency to become more extreme in our beliefs when talking to people that share them; (ii) 'confirmation bias,' meaning, our tendency to accept evidence that proves our premises while rejecting evidence that disproves them; (iii) 'social influences,' meaning, our tendency to agree with what we grasp as the group's main opinion. Put differently, our tendency to self-censor to avoid trouble or shame, especially in cohesive groups in which one may be a lone dissenter; and (iv) 'the common knowledge problem,' meaning, our tendency to focus on data that all (or most) group members share instead of data that just one group member holds.

Conversely, authors such as Fishkin,[177] Landemore,[178] Neblo,[179] Bang & Frith,[180] and Mercier & Sperber[181] are more optimistic about deliberation experiments. For them, whether deliberation aids group accuracy hinges on

170 Hübner Mendes 2015: 67.

171 Id.

172 For overviews of this research, see Mendelberg 2002; Delli Carpini et al 2004; Ryfe 2005, Steiner 2012; Neblo 2015; Fishkin 2018; Smith & Setälä 2018. For an overview of studies on the effects of deliberation in US criminal juries, see Devine 2012: 177–80.

173 2002.

174 2006.

175 2016: ch 3.

176 As many psychologists do, I understand these biases as 'systematic tendenc[ies] to commit some kind of [cognitive] mistakes' (Mercier & Sperber 2017: 207). See also Kahneman et al 1982; Kahneman 2011. For an alternative view that tends to consider these biases as positive traits for deciding, see Gigerenzer et al 1999.

177 2009.

178 2013: 120–30, 136–42.

179 2015: ch 4.

180 2017: 6–7.

181 2017: ch 12, 15, 17.

the structure of the deliberative process—a structure that can curb cognitive biases, or even use them in ways that bolster group judgments. (Though a bit more sceptical, Sunstein argues similarly.)[182]

This being the state of deliberation experiments, once one considers courts' institutional properties, there's a default case for judicial deliberation as a cognitively sound practice for three reasons. First, judges often have different moral views that affect their constitutional interpretations. So, insofar as judges deliberate among themselves, this fact alone checks group polarisation.

Second, Landemore,[183] and Mercier & Sperber,[184] hold that our rational capacities evolved to convince others. Therefore, though one tends to be sloppy at probing one's claims, one tends to be demanding when it comes to probing *others'* claims before accepting them. Thus, confirmation bias actually helps deliberation by working as a 'claims quality control mechanism.' If this is so, when deliberating among themselves, judges may use confirmation bias to refine their claims, hence also refining their decisions. This is plausible considering that constitutional review's procedural rules tend to ensure that judges are even-handedly exposed to contrasting claims.

Lastly, on social influences and the common knowledge problem, these biases may be curbed by the ways in which voting and deliberation are mixed in constitutional courts. (I tackle this issue in Chapter 7.) And these biases are already partially curbed since judges are legal experts—thus being likely confident at making individual judgments—and by the rules governing their office. These rules ensure that judges have a high degree of autonomy from their peers, thus allowing judges not to unduly defer to them, and to reveal private data that judges may find relevant for deciding. So, in this book, I assume that judicial deliberation is a cognitively sound practice since it boosts the rule of law, and since, when facing sketchy evidence, there are good reasons for undertaking it considering courts' institutional properties. At best, judicial deliberation produces sincere agreements on the constitutionality of legislation. At worst, judicial deliberation clarifies the issues at stake, thus revealing judges' grounds for disagreement.

Ceteris Paribus

Last but not least, I only examine constitutional courts' voting rules, not other institutional variables. I only analyse voting rules: I don't analyse other aspects of their institutional design, such as the number of judges, appointment procedures, minimum office requirements, tenure, compensation, evidence, written and oral presentations, etc. So, most of the claims I make here assume that all the institutional variables that shape constitutional courts stay constant

182 2006: 200–1.
183 Landemore 2013: 124–30, 140–2.
184 Mercier & Sperber 2017: ch 12, 15, 17.

except their voting rules. In sum, I mainly work on a ceteris paribus or 'all else equal' basis.

Granted, institutional variables outside voting rules may be as relevant as them for assessing constitutional courts' performance. This seems especially true regarding judicial selection methods and term limits. For example, it's likely that many of the controversies surrounding the US Supreme Court's decisions are amplified by the US method of choosing federal judges,[185] combined with the fact that—unlike other constitutional courts[186]—these judges neither have term limits nor a mandatory retirement age.[187] But here I face a 'depth versus breadth' trade-off. To deeply examine voting rules' effects on costitutional review, I should mainly focus on this variable, which means that (at least in this book) I must ignore other variables. Further, constitutional review systems are arguably complex systems.[188] Thus, if I simultaneously analyse more than one variable, I am more likely to err than if I just focus on one of them.[189]

My ceteris paribus assumption implies that, if a constitutional court decides its cases as a plenary or split into panels, most of my claims apply to this court's plenary or panels, respectively. This assumption also implies that, if a constitutional court has quorum requirements, most of my claims apply once the quorum is met. For example, if a court has nine judges, a quorum requirement of seven judges, and only seven judges decide a case, my claims apply to the seven judges even though, in other cases, they may also apply to more judges than those needed to fulfil the quorum requirement.

Now that I have established the scope of this book, let's develop its claims.

References

Ackerman BA, *We the People, vol 1: Foundations* (Harvard University Press 1993)

Al-Dulaimi AO, *From Negative to Positive Legislator? Response to Unconstitutional Legislative Omission As a Case Study in the Changing Roles of Constitutional Courts* (DPhil thesis, Griffiths University 2018) https://doi.org/10.25904/1912/3526

Appleby G & Roberts H, 'He who would Not be Muzzled: Justice Heydon's Last Dissent in Monis v The Queen (2013)' in Andrew Lynch (ed), *Great Australian*

185 Baum 2019: 38–44.

186 Stone Sweet 2012: 824–5. For constitutional courts in Asia, see Ginsburg 2013. For constitutional courts in Europe, see Kelemen 2019. For constitutional courts in Latin America, see Ferrer Mac-Gregor 2009.

187 Baum 2019: 64–9.

188 Complex systems are systems whose behaviour can't be accurately forecasted due to the interactions between their parts or with their environments (eg, the economy, the human body). Thurner et al 2018: 22–5. In human-made systems, complexity is joined by the fact that we can react to predictions on how the system will behave. In a classic example, communism didn't arrive partly because elites read Marx and reacted to his forecasts. Merton 1936: 903–4. See also Luhmann 2020: 120–31.

189 For a defence of this method, see Lindblom 1959: 79–81.

Dissents (Cambridge University Press 2016) https://doi.org/10.1017/CBO9781316665824.018
Bächtinger A, Dryzek JS, Mansbridge J & Warren ME, 'Deliberative Democracy: An Introduction' in Bächtinger A, Dryzek JS, Mansbridge J & Warren ME (eds), *The Oxford Handbook of Deliberative Democracy* (Oxford University Press 2018) https://doi.org/10.1093/oxfordhb/9780198747369.013.10
Bang D & Frith CD, 'Making better decisions in groups' (2017) 4 *Royal Society Open Science* http://dx.doi.org/10.1098/rsos.170193
Barry BM, *How Judges Judge: Empirical Insights into Judicial Decision-Making* (Routledge 2021) https://doi.org/10.4324/9780429023422
Baum L, *The Supreme Court* (13th edn, CQ Press 2019)
Bellamy R, *Political Constitutionalism: A Republican Defence of the Constitutionality of Democracy* (Cambridge University Press 2007) https://doi.org/10.1017/CBO9780511490187
Binmore K, *Rational Decisions* (Princeton University Press 2011) https://doi.org/10.1515/9781400833092
Berlin I, 'Two Concepts of Liberty' in Hardy H (ed), Liberty: *Incorporating Four Essays on Liberty* (Oxford University Press 2002) https://doi.org/10.1093/019924989X.001.0001
Bobbitt P, *Constitutional Fate: Theory of the Constitution* (Oxford University Press 1984)
Brewer-Carías AR, *Judicial Review in Comparative Law* (Cambridge University Press 1989)
——— *Constitutional Courts as Positive Legislators: A Comparative Law Study* (Cambridge University Press 2011) https://doi.org/10.1017/CBO9780511994760.002
Brennan G & Pettit P, 'Unveiling the Vote' (1990) 20 *British Journal of Political Science* 311 https://doi.org/10.1017/S000712340000586X
Bickel A, *The Least Dangerous Branch: The Supreme Court at the Bar of Politics* (Bobbs-Merrill 1962)
Caviedes C, 'Chang's Parity: An Alternative Way to Challenge Balancing' (2017) 62(2) *American Journal of Jurisprudence* 165 https://doi.org/10.1093/ajj/aux018
Cappelletti M, *Judicial Review in the Contemporary World* (Bobbs-Merrill 1971)
Carroll R & Tiede L, 'Judicial Behaviour on the Chilean Constitutional Tribunal' (2011) 8(4) *Journal of Empirical Legal Studies* 856 https://doi.org/10.1111/j.1740-1461.2011.01243.x
Chambers S, 'Behind Closed Doors: Publicity, Secrecy, and the Quality of Deliberation' (2004) 12(4) *The Journal of Political Philosophy* 389 https://doi.org/10.1111/j.1467-9760.2004.00206.x
Chang R, 'Introduction' in Chang R (ed), *Incommensurability, Incomparability and Practical Reason* (Ruth Chang edn, Harvard University Press 1997)
Colomer J & McLean I, 'Electing Popes: Approval Balloting and Qualified-Majority Rule' (1998) 29 *Journal of Interdisciplinary History* 1 https://doi.org/10.1162/002219598551616
Corley PC, Steigerwalt A & Ward A, *The Puzzle of Unanimity: Consensus on the United States Supreme Court* (Stanford Law Books 2013) https://doi.org/10.1515/9780804786324
Cortés Salinas J, 'Análisis Cualitativo Comparado: las decisiones de la Suprema Corte contra el Ejecutivo en México' ['Qualitative Comparative Analysis: The Supreme

Court Decisions Against the Executive in Mexico'] (2014) 73 *Revista Mexicana de Sociología* 413
Couso J & Hilbink L, 'From Quietism to Incipient Activism' in *Helmke G and Ríos-Figueroa, Courts in Latin America* (Cambridge University Press 2011) https://doi.org/10.1017/CBO9780511976520
Christiano T, *The Constitution of Equality: Democratic Authority and its Limits* (Oxford University Press 2008) https://doi.org/10.1093/acprof:oso/9780198297475.001.0001
da Silva VA, 'Deciding Without Deliberating' (2013) 11(3) *International Journal of Constitutional Law* 557 https://doi.org/10.1093/icon/mot019
Dahl RA, *Democracy and its Critics* (Yale University Press 1989)
De Sousa RB, 'The Good and the True' (1974) 83 *Mind* 534
Devine DJ, *Jury Decision Making: The State of the Science* (New York University Press 2012) https://doi.org/10.18574/9780814704981
Delli Carpini MX, Lomax Cook F & Jacobs LR, 'Public Deliberation, Discursive Participation and Citizen Engagement: A Review of the Empirical Literature' (2004) 7 *Annual Review of Political Science* 315 https://doi.org/10.1146/annurev.polisci.7.121003.091630
Dixon R, 'The Core Case for Weak-Form Judicial Review' (2017) 38(6) *Cardozo Law Review 2193* https://cardozolawreview.com/volume-38-issue-6/
do Vale AR, *La deliberación en los tribunales constitucionales [Deliberation in Constitutional Courts]* (Centro de Estudios Políticos y Constitucionales 2017)
Dorf MC, 'Facial Challenges to State and Federal Statutes' (1994) 46 *Stanford Law Review* 235 https://scholarship.law.cornell.edu/facpub/110
Dworkin R, *A Matter of Principle* (Harvard University Press 1985)
——— *Law's Empire* (Harvard University Press 1986)
——— *Justice for Hedgehogs* (Harvard University Press 2013)
Ely JH, *Democracy and Distrust: A Theory of Judicial Review* (Harvard University Press 1980)
Elster J, *Securities Against Misrule: Juries, Assemblies, Elections* (Cambridge University Press 2013) https://doi.org/10.1017/CBO9781139382762
Epstein L & Knight J, *The Choices Justices Make* (CQ Press 1998)
——— Segal JA & Spaeth HJ, 'The Norm of Consensus in the US Supreme Court' (2001) 45 *American Journal of Political Science* 362 https://doi.org/10.2307/2669346
Epstein L, Landes WM & Posner R, *The Behavior of Federal Judges: A Theoretical and Empirical Study of Rational Choice* (Harvard University Press 2013)
Estlund DM, *Democratic Authority: A Philosophical Framework* (Princeton University Press 2008)
European Parliament, 'Dissenting Opinions in the Supreme Courts of the Member States' (PE 462.470, Directorate-General for Internal Policies. Policy Department C, Citizens' Rights and Constitutional Affairs, November 2012) <http://www.europarl.europa.eu/studies> accessed 30 September 2021
Fallon RH, 'The Core of an Uneasy Case for Judicial Review' (2008) 121 *Harvard Law Review* 1694 https://harvardlawreview.org/2008/05/the-core-of-an-uneasy-case-for-judicial-review/
Ferejohn J & Pasquino P, 'Constitutional Adjudication: Lessons from Europe' (2004) 82 *Texas Law Review 1671* https://heinonline.org/HOL/P?h=hein.journals/tlr82andi=1687

Ferrer MacGregor E & Herrera García A. (2009), 'Suprema Corte de Justicia de la Nación (México)' ['Supreme Court of the Nation (Mexico)'] in Ferrer MacGregor E (coord), *Crónica de Tribunales Constitucionales en Iberoamérica [Chronicle of Constitutional Courts in Iberian America]* (UNAM Marcial Pons 2009)

Ferreres Comella V, *Constitutional Courts and Democratic Values: A European Perspective* (Yale University Press 2009)

Fishkin JS, *When the People Speak: Deliberative Democracy and Public Consultation* (Oxford University Press 2009) https://doi.org/10.1093/acprof:osobl/9780199604432.001.0001

——— 'Deliberative Polling' in Bächtinger A, Dryzek JS, Mansbridge J, & Warren ME (eds), *The Oxford Handbook of Deliberative Democracy* (Oxford University Press 2018) https://doi.org/10.1093/oxfordhb/9780198747369.013.10

Freedom House, 'Marking 50 Years in the Struggle for Democracy' (Freedom House 2023a) <https://freedomhouse.org/report/freedom-world> accessed 16 November 2023

——— 'Nations in Transit 2023: War Deepens a Regional Divide' (Freedom House 2023b) <https://freedomhouse.org/report/nations-transit> accessed 16 November 2023

Fuller LL, 'The Forms and Limits of Adjudication' (1978) 92 *Harvard Law Review* 353 https://doi.org/10.2307/1340368

Gageler S, 'Why Write Judgments?' (2014) 36 *Sydney Law Review* 189

Gardbaum S, *The New Commonwealth Model of Constitutionalism: Theory and Practice* (Cambridge University Press 2013) https://doi.org/10.1017/CBO9780511920806

Garoupa N, Gomez-Pomar F & Grembi V, 'Judging under Political Pressure: An Empirical Analysis of Constitutional Review Voting in the Spanish Constitutional Court' (2013) 29(3) *The Journal of Law, Economics and Organization* 513 https://doi.org/10.1093/jleo/ewr008

——— & Grembi V, 'Judicial review and political partishanship: Moving from consensual to majoritarian democracy' (2015) 43 *International Review of Law and Economics* 32 http://dx.doi.org/10.1016/j.irle.2015.04.002

Gaudemet J, Dubois J, Duval A and Champagne J, *Les Elections dans L'Eglise Latine des Origines au XVI Siècle [Elections in the Latin Church since its Origins to the XVI Century]* (Fernand Lanore 1979)

Gigerenzer G, Todd PM and The ABC Research Group, *Simple Heuristics that Make Us Smart* (Oxford University Press 1999)

Ginsburg T, *Judicial Review in New Democracies: Constitutional Courts in Asian Cases* (Cambridge University Press 2013) https://doi.org/10.1017/CBO9780511511189

——— & Huq AZ, *How to Save a Constitutional Democracy* (University of Chicago Press 2019)

Griffin J, *Well-Being: its Meaning, Measurement and Moral Importance* (Oxford University Press 1988) https://doi.org/10.1093/0198248431.001.0001

Habermas J, *The Theory of Communicative Action,* vol 2: Lifeworld and System: A Critique of Functionalist Reason (Beacon Press 1987)

——— *Between Facts and Norms: Contributions to a Discourse Theory of Law and Democracy* (MIT Press 1996)

Haidt J, *The Righteous Mind: Why Good People are Divided by Politics and Religion* (Pantheon Books 2012)

Hamilton A, 'Federalist No 78. The Judiciary Department' in *The US Constitution and Other Key American Writings (first published 1878*, Canterbury Classics 2015)
Harari YN, *Sapiens: Brief History of Humankind* (Signal 2014)
——— *Homo Deus: A Brief History of Tomorrow* (Signal 2016)
Harel A & Kahana T, 'The Easy Core Case for Judicial Review' (2010) 2 *Journal of Legal Analysis* 227 https://doi.org/10.1093/jla/2.1.227
Heerey P, 'The Judicial Herd: Seduced by Suave Glittering Phrases?' (2013) 87 *Australian Law Journal* 460
Heydon D, 'Threats to Judicial Independence: The Enemy Within' (2013) 129 *Law Quarterly Review* 205
Hickey T, 'The Republican Core of the Case for Judicial Review' (2019) 17(1) *International Journal of Constitutional Law* 288 https://doi.org/10.1093/icon/moz007
Hübner Mendes C, *Constitutional Courts and Deliberative Democracy* (Oxford University Press 2015) https://doi.org/10.1093/acprof:oso/9780199670451.001.0001
Kahana T, 'The Notwithstanding Mechanism and Public Discussion: Lessons from the Ignored Practice of Section 33 of the Charter' (2001) 44(3) *Canadian Public Administration/Administration Publique du Canada* 255 https://doi.org/10.1111/j.1754-7121.2001.tb00891.x
Kahneman D, *Thinking, Fast and Slow* (Farrar, Straus and Giroux 2011)
——— Slovic P & Tversky A (eds), *Judgment Under Uncertainty: Heuristics and Biases* (Cambridge University Press 1982) https://doi.org/10.1017/CBO9780511809477
Kay J & King M, *Radical Uncertainty: Decision-Making Beyond the Numbers* (WW Norton 2020)
Kelemen K, *Judicial Dissent in European Constitutional Courts: A Comparative and Legal Perspective* (Routledge 2019) https://doi.org/10.4324/9781315590769
Kelsen H 'The Nature and Development of Constitutional Adjudication' in Lars Vinx (ed), *The Guardian of the Constitution: Hans Kelsen and Carl Schmitt on the Limits of Constitutional Law (first published 1928*, Cambridge University Press 2015) https://doi.org/10.1017/CBO9781316136256
——— 'Judicial Review of Legislation: A Comparative Study of the Austrian and the American Constitution' (1942) 4 *Journal of Politics* 183 https://doi.org/10.2307/2125770
Kiefel S, 'The Individual Judge' (2014) 88 *Australian Law Journal* 554
King JA, 'Institutional Approaches to Judicial Restraint' (2008) 28 *Oxford Journal of Legal Studies* 409 https://doi.org/10.1093/ojls/gqn020
Knight F, Risk, *Uncertainty* and Profit: The Economic Theory of Uncertainty in Business Enterprises, and its Connection to Profit and Prosperity in Society (Adansonia Press 2018)
Kornhauser LA, 'Aggregate rationality in adjudication and legislation' (2008) 7(1) *Politics, Philosophy and Economics* 5 https://doi.org/10.1177/1470594X07085149
——— & Sager LG, 'Unpacking the Court' (1986) 96(1) *Yale Law Journal* 82 https://www.jstor.org/stable/796436
——— & Sager LG, 'The One and the Many: Adjudication in Collegial Courts' (1993) 81(1) *California Law Review* 1 https://doi.org/10.15779/Z38C43K

——— & Sager LG, 'The Many as One: Integrity and Group Choice in Paradoxical Cases' (2004) 32(3) *Philosophy and Public Affairs* 249 https://www.jstor.org/stable/3557987

Kreit A, 'Making Sense of Facial and As-Applied Challenges' (2010) 18(3) *William & Mary Bill of Rights Journal* 657 https://scholarship.law.wm.edu/wmborj/vol18/iss3/4/

Lagerspetz E, 'Wisdom and numbers' (2010) 49(1) *Social Science Information* 29 https://doi.org/10.1177/0539018409354475

——— *Social Choice and Democratic Values* (Springer 2016) https://doi.org/10.1007/978-3-319-23261-4

Landemore H, *Democratic Reason: Politics, Collective Intelligence and the Rule of the Many* (Princeton University Press 2013)

Levitsky S & Ziblatt D, *How Democracies Die* (Crown 2018)

Lindblom C, 'The Science of "Muddling Through"' (1959) 19 *Public Administration Review* 79 https://doi.org/10.2307/973677

Linz JJ & Stepan A, 'Towards Consolidated Democracies' (1996) 7 *Journal of Democracy* 14 https://doi.org/10.1353/jod.1996.0031

List C & Pettit P, 'Aggregating Sets of Judgments: An Impossibility Result' (2002) 18 *Economics and Philosophy* 89 https://doi.org/10.1017/S0266267102001098

——— 'Aggregating Sets of Judgments: Two Impossibility Results Compared' (2004) 140 *Synthese* 207 https://doi.org/10.1023/B:SYNT.0000029950.50517.59

——— *Group Agency: The Possibility, Design, and Status of Corporate Agents* (Cambridge University Press 2011) https://doi.org./10.1093/acprof:oso/9780199591565.001.0001

Luhmann N, *Introduction to Systems Theory* (Dick Baker ed, Peter Gilgen tr, Polity Press 2020)

Manin B, *The Principles of Representative Government* (Cambridge University Press 1997) https://doi.org/10.1017/CBO9780511659935

Mansbridge J, Bonham J, Chambers S, Estlund D, Føllesdal A, Fung A, Lafont C, Manin B & Martí JL, 'The Place of Self-Interest and the Role of Power in Deliberative Democracy' (2010) 18 *Journal of Political Philosophy* 64 https://doi.org/10.1111/j.1467-9760.2009.00344.x

Mason A, 'Reflections on the High Court: Its Judges and Judgments' (2013) 37 *Australian Bar Review* 102

Mendelberg T, 'The Deliberative Citizen: Theory and Evidence' in Delli Carpini M, Huddy L and Shapiro RY (eds), *Research in Micropolitics*, vol 6 (Elsevier Press 2002)

Mercier H & Sperber D, *The Enigma of Reason* (Harvard University Press 2017)

Merton RK, 'The Unanticipated Consequences of Purposive Social Action' (1936) 1(6) *American Sociological Review* 894 https://doi.org/10.2307/2084615

Mounk Y, *The People vs Democracy: Why Our Freedom is in Danger and How to Save It* (Harvard University Press 2018)

Neblo MA, *Deliberative Democracy between Theory and Practice* (Cambridge University Press 2015) https://doi.org/10.1017/CBO9781139226592

Ottonelli V, 'What Does the Discursive Paradox Really Mean for Democracy?' (2010) 58 *Political Studies* 666 https://doi.org/10.1111/j.1467-9248.2010.00821.x

Pasquino P, 'E Pluribus Unum: Disclosed and Undisclosed Votes in Constitutional/Supreme Courts' in Elster J (ed), *Secrecy and Publicity in Votes and Debates* (Cambridge University Press 2015) https://doi.org/10.1017/CBO9781316015360

Paterson A, *Final Judgment: The Last Law Lords and the Supreme Court* (Hart 2013)
Peirce CS, 'Deduction, Induction, and Hypothesis' in Houser K and Kloessel C (eds), *The Essential Peirce: Selected Philosophical Writings,* vol 1 (first published 1878, Indiana University Press 1992)
Pettit P, 'Deliberative Democracy and the Discursive Dilemma' (2001) 11 *Philosophical Issues* 268 https://doi.org/10.1111/j.1758-2237.2001.tb00047.x
Popper K, *The Logic of Scientific Discovery (first published 1935*, Routledge 2002)
Pou Giménez F, 'Changing the Channel: Broadcasting Deliberations in the Mexican Supreme Court' in David R & Taras D (eds), *Justices and Journalists: The Global Perspective* (Cambridge University Press 2017) https://doi.org/10.1017/9781316672228
Rawls J, *A Theory of Justice* (Revised edn, Harvard University Press 1999)
——— *Political Liberalism* (Expanded edn, Columbia University Press 2005)
Raz J, *The Morality of Freedom* (Reprinted edn, Oxford University Press 2009) https://doi.org/10.1093/0198248075.001.0001
Rodrik D, *Economics Rules: The Rights and Wrongs of the Dismal Science* (WW Norton 2016)
Roux T, 'In Defence of Empirical Entanglement: The Methodological Flaw in Waldron's Case Against Judicial Review' in Levy R and others (eds), *The Cambridge Handbook of Deliberative Constitutionalism* (Cambridge University Press 2018) https://doi.org/10.1017/9781108289474
Ryfe DM, 'Does Deliberative Democracy Work?' (2005) 8 *Annual Review of Political Science* 49 https://doi.org/10.1146/annurev.polisci.8.032904.154633
Sadurski W, *Poland's Constitutional Breakdown* (Oxford University Press 2019) https://doi.org/10.1093/oso/9780198840503.001.0001
Saks MJ, 'What Do Jury Expertiments Tell Us about How Juries (Should) Make Decisions' (1997) 6 *Southern California Interdisciplinary Law Journal* 1
Sánchez A, Magaloni B & Magar E, 'Legalist versus Interpretativist: The Supreme Court and the Democratic Transition in Mexico' in Helmke G and Ríos-Figueroa J (eds), *Courts in Latin America* (Cambridge University Press 2011) https://doi.org/10.1017/CBO9780511976520
Schwartzberg M, *Counting the Many. The Origins and Limits of Supermajority Rule* (Cambridge University Press 2013) https://doi.org/10.1017/CBO9781139013970
Segal JA & Spaeth HJ, *The Supreme Court and the Attitudinal Model Revisited* (Cambridge University Press 2002) https://doi.org/10.1017/CBO9780511615696
Seok Hong J, 'Signalling the Turn: The Supermajority Requirement and Judicial Power on the Constitutional Court of South Korea' (2019) 67 *American Journal of Comparative Law* 177 https://doi.org/10.1093/ajcl/avz008
Shapiro I, 'Optimal Deliberation' (2002) 10 *The Journal of Political Philosophy* 196 https://doi.org/10.1111/1467-9760.00149
Staveley ES, *Greek and Roman Voting and Elections* (Cornell University Press 1972)
Steiner J, *The Foundations of Deliberative Democracy: Empirical Research and Normative Implications* (Cambridge University Press 2012) https://doi.org/10.1017/CBO9781139057486
Songer DR, Johnson SW, Ostberg CL & Wetstein ME, *Law, Ideology and Collegiality: Judicial Behaviour in the Supreme Court of Canada* (McGill-Queen's University Press 2012)

Stone Sweet A, 'Constitutional Courts' in Rosenfeld M and Sajó A (eds), *The Oxford Handbook of Comparative Constitutional Law* (Oxford University Press 2012) https://doi.org/10.1093/oxfordhb/9780199578610.013.0040

Sunstein CR, *Infotopia: How Many Minds Produce Knowledge* (Oxford University Press 2006)

——— Schkade D, Ellman LM & Sawicki A, *Are Judges Political? An Empirical Analysis of the Federal Judiciary* (Brookings Institution Press 2006)

Sinnott-Armstrong W, 'Moral Dilemmas and Incomparability' (1985) 22 *American Philosophical Quarterly* 321 https://www.jstor.org/stable/20014112

Smith G & Setälä M, 'Mini-Publics and Deliberative Democracy' in Bächtinger A, Dryzek JS, Mansbridge J and Warren ME (eds), *The Oxford Handbook of Deliberative Democracy* (Oxford University Press 2018) https://doi.org/10.1093/oxfordhb/9780198747369.013.27

Steiner J, *The Foundations of Deliberative Democracy: Empirical Research and Normative Implications* (Cambridge University Press 2012) https://doi.org/10.1017/CBO9781139057486

Taleb NN, *Antifragile: Things that Gain from Disorder* (2019 Box Set edn, Random House 2012)

Thayer JB, *The Origin and Scope of the American Doctrine of Constitutional Law* (Little, Brown, and Company 1893) https://openlibrary.org/books/OL23449489M/The_Origin_and_Scope_of_the_American_Doctrine_of_Constitutional_Law

Thurner S, Hanel R & Klimek P, *Introduction to the Theory of Complex Systems* (Oxford University Press 2018) https://doi.org/10.1093/oso/9780198821939.001.0001

Tiede LB & Ponce AF, 'Evaluating Theories of Decision-making on the Peruvian Constitutional Tribunal' (2014) 6(2) *Journal of Politics in Latin America* 139 https://doi.org/10.1177/1866802X1400600205

Tomkins A, *Our Republican Constitution* (Hart Publishing 2005) https://doi.org/10.5040/9781472559678

Tushnet M, 'Alternative Forms of Judicial Review' (2003) 101 *Michigan Law Review* 2781 https://scholarship.law.georgetown.edu/facpub/259

——— 'Constitutional Hardball' (2004) 37 *John Marshall Law Review* 523 http://repository.jmls.edu/lawreview/vol37/iss2/7

Vacca R, 'Individual Opinions and Collective Deliberations' (first published 1921, Diego Hammerschlag y Alvaro Nazer trs, 2013) 14(1) *Revista Argentina de Teoría Jurídica* http://repositorio.utdt.edu/handle/utdt/10646

Verdugo Ramírez S, 'Inconstitucionalidad por omisión del legislador' [Unconstitutional Legislative Omissions] (2009) 19 *Actualidad Jurídica* 373

Vermeule A, 'Collective Wisdom and Institutional Design' in Landemore H & Elster J (eds), *Collective Wisdom: Principles and Mechanisms* (Cambridge University Press 2014) https://doi.org/10.1017/CBO9780511846427

Vidmar N & Hans VP, *American Juries: The Verdict* (Prometheus Books 2007)

Viehweg T, *Tópica y Jurisprudencia [Topics and Jurisprudence]* (Luis Díez Picazo tr, 2nd edn, Thomson Reuters 2016)

Waldron J, *Political Political Theory: Essays on Institutions* (Harvard University Press 2016) https://doi.org/10.4159/9780674970342

Webber GCN, Yowell P, Ekins R, Köpcke M, Miller BW, & Urbina FJ, *Legislated Rights: Securing Human Rights through Legislation* (Cambridge University Press 2018) https://doi.org/10.1017/9781108551069

——— & Yowell P, 'Legislated Rights in the Real World' (2020) 21(1) *Jerusalem Review of Legal Studies* 145 https://doi.org/10.1093/jrls/jlaa002

Weill R, 'Hybrid Constitutionalism: The Israeli Case for Judicial Review and Why We Should Care' (2012) 30 *Berkeley Journal of International Law* 349 https://doi.org/10.15779/Z384D36

Weinrib J, *Dimensions of Dignity: The Theory and Practice of Modern Constitutional Law* (Cambridge University Press 2016) https://doi.org/10.1017/CBO9781316026663

Yowell P, *Constitutional Rights and Constitutional Design: Moral and Empirical Reasoning in Judicial Review* (Hart Publishing 2018) https://doi.org/10.5040/9781509913626

3 A Brief History of Voting Rules in the West

Before analysing voting rules' traits, it's worth giving a brief historical account of voting rules in the West, from the Ancient World to the Enlightenment. History provides clues for identifying at least some of these traits, along with helping us identify how voting rules work in addition to other institutional arrangements. Voting rules are always part of a wider institutional context. What history shows is that this institutional context matters since it may influence whether the respective voting rule accomplishes the aims for which it was adopted. Thus, the historical study of voting rules—alongside these other institutional arrangements—provides ways of tackling the challenges posed by the practical application of such rules to specific cases.

History encourages us to use our institutional imagination. As Harari states, '[w]e study history not to know the future but to widen our horizons, to understand that our present situation is neither natural nor inevitable, and that we consequently have many more possibilities before us than we imagine.'[1] Following Ortega y Gasset,[2] at the individual and the group level, history allows us to know who we are by examining what we've done. And since history allows us to do this, when facing problems akin to those we've faced in the past, history at least helps us realise that we may choose whether to do the same thing or change course.

One of the main problems of historically studying a phenomenon is that one is prone to make 'narrative fallacies;'[3] meaning, one is prone to see the studied phenomenon—in this case, some voting rules—as caused by crisp, linear chains of events with little influence by random factors. Historical narratives tend to be deterministic: they tend to ignore the odds that things could have evolved otherwise. Thus, though historically studying a phenomenon is valuable, it's worth joining that view with other approaches. So, this chapter mainly assesses voting rules from a historical standpoint, while the next

1 Harari 2014: 241.
2 Ortega y Gasset 1964: 11–50.
3 Taleb 2010: ch 6.

DOI: 10.4324/9781032723952-3

chapter mainly assesses them from a social choice standpoint and political philosophy standpoint.

In this chapter, I only address the history of voting rules in the West. Though I'm aware that this shows a Eurocentric view, according to available evidence, the ideas that grounded different voting rules and constitutional review originated mainly in the West, thus justifying my narrow focus. Specifically, in this chapter, I analyse voting rules in Ancient Greece, the Roman Republic, the Latin Catholic Church,[4] and the Italian city-states during the Middle Ages. Additionally, I examine the ideas of some of the main Enlightenment philosophers—particularly Pufendorf and Condorcet—on unanimity rule, majority rule, and supermajority rules. More than focusing on historical events, I focus on the ideas behind the application of different voting rules in certain contexts. Thus, I tackle voting rules in Ancient Greece, the Roman Republic, the Latin Church, and the Italian city-states since there's detailed data on how these rules were applied—and, in the Church's case, how they *are* applied—in such contexts; and on these rules' underlying logics. In turn, I stop at the Enlightenment since, arguably, beyond the discoveries made by social choice theorists in the 20th century,[5] our general way of thinking about voting rules hasn't greatly changed since this period.

Voting Rules in the Ancient World

Currently, we assume almost as self-evident that groups must decide by voting. But this hasn't always been the case. In Ancient Greece, before the Classical Period, group decisions were mainly made through 'acclamation.' That is, by roughly estimating the presence of an agreement after watching a group's spontaneous reaction to a proposal (eg, shouting, applauding, etc.). Conversely, voting originally emerged in small aristocratic councils such as the Spartan *Gerousia* and the Athenian *Areopagus*.[6] This difference had to do with who was considered to have the necessary intelligence, knowledge, and skills to engage in political life. Put differently, it had to do with who was considered politically capable.[7]

Acclamation was used in popular assemblies since these assemblies were made of the impoverished masses (the *demos*),[8] whose members weren't considered able enough to count their judgments. Contrariwise, voting was used in small aristocratic councils because these councils were made of 'the best'

4 I use the term 'Latin Catholic Church' since I am only referring to the Roman Catholic Church that uses Latin liturgical rites—not the Eastern Catholic Churches that recognise the pope's authority.
5 For an overview of these discoveries, see Lagerspetz 2016.
6 Glotz 2013: 50-60; Staveley 1972: ch 1; de Ste Croix 2004: 73–5.
7 Lagerspetz 2010: 29, 31; Schwartzberg, 2013: 19–22.
8 Cartledge 2016: 17–20.

(the *aristoi*).[9] So, voting wasn't democratic but aristocratic in origin.[10] This is shown by the fact that, unlike acclamation, which is about roughly estimating 'the dominant view of the crowd qua totality,'[11] voting is about counting group members' judgments, hence signalling that such judgments merit to be counted, hence also signalling respect for the group members that render such judgments.[12]

Now, having one's ability recognised means that one's vote is worth being counted—not that it's worth being counted equally. As Mill holds, the fact that all group members can vote doesn't mean that their votes should count the same. One may claim that, beyond a minimum ability level (which would grant at least one vote) the more able a person is, the more votes that person should have.[13] If one's power to vote is based on one's ability, the only way to hold that such a vote should be equal to other people's is by arguing that one is as able as them, at least presumably. Thus, the Ancient Greek case is especially interesting not only since the aristocrats (and later on, Athenian citizens) could vote, but also since they were considered equally able, which meant that majority rule sufficed to decide.

According to Glotz[14] and Schwartzberg,[15] a main reason for assuming equal ability among Ancient Greek aristocrats was preventing inner strife. Specifically, the Greeks tried to minimise the risk of civil war; a phenomenon 'more or less endemic in the Greek *polis*-world.'[16] The equal vote was adopted as a remedy against inner strife since it signalled equal respect for group members.[17] After all, the aristocrats in the *Gerousia* and the *Areopagus* 'wouldn't have accepted the affront if asked to weigh some members' judgment over their own;'[18] particularly in 'decisions for which individual judgments were pivotal.'[19] Actually, even with the equal vote, in Ancient Greece the danger of inner strife was always latent. When the issues over the table were of major importance, the equal vote itself carried the danger of inner strife since—by its

9 Voting became a popular decision procedure since, in Athens, Cleisthenes' reforms extended the vote (along with other political rights) to the *demos*, thus giving birth to Athenian democracy. Due to these reforms, acclamation was progressively replaced by majority rule. Staveley 1972: 23–7; Glotz 2013: 117–28; Cartledge 2016: ch 3–5. Hansen 1999: 34–6.

10 This is akin to Manin's (1997) account of elections as an originally aristocratic procedure for choosing officials. But the parallel isn't fully applicable once we consider that elections didn't proceed by vote counting but by 'estimation', meaning, by an imprecise aggregation of hands. Schwartzberg 2013: 28–34.

11 Schwartzberg 2013: 33–4.

12 Id 28–34.

13 Mill [1861] 1948: ch 8.

14 2013: 56–7.

15 2013: 21–2.

16 Cartledge 2016: 226.

17 Glotz 2013: 56–7.

18 Schwartzberg 2013: 106–7.

19 Id.

very nature—voting underlines the differences among group members.[20] So, it would likely have been inconvenient to agitate the waters further by suggesting that ability among group members diverged, and that hence not all votes should count the same.

This logic linking voting and ability wasn't affected by the extension of political rights (including the right to vote) to all Athenian citizens. For Athenians, citizenship itself was a matter of ability. Not all of Athens' inhabitants were citizens. Women, children, foreigners, and slaves were excluded—an exclusion explained by the fact that they were considered unable. And though citizenship was automatically conferred on all males over eighteen years old, citizens were regularly checked and their citizenship could be revoked if they showed clear inability.[21] Therefore, Athenians' idea of citizenship was somewhat akin to that of 'nobility' in medieval Europe. It wasn't just a matter of being male and free, but also a matter of *noblesse oblige*: a matter of behaving in ways worthy of citizens.

Voting's origins, especially its links with the ideas that: (i) each citizen is assumed able (which explains why their judgments must be counted); and (ii) each citizen is assumed *equally* able (which explains why their judgments must be counted equally), grounds much of the traditional bonds in Western philosophy between majority rule and respect for individuals. Specifically, this origin explains a unique trait of majority rule: the fact that majority rule works as 'a metaphorical badge of equality'[22] among group members.

Additionally—and in a way similar to that of Ancient Greek city-states—in the Roman Republic's representative assemblies, decision processes also evolved from acclamation to voting,[23] and decisions were made by majority rule.[24] Further, the Roman Republic offers one of the first proofs of the use of supermajority rules, especially in the process called *ampliatio*. In Roman criminal trials, whenever more than 1/3 of the jurors held that the available evidence was insufficient to issue a verdict *(non-liquet)*, these jurors could request an *ampliatio*. That is, they could request up to two further hearings. Yet if the remaining 2/3 of the jurors decided that available evidence was

20 This also explains that, in many Greek cities, voting was called *diaphora*, which means 'dividing up' or 'disagreeing.' Schwartzberg 2013: 22. Akin phenomena have been observed in some indigenous communities. According to Hébert, in some communities, deciding by unanimity is 'an imperative to which the community must submit … [since] the cost of not reaching [unanimity] would be factionalism and potentially the scission of the group' (2018: 104-5). See also El-Hakim 1978; Steiner & Dorff 1980; Urfalino 2014a.

21 Schwartzberg 2013: 28–30.

22 Schmidtz & Brennan 2010: 189.

23 Staveley 1972: 157–8.

24 Still, in these assemblies, the majority wasn't gauged considering each member. Rather, it was gauged considering sub-groups of members, such as the *curiae*, the *centuriae*, and the tribe. For an overview of these assemblies and their decision procedures, see Staveley 1972: ch 6–10; Ribas Alba 2008: ch 5–7; Fernández de Buján 2020: 108–9, 147–52.

enough, the jurors that refused to issue a verdict were removed and the trial continued with the remaining jurors.[25]

The Roman context in which supermajority rules were applied is a context in which what matters the most is a group's skill at deciding rightly, such as deciding whether the group has enough evidence to issue a verdict. In what follows, I show that the Church and the Italian city-states applied these rules in similar contexts. Unfortunately, as Lagerpetz states, after the fall of the Western Roman Empire, 'the practice of vote counting lost its significance and was more or less forgotten.'[26] Yet during the Middle Ages, this practice would strongly re-emerge in the Church and the Italian city-states.

Voting Rules in the Middle Ages

The Latin Catholic Church

Through the Middle Ages, the Latin Catholic Church was Europe's most powerful organisation, alongside being the custodian of the political, intellectual, and spiritual legacy of the Ancient World.[27] As in pre-classical Greece, in the Church, group decisions originally followed the logic of acclamation instead of that of voting. In its decision processes, the Church expected unanimous agreements. Actually, the word 'unanimity' comes from the Latin *unanimitas,* which means 'oneness of spirit.' Naturally, this expectation of unanimity was particularly significant in the most important decision inside the Church: the election of a new Roman pontiff or 'pope.'[28]

Unanimity was expected since, in the Church's conception, group decisions were divinely inspired. Thus, all decision-makers had to surrender their wills to the revelations of the Holy Spirit. In this conception, disagreement was deeply frowned upon. It was a sign that at least some decision-makers were surely acting in error or bad faith and hence a sign that the Holy Spirit wasn't present.[29] Unfortunately, unanimity was rarely attained. So, there were a series of schisms that usually left the Church under the influence of other powers, particularly Carolingian emperors and Merovingian kings during the High Middle Ages, and Holy Roman emperors and Italian noble families during the Late Middle Ages.[30] In this context, the first attempt to tackle inner strife was the 'greater and sounder part' doctrine (*sanior et maior pars,* also translated as 'greater and wiser' part) proposed in *The Rule of Saint Benedict.*[31]

25 Schwartzberg 2013: 44-6.
26 Lagerspetz 2010: 31.
27 Id 31–2.
28 Colomer & McLean 1998: 2-5; Lagerspetz 2010: 31; Schwartzberg 2013: 49-52; Urfalino 2014b: 177–9.
29 Colomer & McLean 1998: 2-5; Lagerspetz 2010: 31; Schwartzberg 2013: 49-52; Urfalino 2014b: 177.
30 Gaudemet et al 1979: 49, 166–7, 193–4; Colomer & McLean 1998: 3.
31 Benedict of Nursia 2018: ch 64.

According to this doctrine, when a decision had to be made and unanimity wasn't reached, in principle the judgment of the majority (the 'greater part' or *pars maior*) prevailed. Still, if the minority claimed to a higher authority (meaning bishops, archbishops, and, ultimately, the pope) that its judgment was sounder than that of the majority—put differently, that though the majority was the greater part, it wasn't 'the sounder part' (or *pars sanior*)—and gave enough proof of its claims, the higher authority could replace the majority's decision by that of the minority.[32] Predictably though, the greater and sounder part doctrine became inadequate for resolving inner strife where it mattered the most: namely, in papal elections. This happened for two reasons: first, endemic disagreements on the reasons for considering a minority sounder than a majority; and second, the fact that, in papal elections, there was just no higher spiritual authority to turn to (at least not within this realm). With time, these insufficiencies led to the development of the current 2/3 rule in the electoral procedure known as 'the Conclave.'[33]

To determine whether the minority had a level of wisdom *(sanioritas)* strong enough to void a majority judgment, 12th century canonists (such as Rufinus and Huguccio) suggested two standards that joined numbers. These standards were: (i) authority (*auctoritas,* also translated as 'merit'); and (ii) zeal (*zelus,* also translated as 'intentions'). Once these standards were suggested, canonists generally worked by proposing solutions to hypothetical cases. Unfortunately, when applying these standards to similar cases, different canonists arrived at different solutions. Thus, after lengthy discussions, most canonists concluded that, when an election was disputed, all else being equal, the party that complied the most with two of the three standards—meaning, numbers, authority, and zeal—had to be the one whose opinion should prevail.[34] For example, if in a disputed episcopal election a faction had a numerical majority, but the other faction was more authoritative or had a higher zeal, the minority faction's opinion should prevail.

The canonists' consensus ended up being question begging. The problem was that, just like wisdom, standards such as authority and zeal have qualitative aspects while numbers are just a quantitative standard. Since authority and zeal have qualitative aspects, comparisons operating in terms of 'more' or 'less' often don't apply. So, in many church disputes, appeals to authority

32 Colomer & McLean 1998: 6–7; Lagerspetz 2010: 32–4; Schwartzberg 2013: 55–8; Urfalino 2014b: 177–9.

33 Alongside the 2/3 rule—which works 'by scrutiny' or *per scrutinium*—the Conclave rules also allowed for the election of a pope by acclamation *(per acclamationem)* and by compromise (*per compromissum);* meaning, by delegating the choice to a smaller group of cardinals. These alternative rules stayed active until Pope John Paul II derogated them in 1996. Apostolic Constitution *Universi Dominici Gregis* on the Vacancy of the Holy See and the Election of the Roman Pontiff, para 62.

34 Lagerspetz 2010: 32–3; Schwartzberg 2013: 53–6; Urfalino 2014b: 177–9.

and intentions were useless. And most attempts to specify these standards also faced the same challenge, hence kicking the can down the road a bit further.[35]

Despite the greater and sounder part doctrine's problems, these problems weren't unsolvable when there was a higher spiritual authority to turn to, such as bishops, archbishops, or the pope. Yet, the doctrine couldn't be applied when the election of the pope was at stake.[36] In this context, the Church established the current 2/3 rule for papal elections in the first canon of the Third Lateran Council of 1179, called *Licet de evitanda*.[37] It isn't clear why the cardinals agreed on a 2/3 rule, nor is it clear the role that the greater and sounder part doctrine played in developing the rule.[38] Yet, what seems clear is that the 2/3 rule tried to accommodate three ideas. First, the idea that, regardless of his rank, each cardinal was as wise as his peers. Thus, each cardinal had one vote. Second, the idea that a widespread agreement among cardinals was proof that unanimity had been reached, though the voting rule itself didn't require unanimity in a strict mathematical sense. Finally, the idea that future schisms should be halted.

Despite the hierarchal differences among cardinals, all cardinals were ultimately considered equally sound in judgment, thus receiving one vote each. What seems to have happened is the following. Since its creation, the College of Cardinals has three types of members: cardinal-bishops, cardinal-priests, and cardinal-deacons. Cardinal-bishops are hierarchically superior to cardinal-priests, who in turn are hierarchically superior to cardinal-deacons.[39] Originally, whenever the cardinals of a higher rank found themselves in a minority, those cardinals (following the greater and sounder part doctrine) tended to lean on their hierarchical authority to question the majority. Still, from the 12th century onwards, this purely hierarchical conception of authority eroded since popes progressively appointed cardinals known for traits such as knowledge, morality, or religiosity.[40] In this new conception of authority, having these traits signalled that these cardinals' judgments were allegedly as high as their peers'. When this view was joined with the fact that a schism would likely follow cardinals' disagreements on who should become pope,[41] the result was that all cardinals were considered equals in the proceedings of the college, including papal elections. This explains why each cardinal has one vote in the Conclave.

35 Lagerspetz 2010: 32–4; Schwartzberg 2013: 53–6; Urfalino 2014b: 178.

36 Colomer & McLean 1998: 6–7; Lagerspetz 2010: 32–4; Schwartzberg 2013: 53–6.

37 Papal Encyclicals Online nd-a.

38 Some authors claim that the rule was a child of the doctrine, whereas others claim that the doctrine was practically abandoned. Colomer & McLean 1998: 9–10; Lagerspetz 2010: 34; Schwartzberg 2013: 59–62.

39 Code of Canon Law c 350.

40 Schwartzberg 2013: 55–7.

41 Colomer & McLean 1998: 3–5; Lagerspetz 2010: 33; Schwartzberg 2013: 55; Urfalino 2014b: 177.

Moreover, though the Church didn't give up on unanimity as an idea, it gave up on unanimity as a voting rule. In principle, unanimous agreements were desirable. But unanimity rule was too stringent since it considered neither moral disagreements among cardinals, nor the possibility that at least one cardinal may act in bad faith.[42] As *Licet de evitanda* states, the pretension of 'avoiding dissension in the choice of a sovereign pontiff'[43] generally led to the church suffering 'serious divisions'[44] due to some cardinals' 'wicked and reckless ambition.'[45] So, the church tried to design a decision procedure that—considering how humans usually behave—showed a level of agreement among cardinals that was strong enough to justify the election of a new pope.

What seems to have produced the 2/3 rule then is a cognitive intuition: the intuition that, given some conditions—namely, the conditions in which conclaves unfold—a widespread agreement among cardinals is evidence of a right decision, in the sense that such an agreement proves that the Holy Spirit's will on who should become pope was rightly tracked.[46] I call this motive an intuition since probabilistic mathematics hadn't yet been invented.[47] And I use the caveat 'given certain conditions' since Colomer & McLean argue that the Conclave's rules evolved over centuries to (i) obtain 'quick decisions;'[48] and (ii) prevent 'strategic maneuvering'[49] among cardinals; meaning, preventing cardinals from bargaining and from mis-representing their judgments in their votes. Considering this background, once we include that, in the Conclave, all cardinals were assumed equally sound in judgment, the suggestion that, in the Conclave's conditions, a widespread agreement among the sound proves that the decision is also sound makes intuitive sense. As Pope Pius II said about his own election, '[w]hat is done by the two-thirds of the sacred college, that is *surely* of the Holy Spirit, which may not be resisted.'[50]

Most of the Church's records suggest that the aim of the 2/3 rule was to choose 'the true pope under conditions most likely to promote good judgment, given the desire to ensure a swift and decisive outcome.'[51] In the 1274 Council of Lyons—the council that formalised the Conclave as we currently know it[52]—it was decided that, from that point onwards, the faction of cardinals that in a Conclave reached the 2/3 threshold wouldn't just be the greater

42 Colomer & McLean 1998: 2–5; Lagerspetz 2010: 31–2; Schwartzberg 2013: 49–52; Urfalino 2014b: 177–9.
43 Papal Encyclicals Online nd-a.
44 Id.
45 Id.
46 Lagerspetz 2010: 33–4; Schwartzberg 2013: 60, 68.
47 It's been argued that, before Pascal, the Ancient Greeks, the Romans, and Medieval Europeans had notions of probability, but they didn't gauge them mathematically. See Franklin 2015.
48 Colomer & Mclean 1998: 12.
49 Id.
50 Emphasis added. Pope Pius II, cited in Id 11.
51 Schwartzberg 2013: 60.
52 Papal Enclyclicals Online nd-b.

part, but would also be the sounder part.[53] In Pope Gregory X's words, 'not zeal to zeal, nor merit to merit, but only numbers are to be compared.'[54] Therefore, once the respective numbers were reached, the minority was deprived of 'all power to impute lack of zeal, merit or authority to the majority or their candidate.'[55]

Further, the 2/3 rule also had a political function: curbing future schisms. By establishing a supermajority rule, *Licet de Evitanda* stimulated the formation of large coalitions of cardinals, hence boosting the odds that the chosen pope would have their future support. This happened since, to reach the threshold, cardinals upholding different candidates would likely have to compromise and agree on a pope that—though not their individual 'best' or 'optimal' choice—was still an individual 'good enough' choice, insofar as the chosen candidate would probably not threaten their main interests, preferences, or values.[56] Thus, since the cardinals could at least choose a 'good enough' candidate, they had a stake in the election. And since they had such stake, the new pope would likely have their future support.

The Italian City-States

It's well documented that—especially from the 11th to the 15th century—the medieval Italian city-states used intricate procedures that combined random selection (also called 'sortition' or 'lot')[57] and voting to choose their most important officials.[58] These procedures tried to bolster political authority in a context of soaring class tensions between an ascending mercantile class and an established feudal and ecclesiastical oligarchy.[59]

When analysed through Ancient Greek categories, it's clear that the Italian city-states weren't democracies, but aristocracies. Their political systems weren't a government of the poor (*demos*),[60] but a government of the mercantile, feudal, and ecclesiastical elites whose competing ambitions had to be kept in check. As Manin argues, the underlying theme of the Italian city-states' political history was 'the divisions generated by the desire for public

53 Schwartzberg 2013: 61–2.

54 *Noc zeli ad zelum, nec meriti ad meritum, sed solum numeri ad numerum fiat collatio.* This phrase appears in Pope Gregory X's decree *Ubi Periculum*, which means 'Where Danger' or 'In Case of Danger.' Pope Gregory X, cited in Colomer & McLean 1998: 11; Lagerspetz 2010: 34.

55 Papal Enclyclicals Online nd-a.

56 Colomer & McLean 1998: 9–13; Schwartzberg 2013: 62, 68–70.

57 For justifications of the use of lot as a decision process—particularly for choosing officials—see Duxbury 1999: ch 3–5; Goodwin 2005; Stone 2011a; Stone 2011b.

58 Other places that used lot—either on its own or joined with elections—to choose municipal officials were Aragonese and German cities such as Barcelona, Frankfurt am Main, Gerona, Münster, Lleida, and Zaragoza. Duxbury 1999: 30–2; Van Reybrouck 2016: 73–4.

59 Dowlen 2008: 69–73.

60 Cartledge 2016: 17–20.

office'[61]—divisions worsened by the State's lack of a monopoly in the use of force. Alongside wealth, the main families of the Italian city-states[62] had private armies under their control. Thus, political conflicts easily became family vendettas that regularly resulted in open warfare.[63]

In this context, the main aim of the Italian city-states' political selection procedures was to ensure that those chosen to the highest offices had at least some authority over warring elites. They weren't designed to reflect 'public opinion,'[64] establish 'a system of accountability,'[65] or 'encourage new blood into the political arena.'[66] To accomplish this aim, these selection procedures had to accomplish two secondary aims: first, they had to be impartial, in the sense of being impervious to the elites' corrosive influence;[67] and second, they had to choose able people,[68] in the sense that they had to choose people that were at least 'acceptable to the largest proportion of the elite, as a means of ensuring political stability.'[69] Impartiality was accomplished by lot,[70] and ability was accomplished by supermajority rules.[71]

One of the main political selection procedures used in the Italian city-states was the Venetian Ballot (from the Italian word *ballotta*, which means 'ball'). This procedure was used to choose the doge—the highest Venetian official—and was imitated in Parma, Ivrea, Brescia, and Bologna.[72] The Venetian Ballot shared many traits with the Conclave, such as secrecy of inner discussions, secret voting, and the isolation of the electors.[73] Indeed, it's been argued that Pope Alexander III thought about the 2/3 rule for papal elections during a trip to Venice in 1177, and that Pope Gregory X took the Venetian Ballot

61 1997: 52.

62 Another destabilising factor were the geopolitical games regularly played by the European powers over the Italian peninsula—mainly the Holy Roman Empire, the Papacy, Aragón (which would later become part of Spain), and France—which became linked with the Italian city-states' intra-elite disputes. See generally Elliott 1963; Knecht 1994; Mallett & Shaw 2012.

63 Actually, due to the regularity and severity of inner strife, it wasn't uncommon for the Italian city-states to outsource political authority by bringing in a *Podestà*. That is, by importing a temporary head of state from another city. Manin 1997: 52-3; Dowlen 2008: 72.

64 Dowlen 2008: 88–9.

65 Id.

66 Id.

67 Manin 1997: 51–4; Dowlen 2008: 69–73.

68 Manin 1997: 57; Schwartzberg 2013: 62–7.

69 Schwartzberg 2013: 65.

70 Impartiality was achieved due to lot's 'a-rationality.' That is, lot's capacity to exclude reasons from a decision process. Manin 1997: 51–4; Duxbury 1999: 13–4; Dowlen 2008: 11–6; Stone 2011a.

71 Manin 1997: 57; Schwartzberg 2013: 62–5.

72 Manin 1997: 63-7; Dowlen 2008: 99–105; Schwartzberg 2013: 62–7; Van Reybrouck 2016: 69–75. See also Najemy 1982.

73 Actually, the English word 'ballot' comes from the fact that the doge's electors used balls wrapped in cloth. Manin 1997: 64.

as one of the main models for regulating the Conclave.[74] These similarities highlight that the Venetian Ballot and the Conclave were designed for similar purposes. That is, curbing the effects of inner strife by ensuring that: (i) people chosen as officials were minimally able; and (ii) such people wouldn't likely threaten the main interests, preferences, and values of their electors.

In the Italian city-states, procedures such as the Venetian Ballot were quite effective in securing ample elite support for officials since they gave sufficient guarantees that these officials would be impartial and minimally able. According to Mowbray & Gollman's[75] computerised experiment, the Venetian Ballot generally ensured that 'more popular candidates actually won, while nevertheless giving minorities a chance and neutralising corrupt voting behaviour.'[76] Also, the Ballot 'helped to bring compromise candidates to the fore by amplifying small advantages.'[77] Research in social choice theory by Coggins & Perali shows akin results.[78]

The development of supermajority rules in the Church and the Italian city-states highlights two facts: first, it highlights a basic flaw of unanimity rule. As a voting rule, unanimity is too stringent since it doesn't consider that at least one group member may act in bad faith or out of moral disagreement; and second, it highlights that, given some conditions, sincere agreements among group members on decisions can be considered proof that such decisions are right.

In contrast to the Church and the Italian city-states, the evolution of decision procedures in the representative assemblies of other Medieval European polities isn't very clear.[79] It's known that these assemblies were made of two or more branches, chambers, or houses that represented each estate, but there isn't much detailed data on how these branches decided, nor on how their decisions were counted to produce the final decision.[80] The spread of voting as a decision procedure—and of majority rule as a general voting rule—happened in European representative assemblies mainly in the 19th century.[81] This spread was heavily based on some Enlightenment philosphers' ideas, which I analyse in what follows.

74 Colomer and McLean 1998: 9-12; Schwartzberg 2013: 60–1.
75 Mowbray & Gollman 2007.
76 Van Reybrouck 2016: 69–72.
77 Id.
78 Coggins & Perali 1998.
79 On the evolution of some of these assemblies, see Post 1964: ch 2; Canning 1988: 353–5; González Antón 1989: 101–9.
80 Lagerspetz 2010: 34–5.
81 Id 35–8.

Voting Rules in the Enlightenment

Enlightenment Philosophers' Rejection of Unanimity Rule

In the 18th century, a main ramification of the Enlightenment's spirit was the idea that voting rules could track the truth—an idea bolstered by the development of probabilistic mathematics, as symbolised in the works of Condorcet[82] and Laplace.[83] Yet, unlike the Catholic Church, this 'truth' wasn't the will of the Holy Spirit, but the objective, inherent truth of the world that could be discovered only by reason. As Schwartzberg indicates, 'Leibniz, for instance, imagined a day in which disagreement could be settled by computation: "Let us calculate, sir!" would be the gauntlet, and once proven mathematically, all would immediately concur.'[84]

Given this background, one may have expected a strong defence of unanimity rule as a general voting rule. After all, just as in the Middle Ages unanimity was taken as signalling the right identification of the Holy Spirit's will, in the Enlightenment, unanimity rule may have been taken as signalling 'the consensus of the enlightened.'[85] That is, it may have been taken as proof that objective truth was identified by those trained in using reason. This expectation for 'enlightened' defences of unanimity rule makes even more sense considering that, during the Enlightenment, the main contractual theories of society's origins (such as Pufendorf's,[86] Locke's,[87] and Rousseau's)[88] appeared for the first time—theories that were largely inspired by Roman private law.

Enlightenment philosophers were quite versed in Roman private law. And some of them were highly involved in the codification of private law, following Roman, Byzantine, and ecclesiastical examples. A main principle of Roman private law (present both in Ulpian and in the *Corpus Iuris Civilis*) is that 'what touches all should be considered and approved by all' (*quod omnes tangit, ab omnibus tractari et aprobari debet,* also called 'QOT').[89] This principle has been—and still is—expounded as supporting unanimity rule when managing common goods, such as water, land, etc.[90]

When describing society's origins, many Enlightenment philosophers drew on the QOT principle. As Pufendorf claims, natural law prescribes the autonomy of individuals, which means that natural law demands their consent to

82 [1785] 2014.
83 [1825] 2009.
84 2013: 75.
85 Id.
86 1703.
87 [1689] 1980.
88 1762.
89 Manin 1997: 87-8; Schwartzberg 2013: 57–8.
90 During medieval times though, there was an alternative interpretation of the *QOT* principle as not requiring mathematical unanimity. In this second conception, as Ulpian states '[a]nything publicly done by the majority is ascribed to everyone.' Ulpian, cited in Schwartzberg 2013: 57-8.

acquire obligations. For Pufendorf, no individual may 'be obliged by [anything] to which he does not give his [c]onsent.'[91] Thus, 'the [d]ecrees of the majority will not, in the least, affect him or force his compliance.'[92] So, it's strange that, once civil society is established, Enlightenment philosophers rejected unanimity rule as a general voting rule, favouring majority rule instead. Put differently, it's paradoxical that, for Enlightenment philosophers, the only 'single law that by its nature requires unanimous consent' is the social contract.[93]

A common explanation as to why Enlightenment philosophers rejected unanimity rule as a general voting rule is that, though in principle they considered unanimity rule as ideal, in practice, unanimity is seldom achievable. Thus, groups should decide by majority rule on expediency grounds.[94] But, following Schwartzberg,[95] this explanation is incomplete. There's evidence that Enlightenment philosophers not only rejected unanimity rule since it was impractical, but also since (i) it 'was not necessary on epistemic grounds and could actually subvert the effort to reach moral certainty,'[96] and (ii) it 'did not ensure freedom but encouraged coercion.'[97] An akin conclusion can be inferred from Pasquino's,[98] Lagerspetz's,[99] and Landemore's[100] reviews of Enlightenment philosophers' ideas on voting rules. I address these ideas in the following paragraphs.

In Schwartzberg's view, during the Enlightenment, the only real supporter of unanimity rule was Voltaire, and only in the context of criminal juries. Yet Voltaire's claims that unanimity rule boosted the odds of rightly deciding criminal cases were intuitive—not mathematical.[101] According to McLean & Hewitt, though Condorcet upheld Voltaire's campaign for reforming criminal juries, he regretted that Voltaire 'lacked the mathematical background needed to furnish a constructive alternative.'[102] Conversely, Enlightenment

91 Pufendorf 1703: 153.
92 Id.
93 Rousseau 1762: 245–6.
94 Pufendorf held that institutions should decide by majority rule 'not because there is a [n]ecessity of this by … [n]ature, but because there is hardly any other possible means of transacting [b]usiness among [n]umbers' (1703: 153). And Condorcet claims that majority rule was mainly introduced for the sake of peace and general utility—not for avoiding mistakes or acting according to truth ([1785] 2014: cxxxvii–cxlii).
95 Schwartzberg 2013: 73.
96 Id.
97 Id.
98 2010: 99–103.
99 2010: 38–41.
100 2013: 69–75.
101 2013: 79, 87–8.
102 1994: 33.

philosophers involved in probabilistic mathematics (such as Condorcet and Laplace) rejected that unanimity rule had epistemic properties.[103]

Through the Enlightenment, an urgent political campaign was reforming the criminal justice system. Voltaire was obsessed with the so-called 'famous cases' (*causes célèbres*): a number of 18th century criminal cases in which the accused—all of whom were Huguenots—were convicted to death in predominantly Catholic France.[104] For Voltaire, the fact that criminal juries could punish by majority rule was a perfect excuse for religious intolerance. Voltaire's defence of unanimity rule rested on the modern idea that convicting the innocent is worse than acquitting the guilty. Yet for Schwartzberg, this modern idea was likely mixed with a conviction that unanimity rule promoted criminal juries' accuracy.[105]

Unlike Voltaire though, Condorcet[106] and Laplace[107] held that unanimity rule doesn't promote criminal juries' accuracy. Their objection is that unanimity rule boosts coercion against dissenters, hence offsetting the odds that unanimous decisions are right. For Condorcet and Laplace, unanimity rule boosts coercion against dissenters by stimulating peer pressure and social influences. Thus, unanimity rule curbs the odds that group members vote according to what they really think.

In Condorcet's 'Essay on the Application of Mathematics to the Theory of Decision-Making,'[108] Condorcet rejected unanimity rule in English criminal juries. Though Condorcet recognises that requiring this rule signals an attempt to decide correctly, he still claims that unanimity rule doesn't boost juries' accuracy since the sole fact that the jurors are obligated to 'stay in the same place until they are in agreement … privileges strong and mischievous juror[s] over honest but weak one[s].'[109] For Cordorcet, unanimity rule boosts coercion against dissenters for 'not only does hunger become a real torment, but the boredom, the disagreement, the malaise brings [the jurors] to a certain point, thus constituting a veritable torture device.'[110] Hence, since unanimity rule boosts coercion against dissenters,[111] this rule erodes two conditions for group accuracy that I analyse extensively in the next chapter: namely, statistical

103 Schwartzberg 2013: 79, 87–8.

104 McLean & Hewitt 1994: 33; Schwartzberg 2013: 74–9. The French religious wars happened two centuries ago, and religious tolerance in France was fragile, as shown by the enactments and revocations of tolerance edicts. On the French religious wars, see Holt 2005; Knecht 2014. On 16th century religious wars generally, see Elliot 2000.

105 2013: 77–9.

106 [1785] 2014: cxxxix–cxlii.

107 [1825] 2009: 171–4.

108 [1785] 2014.

109 Condorcet, cited in Schwartzberg 2013: 87.

110 Condorcet, cited in Schwartzberg 2013: 87.

111 Condorcet [1785] 2014: cxxxix–cxlii.

independence and sincere voting.[112] And since unanimity rule erodes these conditions, it's unlikely that the decisions made under this rule are right.

Laplace reasoned similarly.[113] Though Laplace holds that: (i) 'the correctness of judgments is as much more probable as the judges are more numerous and more enlightened;'[114] (ii) 'to condemn an accused it is necessary without a doubt that the judges should have the strongest proof of his offence;'[115] (iii) conviction by 'a single majority vote in a numerous tribunal indicates that the affair in question is *very doubtful*;'[116] and (iv) '[i]n a jury of twelve members, if the plurality demanded for condemnation is [unanimity] the probability of error to be feared is 1/8192;'[117] he still rejects applying unanimity rule in criminal juries. Despite all these clues that lead the reader to expect a strong support of unanimity rule, Laplace doesn't uphold such rule. As in the case of Condorcet, this lack of support is based on Laplace's insights on how unanimity rule alters social dynamics for the worse.

For Laplace, jurors don't base their decisions solely on '[the] proofs favourable or contrary to the accused,'[118] but on their 'temperament … character, [and] habits,'[119] traits that are 'sometimes contrary to the decisions which the majority of the jury *would have made* if they had listened *only to the proofs*.'[120] In Laplace's view, since unanimity rule tinkers with group members' temperament, character, and habits, unanimity rule encourages coercion among them. And since unanimity rule encourages coercion among them, unanimity rule stimulates jurors to agree on decisions for the wrong reasons rather than for the right reasons, hence eroding the alleged cognitive benefits of the rule.[121]

Condorcet's and Laplace's analysis of unanimity rule questions the idea that this rule boosts group accuracy. For Condorcet and Laplace, unanimity rule's coercive potential cancels all cognitive benefits that this rule may have. Studies on US criminal juries suggest that unanimity rule may really coerce dissenters, especially if the jury has a lone holdout.[122] This research consistently shows a strong positive link between the verdict preferred by most jurors

112 For Condorcet, decisions are likely right if they are made under the following conditions: (i) the group must face only two options; (ii) group members must be able; (iii) group members must vote in 'statistically independent' ways, meaning, group members shouldn't blindly follow their peers when voting; and (iv) group members must vote 'sincerely,' meaning, they must show their true opinions in their votes. ([1785] 2014: xxi–xxii).
113 [1825] 2009: 165–74.
114 [1825] 1902: 132.
115 Id 133.
116 Id 135.
117 Id 138–9.
118 Id 139.
119 Id.
120 Id. Emphasis added.
121 Laplace [1825] 2009: 165–74. See also Schwartzberg 2013: 87.
122 Schwartzberg 2013: 95–7.

at the beginning of the jury's decision process with the final verdict issued by the jury.[123] Thus, in many cases, dissenting jurors end up accepting most of their peers' views. And since, in US criminal juries, unanimity is needed to issue verdicts, it's likely that dissenting jurors changed their minds not because they sincerely agreed with their peers, but because they were pressured into 'finishing the job.' Or because they didn't want to cause trouble by opposing what they saw as the jury's prevalent opinion.

So, if unanimity rule is rejected, what voting rule should replace it? Broadly speaking, the position taken by Enlightenment philosophers is that the general voting rule should be majority rule, while supermajority rules should be left for special cases in which a worthy status quo (eg, the presumption of innocence) needs protection.

Enlightenment Philosophers' Case for Majority Rule

Enlightenment philosophers' case for majority rule is based on the Greek idea of equal ability among group members, joined with the idea that there's moral value in accepting a majoritarian decision as a signal of cognitive humility. Put differently, alongside rescuing the idea of alleged equal ability among group members, Enlightenment philosophers—particularly Pufendorf—supported majority rule since, unlike unanimity rule, majority rule gives minority group members a chance to recognise that they may have been wrong.

Pufendorf's analysis focuses on states' main institutions. For Pufendorf, though in principle one may argue that, when deciding, the view of the most able should prevail, the problem is that, when the State's main institution is collective, there's no higher authority to turn to when facing competing ability claims. (Notice the parallel with the Latin Catholic Church's history.)[124] In Pufendorf's words, though 'in determining speculative truths, [o]pinions are not passed by [n]umber, but by [w]eight,'[125] when passing '[b]usiness in an [a]ssembly,'[126] there's no clarity as to 'who shall be the [j]udge … of which [o]pinion is the wiser.'[127] So, since there's no way of judging who the most

123 Due to secrecy, jury debates can't be watched. So, to empirically assess peer pressure and social influences, researchers usually do post-trial interviews, approximate the initial verdict distribution among jurors using the first vote's results, and, in the case of mock juries, compare jurors' preferred hypothetical verdicts at the beginning of the decision process with the jury's actual verdict. Another usual way of studying jury decision processes is through mathematical models. For overviews of this research, see Saks 1997: 37, 39–41; Vidmar & Hans 2007: 142–4; Devine 2012: 156–7, 158–61, 185–6. For empirical studies, see Kalven & Zeisel 1993: 486–91; Hastie et al 1983; Guinther 1988; Waters & Hans 2009. For mathematical studies, see Schwartz & Schwartz 1992: List & Pettit 2011: 119–22.

124 1703: 153–4. See also Lagerspetz 2010: 39; Pasquino 2010: 101–3; Schwartzberg 2013: 81–2.

125 1703: 153.

126 Id 153–4.

127 Id 154.

able group member is, it must be presumed that all group members are equally able, and thus that they have 'an equal [r]ight to influence the [p]roceedings,' hence justifying majority rule.[128] Thus, Pufendorf bases his case for majority rule on the same idea used in Ancient Greece: the idea of a presumptive equal ability among group members.

Further, Pufendorf holds that, since all group members are presumed equally able, the minority should accept the majority's judgment since doing otherwise is a cognitively arrogant act that boosts the risk of arbitrary government.[129] For Pufendorf, given that all group members must be presumed equally able, no group member must have powers that would make them 'the sole and arbitrary [g]overnour of the State.'[130] Pufendorf puts as examples of arbitrary powers the power of a group member to: (i) control 'the [w]hole matter by [their] vote, and declaring which of the [o]pinions is the better;'[131] (ii) prefer 'the judgment of the smaller [p]arty to that of the greater;'[132] and (iii) reject 'both [p]roposals, on [p]retence that neither was good.'[133]

According to Pufendorf, if group members are presumed equally able, each minority member must 'shew [themselves] easily to others, and … conform [themselves] to the good of the whole,'[134] since not doing so means that '[they think themselves] wiser than [their] fellows,'[135] which in turn means that they likely think they should have arbitrary powers.[136] In sum, for Pufendorf, accepting the majority's judgment shows that one accepts one's fallibility; hence showing that one is reasonable; and hence showing that one likely opposes arbitrary government. Conversely, to oppose the majority shows that one doesn't accept one's fallibility; hence showing that one is unreasonable; and hence showing that one likely supports arbitrary government. Rousseau[137] and Condorcet[138] argued similarly.

128 Id 152–4.
129 1703: 152–4. See also Lagerspetz 2010: 39; Schwartzberg 2013: 79–81.
130 1703: 154.
131 Id.
132 Id.
133 Id.
134 Id 153.
135 Id 153.
136 1703: 153–4; Lagerspetz 2010; Schwartzberg 2013: 79–81.
137 For Rousseau, '[when] the opinion contrary to my own prevails, it proves nothing more than *I made a mistake* and that what *I deemed to be the general will was not*' ([1762] 2003: 246). Emphasis added.
138 For Condorcet (cited in McLean & Hewitt 1994: 38), '[e]very man has the right to live by his own reason; but when he joins society he agrees to submit some of his actions to common reason … Thus, when he submits to a law contrary to his opinion, he must say to himself: *This is a question not of myself but of all; therefore, I must not act by what I think reasonable, but what all who, like me, have abstracted from their own opinions must regard as conforming to reason and truth.*'

Enlightenment Philosophers' Case for Supermajority Rules

Though Enlightenment philosophers generally favoured majority rule, they still upheld supermajority rules in one kind of situation: the protection of some status quo or default positions. Specifically, Enlightenment philosophers favoured supermajority rules to guard: (i) the presumption of innocence in criminal trials; and (ii) constitutional provisions. And Condorcet proposed a second argument for supermajority rules based on the idea that, by calibrating the speed of decision processes, supermajority rules boost deliberation.

In Rousseau's case, though in principle he thinks majority rule is the usual rule for tracking the general will, he suggests that, depending on 'the conditions and the needs of the body politic,'[139] it may be necessary to use a voting threshold 'between unanimity and a tie;'[140] meaning, it may be necessary to use a supermajority rule. For Rousseau, whether the general will should be declared by majority rule or by a supermajority rule hinges on two criteria: importance and urgency. Rousseau sees a direct link between importance and voting thresholds. So, 'the more important and serious the deliberations are, the more the [judgment] that prevails should approach unanimity.'[141] But Rousseau also sees an inverse link between urgency and voting thresholds. Thus, 'the greater dispatch the business at hand requires, the smaller the prescribed difference in the division of [judgments] should be.'[142] Rousseau doesn't specify his concepts of 'importance' and 'urgency,' nor does he develop his claims further. Yet Condorcet argues for supermajority rules in a way akin to Rousseau's. More than Rousseau's claims then, Condorcet's argument for supermajority rules better indicates why importance and urgency are key criteria when deciding on a voting rule.

Condorcet's argument for supermajority rules isn't based on probabilistic grounds. Still, Condorcet endorses supermajorities rules in a specific set of cases: namely, cases in which he considers it necessary to guard a status quo or default position. In a relevant passage of his *Plan de Constitution présenté a la Convention Nationale* [Constitutional Plan Presented to the National Convention],[143] Condorcet holds that:

> [T]he objections against [supermajority rules] have force only against those who would propose to apply them in cases where it is necessary to act, where action cannot take place without a new decision, and where *there exist no grounds for preferring one or another of the proposed decisions.* The laws of all civilized peoples require more than a mere majority for the condemnation of an accused person, *because the evil resulting from*

139 Rousseau [1762] 2003: 247.
140 Id.
141 Id.
142 Id.
143 1793.

> *the error of punishing the guilty is greater than that of mistakenly absolving the guilty.* This greater majority can … be required in *important matters that it would be dangerous to decide badly,* when a decision concerning them can be postponed without disadvantages so great as to balance this danger.[144]

Condorcet repeats this rationale in his 'Essay on the Constitution and Functions of the Provincial Assemblies.'[145]

Thus, Condorcet suggests a 'precautionary principle' or 'errors a-symmetry logic' for using supermajority rules, which he then illustrates with specific examples, such as criminal juries. According to this logic, supermajority rules are allowed as a voting rule when the effects of mistakenly changing a certain status quo are worse than the effects of keeping it. Supermajority rules guard a status quo by giving some minority group members—those needed to reach the supermajority threshold—the power to block a majority's proposal to change it.[146] Condorcet claims that bicameralism enables legislative minorities to block bills upheld by legislative majorities. He also states that this effect is akin to using supermajority rules for deciding, but with the difference that bicameralism works 'in an uncertain or bizarre manner.'[147] Hence, though Condorcet rejects bicameralism for blocking majorities' legislative proposals, he *doesn't* reject supermajority rules for that same purpose when his error asymmetry logic applies.

Moreover, Condorcet holds that supermajority rules can boost deliberation among legislators by reducing the speed of legislative processes.[148] For Condorcet, once bicameralism is rejected, its beneficial effects—that is, bicameralism's capacity to slow down the enactment of statutes—should be mimicked. According to Condorcet, in legislatures, one should use procedures that 'even in the most imperious circumstances'[149] guard against the effects of overhasty decisions.[150] Put differently, in legislatures, one should use procedures that ensure that no decision, however quick, is 'made without reflection.'[151] And that provide 'the members of the legislative assembly … [with] the means of forming an opinion … [and the means] to enlighten themselves as to the grounds and consequences of the decision proposed to them.'[152]

144 [1793] 1976: 161. Emphasis added.
145 1788: 120–1.
146 Condorcet 1793: 14, 19. See also Tsebelis 2002: 139–43, 149–51; Schwartzberg 2013: 92–4, 121–3; Lagerspetz 2016: 195–6, 278–83.
147 1793: 14.
148 Id 16.
149 Id 16–7.
150 Id 17.
151 Id.
152 Id.

Supermajority rules reduce the speed of legislative processes in the same way in which they guard a status quo: by granting some minority group members the power to block a majority's decision proposal to change it.[153] Thus, for Condorcet, alongside guarding a status quo, supermajority rules boost deliberation since, if minority group members use a supermajority rule to slow down the decision process, this allows group members to refine or develop better claims on what should be done, which in turn may translate into a sincere agreement. So, as Schwartzberg argues, Condorcet's case for supermajority rules is epistemic 'insofar as it promotes the quality of citizens' judgments through ensuring adequate deliberation.'[154]

Enlightenment philosophers' analysis of voting rules gives us relevant clues on their traits. First, their analysis gives a probabilistic argument that fits with the Church's reasons for abandoning unanimity rule. As we have seen, the Church's experience proved that unanimity rule is too taxing: unanimity rule doesn't consider that group members may act in bad faith or out of moral disagreement. What Enlightenment philosophers included in this analysis is that, due to this flaw, unanimity rule boosts coercion against dissenters. Thus, they generally concluded that unanimity rule's coercive potential offsets its alleged cognitive benefits.

Second, on majority rule, Enlightenment philosophers (particularly Pufendorf) rescued from Greek Antiquity the idea that this voting rule stems from group members' alleged equal ability. Hence, since majority rule stems from this alleged equal ability, this voting rule has a 'semiotic' function,[155] in the sense that it signals this equality to the rest of society.

Third, by claiming that minorities should submit to majority-supported decisions, Enlightenment philosophers show that, unlike unanimity rule, majority rule allows dissent. In this sense, Enlightenment philosophers also direct one's attention to the fact that—unlike unanimity rule—majority rule is flexible since it considers the possibility that group members act in bad faith or out of moral disagreement.

Fourth, on supermajority rules, Enlightenment philosophers (particularly Condorcet) held that these voting rules may guard a status quo against likely negative changes. Enlightenment philosophers were also key in showing why this happens by remarking that supermajority rules give minorities the ability to block majorities' decision proposals.

Lastly, Enlightenment philosophers (and, again, particularly Condorcet) also built a deliberative case for supermajority rules that parallels the way in which these rules were used in the Church and in the Italian city-states. By giving minorities the power to block majorities' decision proposals, supermajority

153 Condorcet 1793: 14, 19. See also Tsebelis 2002: 139–43, 149-51; Schwartzberg 2013: 92–4, 121–3; Lagerspetz 2016: 195–6, 278–83.

154 2013: 94.

155 I took this word from Brennan 2016: ch 5.

rules slow down decision processes; hence boosting deliberation; and hence potentially boosting their decisions' quality.

Conclusion

There are many traits that may be articulated from voting rules' history. For starters, from the Church's bad experience with unanimity rule in papal elections—and from its analysis by Condorcet and Laplace—I infer a major flaw of unanimity rule: namely, its inability to consider bad faith of moral disagreement, hence boosting coercion against dissenters. Historical experience—and research on US criminal juries—suggests that this flaw seems strong enough to void unanimity rule's alleged cognitive benefits. Thus, from this point onwards, I discard unanimity rule from my analysis, hence only focusing on majority rule and supermajority rules.

Further, from supermajority rules' and majority rule's history—particularly supermajority rules' use in the Church and the Italian city-states, and the arguments for majority rule made by Enlightenment philosophers—I articulate a trait shared by these voting rules: their ability to consider how humans generally behave, hence allowing for bad faith or moral disagreement. This trait is a key asset for using these voting rules to replace unanimity rule. I call this trait 'flexibility.'

Moreover, from majority rule's history—particularly its link with voting, and its analysis by Enlightenment philosophers (especially Pufendorf)—I articulate a trait exclusive to majority rule. That is, majority rule's ability to work in society as a symbol of a certain equal status among group members. Specifically, majority rule has historically been used to recognise that, particularly in political matters, group members are presumed equally able. I call this trait 'equality-signal.'

Lastly, from supermajority rules' history—particularly their use by the Church and the Italian city-states, and Enlightenment philosophers' case for supermajority rules (especially Condorcet's)—I articulate three relevant traits of these voting rules. First, supermajority rules may guard a status quo. I call this trait 'non-neutrality.' Second, supermajority rules may boost deliberation by slowing down decision processes. I call this trait 'decelerator.' Third, when groups decide by at least reaching supermajority rules' thresholds, these voting rules tap into a certain intuition that sincere agreements on decisions are evidence that such decisions are right. Thus, as does majority rule, supermajority rules also socially express something: namely, that decisions reached under sincere agreements are likely right and thus are authoritative. I call this trait 'agreement-signal.'

References

Brennan J, *Against Democracy* (Princeton University Press 2016) https://doi.org/10.1515/9781400882939

Canning JP, 'Introduction: Politics, Institutions and Ideas' in Burns JH (ed), *The Cambridge History of Medieval Political Thought* c.350-c.1450 (Cambridge University Press 1988)
Cartledge P, *Democracy: A Life* (Oxford University Press 2016)
Coggins JS & Perali CF, '64% Majority Rule in Ducal Venice: Voting for the Doge' (1998) 97(4) *Public Choice* 709 https://doi.org/10.1023/A:1004947715017
Colomer J & McLean I, 'Electing Popes: Approval Balloting and Qualified-Majority Rule' (1998) 29 *Journal of Interdisciplinary History* 1 https://doi.org/10.1162/002219598551616
Condorcet MJA, *Essai sur l'Application de l'analyse à la probabilité des décisions rendues à la pluralité des voix* [Essay on the Application of Mathematics to the Theory of Decision-Making] (first published 1785, Cambridge University Press 2014)
——— 'On the Principles of the Constitutional Plan Presented to the National Convention' in Keith Michael Baker (ed), *Condorcet: Selected Writings (first published 1793*, Bobbs-Merrill 1976)
——— *Essai sur la constitution et le fonctions des assemblées provinciales* [Essay on the Constitution and Functions of the Provincial Assemblies] (1788) https://gallica.bnf.fr/ark:/12148/bpt6k41723m
——— *Plan de Constitution présenté a la Convention Nationale* [Constitutional Plan Presented to the National Convention] (Paris, Imprimerie Nationale 1793) https://gallica.bnf.fr/ark:/12148/bpt6k73809
de Ste Croix GEM, *Athenian Democratic Origins* (Oxford University Press 2004) https://doi.org/10.1093/acprof:oso/9780199255177.001.0001
Devine DJ, *Jury Decision Making: The State of the Science* (New York University Press 2012) https://doi.org/10.18574/9780814704981
Dowlen O, *The Political Potential of Sortition: A Study of the Random Selection of Citizens for Public Office* (Imprint Academic 2008)
Duxbury N, *Random Justice: On Lotteries and Legal Decision-Making* (Oxford University Press 1999) https://doi.org/10.1093/acprof:oso/9780198268253.001.0001
El-Hakim S, 'The Structure and Dynamics of Consensus Decision-Making' (1978) 13(1) *Man, New Series* 55 https://www.jstor.org/stable/2801065
Elliott JH, *Imperial Spain: 1469-1766 (*Edward Arnold 1963)
——— *Europe Divided:* 1559-1598 (2nd edn, Wiley-Blackwell 2000)
Fernández de Buján A, *Derecho Público Romano [Roman Public Law]* (23rd edn Civitas Thomson Reuters 2020)
Franklin J, *The Science of Conjecture: Evidence and Probability before Pascal* (Johns Hopkins University Press 2015)
Gaudemet J, Dubois J, Duval A and Champagne J, *Les Elections dans L'Eglise Latine des Origines au XVI Siècle [Elections in the Latin Church since its Origins to the XVI Century]* (Fernand Lanore 1979)
González Antón L, *Las Cortes en la España del Antiguo Régimen [The Cortes in Old Regime Spain]* (Siglo XXI 1989)
Goodwin B, *Justice by Lottery* (2nd edn, Imprint Academic 2005)
Glotz G, *The Greek City and Its Institutions (first published 1929*, N Mallison tr, Routledge 2013)
Guinther J, *The Jury in America (*Facts on File Publications 1988)
Hansen MH, *The Athenian Democracy in the Age of Demosthenes: Structure, Principles, and Ideology* (JA Cook tr, University of Oklahoma Press 1999)

Harari YN, *Sapiens: Brief History of Humankind* (Signal 2014)

Hastie R, Penrod SD & Pennington N, *Inside the Jury* (Harvard University Press 1983)

Hébert M, 'Indigenous Spheres of Deliberation' in Bächtinger A, Dryzek JS, Mansbridge J, & Warren ME (eds), *The Oxford Handbook of Deliberative Democracy* (Oxford University Press 2018) https://doi.org/10.1093/oxfordhb/9780198747369.013.10

Holt MP, *The French Wars of Religion*, 1562-1629 (2nd edn, Cambridge University Press 2005) https://doi.org/10.1017/CBO9780511817922

Kalven Jr H & Zeisel H, *The American Jury (special edn*, The Legal Classics Library 1993)

Knecht RJ, *Renaissance Warrior and Patron: The Reign of Francis I* (Cambridge University Press 1994)

——— *The French Wars of Religion* 1559-1598 (3rd edn, Routledge 2014) https://doi.org/10.4324/9781315833583

Lagerspetz E, 'Wisdom and numbers' (2010) 49(1) *Social Science Information* 29 https://doi.org/10.1177/0539018409354475

——— *Social Choice and Democratic Values* (Springer 2016) https://doi.org/10.1007/978-3-319-23261-4

Laplace PS, *A Philosophical Essay on Probabilities (first published 1825*, Frederick Wilson Truscott Frederick Lincoln Emory tr, Chapman and Hall 1902) https://bayes.wustl.edu/Manual/laplace_A_philosophical_essay_on_probabilities.pdf

——— *Essai philosophique sur les probabilités* [Philosophical Essay on Probabilities] (first published 1825, Cambridge University Press 2009)

List C & Pettit P, *Group Agency: The Possibility, Design, and Status of Corporate Agents* (Cambridge University Press 2011) https://doi.org./10.1093/acprof:oso/9780199591565.001.0001

Locke J, *Two Treatises of Government (first published 1689*, Hacket 1980)

Mallett ME & Shaw C, *The Italian Wars, 1494-1559: War, State and Society in Early Modern Europe* (Pearson 2012).

Manin B, *The Principles of Representative Government* (Cambridge University Press 1997) https://doi.org/10.1017/CBO9780511659935

McLean I & Hewitt F, 'Section 2: The Theory of Voting' in McLean I and Hewitt F (eds), *Condorcet: Foundations of Social Choice and Political Theory* (Edward Elgar 1994)

Mill JS, 'Considerations on Representative Government' in McCallum RB (ed), *On Liberty and Considerations on Representative Government (first published 1861*, Basil Blackwell 1948)

Mowbray M & Gollman D, 'Electing the Doge of Venice: Analysis of a 13th Century Protocol' (IEE Computer Security Foundations Symposium, Venice, Italy 6-8 July 2007) <https://www.hpl.hp.com/techreports/2007/HPL-2007-28R1.pdf> accessed 9 July 2019.

Najemy JM, *Corporatism and Consensus in Florentine Electoral Politics*, 1280-1400 (University of North Carolina Press 1982)

of Nursia B, *The Rule of St Benedict in English* (Timothy Fry ed, Liturgical Press 2018)

Ortega y Gasset J, 'Historia como sistema' [History as a System] in Ortega y Gasset J, *Obras Completas de José Ortega y Gasset [The Complete Works of José Ortega y Gasset]*, vol 6 (first published 1923, 6th edn, Revista de Occidente 1964)

Papal Encyclicals Online: Church Councils, 'Third Lateran Council—1179 AD' (nd-a) <www.papalencyclicals.net/councils/ecum11.htm> accessed 9 June 2019.

Papal Enclyclicals Online: Church Councils, 'Second Council of Lyons—1274 AD' (nd-b) <https://www.papalencyclicals.net/councils/ecum14.htm> accessed 9 June 2019.
Pasquino P, 'Samuel Pufendorf: majority rule (logic, justification and limits) and forms of government' (2010) 49(1) *Social Science Information* 99 https://doi.org/10.1177/0539018409354476
Post G, *Studies in Medieval Legal Thought: Public Law and the State 1100-1322* (Princeton University Press 1964)
Pufendorf S, *Of the Law of Nature and Nations: Eight Books. Book the Seventh* (Oxford 1703)
Ribas Alba JM, *Democracia en Roma. Introducción al Derecho Electoral Romano* [Democracy in Rome. Introduction to Roman Electoral Law] (Comares 2008)
Rousseau JJ, *Du contrat social, ou principes du droit politique [On the Social Contract; or, Principles of Political Right]* (Leipzig, Gerard Fleischer 1762)
——— 'On the Social Contract; Or, Principles of Political Right' in John T Scott (ed), *The Major Political Writings of Jean-Jacques Rousseau: The Two Discourses and the Social Contract (first published 1762*, University of Chicago Press 2003).
Saks MJ, 'What Do Jury Expertiments Tell Us about How Juries (Should) Make Decisions' (1997) 6 *Southern California Interdisciplinary Law Journal* 1
Schmidtz D & Brennan J, *A Brief History of Liberty* (Wiley-Blackwell 2010) https://doi.org/10.1002/9781444318289
Schwartz EP & Schwartz WF, 'Decisionmaking by Juries under Unanimity and Supermajority Voting' (1992) 80 *Georgetown Law Journal* 775
Schwartzberg M, *Counting the Many. The Origins and Limits of Supermajority Rule* (Cambridge University Press 2013) https://doi.org/10.1017/CBO9781139013970
Staveley ES, *Greek and Roman Voting and Elections* (Cornell University Press 1972)
Steiner J & Dorff RH, 'Decision by Interpretation. A New Concept for an Often Overlooked Decision Mode' (1980) 10(1) *British Journal of Political Science* 1 http://www.jstor.org/stable/193446
Stone P, *The Luck of the Draw: The Role of Lotteries in Decision Making* (Oxford University Press 2011a) https://doi.org/10.1093/acprof:oso/9780199756100.001.0001
——— (ed), *Lotteries in Public Life: A Reader* (Imprint Academic 2011b)
Taleb NN, *The Black Swan: The Impact of the Highly Improbable* (2019 Box Set edn, Random House 2010)
Tsebelis G, *Veto Players: How Political Institutions Work* (Princeton University Press 2002) https://doi.org/10.1515/9781400831456
Urfalino P, 'The Rule of Non-Opposition: Opening Up Decision-Making by Consensus' (2014a) 22(3) *The Journal of Political Philosophy* 320 https://doi.org/10.1111/jopp.12037
——— 'Reasons and Preferences in Medicine Evaluation Committees' in Landemore H and Elster J (eds), *Collective Wisdom: Principles and Mechanisms* (Cambridge University Press 2014b) https://doi.org/10.1017/CBO9780511846427
Van Reybrouck D, *Against Elections: The Case for Democracy (Seven Stories* 2016)
Vidmar N & Hans VP, *American Juries: The Verdict* (Prometheus Books 2007)
Waters NL & Hans VP, 'A Jury of One: Opinion Formation, Conformity, and Dissent on Juries' (2009) 6 *Journal of Empirical Legal Studies* 513 https://doi.org/10.1111/j.1740-1461.2009.01152.x

4 The Traits of Majority Rule and Supermajority Rules

In this chapter, I present the main traits of majority rule and supermajority rules. Alongside the traits derived from voting rules' history, I include traits articulated by social choice scholars and political philosophers. The idea is to present a thorough (though not exhaustive) map of voting rules' traits—a map that allows us to compare majority rule and supermajority rules to determine which voting rule is best suited for declaring statutes unconstitutional.[1] This chapter is split into two sections. First, I show some traits shared by majority rule and supermajority rules. These traits are 'Condorcet accuracy,' 'flexibility,' and 'anonymity.' Second, I show the traits that only majority rule has (that is, 'neutrality,' 'decisiveness' and 'equality-signal'), and the traits that only supermajority rules have (that is, 'non-neutrality,' 'decelerator,' and 'agreement-signal'), respectively.

Shared Traits

There are three traits shared by majority rule and supermajority rules. First, 'Condorcet accuracy.' That is, the trait by which majority rule and supermajority rules boost group accuracy according to the Condorcet Jury Theorem. Second, 'flexibility.' That is, the trait by which majority rule and supermajority rules consider dissent. Finally, 'anonymity.' That is, the trait by which majority rule and supermajority rules render group members' identity irrelevant for deciding.

Let's analyse these traits in detail.

1 I don't analyse what could be called 'Hong-Page accuracy.' This is the trait by which majority rule may boost group accuracy according to the 'Hong-Page theorem.' This theorem was developed by mathematician Lu Hong and political scientist Scott Page to prove that, under certain conditions, diverse groups may outperform homogeneous groups. I exclude this theorem since this theorem only works in 'cognitively diverse groups;' meaning, it only works in groups whose members are knowledgeable in different disciplines and belong to different demographics. This theorem doesn't apply to constitutional courts since judges are relatively homogeneous groups insofar as they are mainly (or solely) made of legal experts. Notice though that the Hong-Page theorem gives arguments for including lay judges in constitutional courts. Hong & Page 2004; Page 2007: 139–43, 149–51. For a critique of the theorem, see Thompson 2014.

DOI: 10.4324/9781032723952-4

Condorcet Accuracy

Condorcet accuracy is the trait by which majority rule boosts group accuracy: it's the trait by which majority rule boosts the odds that groups decide rightly subject to substantive standards. Condorcet accuracy is based on the Condorcet Jury Theorem. This theorem—made by Condorcet[2] and re-discovered by Black[3]—is one of the oldest mathematical proofs of group decisions' cognitive soundness. According to this theorem, if four conditions hold, the larger the number of group members supporting a decision, the higher the odds that such a decision is right.[4] The theorem isn't bound by substantive standards' specificity. Given a substantive standard, and if its conditions hold, the theorem applies. For example, the theorem applies among physicians deciding under medical standards, engineers deciding under engineering standards, etc.

Condorcet claimed that the ***absolute margins*** generated by majority rule boosted accuracy. The absolute margins are the ***differences*** between majorities and minorities generated in each decision.[5] For example, if, in a nine-judge court, five judges are for declaring a statute unconstitutional while four judges are against declaring it unconstitutional, the absolute margin for this decision is one since five minus four equals one. For Condorcet, if the theorem's conditions hold, the larger the absolute margin produced on a specific decision, the higher the odds that such a decision is right.

Condorcet's formula is as follows:[6]

$$\frac{A^M}{A^M + (1 - A)^M}$$

2 [1785] 2014.
3 1971: 159–65.
4 Condorcet [1785] 2014.
5 McLean & Hewitt 1994: 35–7; List & Pettit 2011: 91.
6 List changed the theorem to consider 'base rates.' Base rates are the unconditional odds that some facts happen. Base rates are unconditional since they are 'the true state of the world': they don't stem from opinions made by individuals or groups. When considering base rates, the theorem is:

$$\frac{PA^M}{PA^M + (1 - P)(1 - A)^M}$$

where 'P' is the base rate, and (1 — P) are the unconditional odds that the respective fact *won't* happen. When making factual judgments, one should consider base rates since not doing so can skew results even when most group members are able. (This happens in medical diagnoses.) I kept Condorcet's formula for two reasons: first, due to reasonable disagreement, in constitutional review, we don't know what 'the true state of the world' is; and second, if due to reasonable disagreement, we assume that the base rate of unconstitutionality of statutes is 50%, the results are the same as with Condorcet's formula. List 2004: 522-30; List & Pettit 2011: 82–6, 91. On base rates, see also Hastie & Dawes 2001.

where 'A' represents ability—that is, each group member has above 50% odds of deciding rightly (I analyse this concept later on)—'M' represents the absolute margin—that is, the difference between a majority and a minority—and (1 — A) represents inability. That is, each group member's odds of deciding wrongly.

For example, suppose that Weirdland's constitutional court has nine judges, and the court decides its cases as a plenary and with all its judges present. And suppose that the court decides on the validity of 'statute X,' that it declares such statute unconstitutional, and that each judge is 60% able.[7] That is, each judge has a 60% probability of deciding rightly. In this case, the theorem goes:

$$\frac{0.6^M}{0.6^M + (1-0.6)^M}$$

Assuming that the judges do not unanimously find statute X unconstitutional, there are five possible voting results in this case: first, a majority decision; second, a six-to-three decision; third, a seven-to-two decision; and last, an eight-to-one decision. Hence, when applying the theorem, we get the following accuracy results:

Voting Results	Absolute Margin	Group Accuracy
Majority Decision	One	60%
Six-to-Three	Three	77%
Seven-to-Two	Five	88%
Eight-to-One	Seven	94%

Figure 4.1 The Condorcet Jury Theorem applied to our example

7 I gave judges a 60% individual ability since: (i) an individual ability below 60% would be too close to randomness; and (ii) a higher individual ability may be too controversial, especially for scholars critical of constitutional review. Some may object that I'm being too generous. But if judges can't be considered at least 60% able (or at least *around* 60% able), this isn't a problem of constitutional courts' voting rules, but a problem of judicial education and judicial selection.

In the theorem, what matters most is neither group size, nor the proportion of the majority to group size: what matters most is ***absolute margin size.*** Thus, even if groups become larger or smaller, absolute margin size may stay equal, which means that group accuracy may stay equal as well.[8] For example, the accuracy of Weirdland's court declaring statute X unconstitutional by a five-to-four vote is the same as the accuracy of a five-member court declaring that statute unconstitutional by a three-to-two vote. So, as McLean & Hewitt argue, in the theorem, 'we should talk about "a majority of [eight]," "a majority of 20," etc., not "a [2/3] majority" or a "[3/4] majority."'[9]

The Condorcet Jury Theorem works if four conditions hold. First, the group must face binary or pairwise options:[10] they must only face two possible decisions ('binary choice'). Second, group members must be able, capable, competent, or skilled: their odds of deciding rightly must be above 50% ('ability'). Third, group members must vote independently of each other ('statistical independence'). Finally, group members mustn't misrepresent their opinions ('sincere voting'). The binary choice condition is self-explanatory. The rest of the conditions though need more analysis.

1. Ability

Ability means that group members' odds of deciding rightly are above 50%. Put differently, group members' odds of being right must be better than a coin-flip.[11] There's a tight and a loose version of this condition. In the tight version, each group member must have above 50% odds of deciding rightly. This is Condorcet's view.[12] Conversely, in the loose version, the ***average group member*** must have above 50% odds of deciding rightly.[13] This second version allows groups to have unable members if the ***average ability*** stays above 50%. In both interpretations, one can increase group accuracy by (i) boosting group members' ability, (ii) boosting absolute margins, or (iii) boosting group members' ability ***and*** absolute margins.

8 McLean & Hewitt 1994: 35–7; List &Pettit 2011: 91.

9 McLean & Hewitt 1994: 37.

10 In this book, ***not deciding*** isn't considered an 'option.' Thus, if one must choose between Jane and Mary for mayor, Jane and Mary are the only options. Naturally, one may abstain from voting, cast a blank vote, etc., but formally speaking, such actions wouldn't be 'options.' Hence, in this example, the group still faces a binary choice.

11 Condorcet [1785] 2014: xxi–xxii.

12 Id.

13 Grofman et al 1983: 261, 268–70. See also Estlund 2008: 225; Landemore 2013: 73; Lagerspetz 2016: 307.

Unfortunately, due to distributions of information, skills, knowledge, and traits generally[14]—and due to people's cognitive biases[15]—it's doubtful that the ability condition holds once group size increases. As Condorcet[16] claimed, many times, things seem to go the other way around. That is, the larger the group, the lower the odds that its members are able. Thus, the larger the group, the more it's exposed to deciding wrongly.

2. *Statistical Independence*

Statistical independence means that a group member's ability mustn't be affected by their peers' ability. As Landemore claims, 'the probability of one person being right … should be the same regardless of the probability of another person being right for that same question.'[17] Or, as Brennan holds, '[group members] cannot just be copying each other's votes.'[18]

It's quite debated whether statistical independence is hindered by communication among group members. This debate is tainted by the sketchiness of empirical research on deliberation. For Miller,[19] Panning,[20] and Grofman & Feld,[21] any share of information hinders statistical independence. Thus, any sort of discussion prior to voting should be banned. Conversely, for Lahda,[22] Estlund,[23] Landemore,[24] and Schwartzberg,[25] though statistical independence excludes 'blind deference to someone else's authority,'[26] it doesn't exclude 'communication among group members, information sharing, or any kind of pre-voting [discussion].'[27] In this second version of statistical independence, if group members don't unreflexively follow each other, statistical independence holds even if they previously communicate. Since I assume that judicial deliberation is cognitively sound, I support the second version of statistical

14 Eg, research shows that political ignorance is widespread. This matters since the Condorcet Jury Theorem has been used to claim that democracies usually decide better than other political systems. For overviews of this research, see Converse 1990; Caplan 2008; Achen & Bartels 2016; Brennan 2016: ch 2–3, 187–95.
15 Kahneman et al 1982; Kahneman 2011.
16 Condorcet [1785] 2014: xxiv–xxv.
17 2013: 73.
18 2016: 179.
19 1986.
20 1986.
21 1988.
22 1992: 617, 625–30.
23 2008: 225–26.
24 2013: 153–4.
25 2013: 93–4.
26 Landemore 2013: 154.
27 2013: 153–4.

independence. Yet, there's a phenomenon that's been proven to hinder statistical independence: namely, 'information cascades.'[28]

Information cascades occur when groups must decide and voting is public and sequential. That is, group members may see how their peers vote, and votes are cast one after the other. In these situations, group members may copy each other since they don't just consider their own judgment, but also their peers' judgments, as shown in their votes. This gives the first voter an excessive influence, hence producing a 'snowball' or 'bandwagon' effect.[29] The farther a voter is in the queue, the likelier it is that they'll defer to their peers. Further, this effect is stronger when previous voters have a higher social status—however measured—than later voters.[30] This happens due to peer pressure and social influences.[31] There are ways to tackle information cascades, which I examine in Chapter 7.

3. Sincere Voting

Sincere (or 'truthful') voting consists in voting for the option one judges as right considering the available options and data. Put differently, sincere voting consists in *not* misrepresenting one's votes.[32] According to social choice research, two typical behaviours erode this condition: bargaining and manipulation.[33]

Bargaining is about trying to change group members' minds by making credible threats or promises.[34] Bargaining erodes sincere voting since one may misrepresent one's vote due to threats or promises made by peers or by third parties. In turn, manipulation is about trying to mould a voting process' result.[35] Manipulation erodes sincere voting since one may try to mould this result by misrepresenting one's votes. Some common kinds of bargaining are 'vote-selling'—that is, voting against one's judgment to get a pecuni-

28 One of the first scholars that identified information cascades—though he didn't exactly call them that—is Jeremy Bentham ([1843] 1999: 106–7, 150).

29 For overviews of studies on information cascades, see Sunstein 2006: 88-92; Farnsworth 2007: 136–9; Devine 2012: 169–71; Barry 2021: 218–9. For mathematical research on information cascades, see Banerjee 1992; Bickchanandi et al. 1998; Daughety & Reinganum 1999; Hung & Plott 2011; Callender 2007: 74. For empirical research on information cascades, see Anderson & Holt 1997; De Vany & Walls 1999; Walden & Browne 2002; Urfalino & Costa 2015.

30 Sunstein 2006: 67–9, 86-8; Devine 2012: 163–6. See also Stasser & Titus 1985; Liu et al 2012.

31 Sunstein 2006: ch 2–3.

32 Landemore 2013: 154–6; Lagerspetz 2016: 217–29.

33 As do most social choice scholars, I assume that, generally speaking, sincere voting is moral while bargaining and manipulation are immoral. Still, it has been questioned whether manipulation is immoral, especially when one manipulates for altruistic reasons. Kornhauser & Sager 1993: 53–4; Carminker 1999; Dowding & van Hees 2007; Lagerspetz 2016: 229–35.

34 Elster 2013: 30–6.

35 Lagerspetz 2016: 217–29.

ary benefit—and 'logrolling,' that is, voting against one's mind in exchange for a reciprocal response by one's peers. For its part, some common kinds of manipulation are: (i) supporting an option one doesn't like to boost the odds that one's favoured option is chosen; (ii) proposing a procedural change to boost the odds that one's favoured option is chosen; and (iii) introducing new options to boost (or hinder) the odds that the other options are chosen.[36]

Two main causes of manipulation are the doctrinal paradox and possible cycles. As seen in Chapter 1, the doctrinal paradox can boost manipulation since group members may misrepresent their conclusions to ensure that such conclusions are supported by premises they endorse. Or vice versa, they may misrepresent their premises to advance a conclusion they endorse.[37]

Further, when groups face multiple—meaning, more than two—options, cycles may occur.[38] Possible cycles give manipulators relevant chances at influencing voting processes to get the results they like. Cycles are decision making situations in which transitivity is violated. Transitivity is an element of rational choice. In short, transitivity means that, if a person or group faces options A, B, and C, and chooses A over B, and B over C, they should also choose A over C. So, all else equal, A should always defeat B (or C) if it competes against B (or C) in binary choice situations.[39] Yet, when cycles occur, there's no option like A; meaning, there's no option that can defeat all the other options if they compete against each other in binary choice situations. So, in cycles, the respective person or group chooses almost at random: they may choose any option, but that option isn't necessarily favoured over all its competitors. Thus, when cycles happen, individuals or groups behave irrationally in the sense that they don't have a stable ranking of options.

When groups face multiple options, cycles may occur unless the decision procedure gives more weight to some individual judgments over others. Some ways of doing this are by: (i) using runoff (also called 'two-rounds') voting to reduce multiple options into binary options (this usually happens in many presidential elections); (ii) making an individual or group the agenda setter (this usually happens in deliberative assemblies);[40] and (iii) using supermajority rules.[41]

36 Carminker 1999; Elster 2013: 72–84.

37 Kornhauser & Sager 1993: 53–5; List & Pettit 2011: 58, 110–4.

38 Cycles were discovered by Condorcet ([1785] 2014: lviii–lx, 119–20). Kenneth Arrow rediscovered them in the 1950s (1963). Further, Allan Gibbard (1973), Mark Satterthwaite (1975), and Richard McKelvey (1979) reached akin conclusions.

39 In social choice terms, option A is a 'Condorcet winner.' Lagerspetz 2016: 78.

40 Elster 2013: 76–7; Landemore 2013: 149–50.

41 For Caplin & Nalebuff, 64% rules are immune to cycles (1988). This rule is akin to the rule used to choose the Venetian Doge (Coggins & Perali 1998). Other social choice research reached akin results. See Saari 1997; Colomer & McLean 1998; Tsebelis 2002: 139–43, 149–51; Lagerspetz 2016: 195–6, 278–83.

No voting rule is fully 'strategy-proof;' meaning, no voting rule can eliminate bargaining and manipulation.[42] Specifically, it's hard to curb logrolling and the kind of manipulation allowed by the doctrinal paradox. Still, some voting rules are more strategy-proof than others. In particular, supermajority rules are more strategy-proof than majority rule. This happens since—as we shall see below—supermajority rules guard a status quo.[43] Under majority rule, one may bargain or manipulate for and against a status quo. Conversely, under supermajority rules, the possibility to bargain and manipulate against a status quo is bounded, while the possibility to bargain and manipulate for the status quo stays constant.

The Condorcet Jury Theorem applies to majority rule and supermajority rules. Actually, supermajority rules may boost group accuracy more than majority rule when groups are relatively small (of around the size of a criminal jury or less) and errors are asymmetrical. That is, the group wants to avoid particularly serious errors, such as convicting the innocent. In these cases, supermajority rules may boost group accuracy indirectly: they don't boost group accuracy by directing the group to the 'best' or 'optimal' decision, but by avoiding the worst decision.[44] This also happens since supermajority rules guard a status quo.[45] Yet unlike majority rule, supermajority rules are indeterminate:[46] they are a gamut, range, or spectrum of voting rules. This is problematic since the more a supermajority rule departs from majority rule, the more a supermajority rule resembles unanimity rule. And the more a supermajority rule resembles unanimity rule, the more a supermajority rule boosts coercion against dissenters,[47] hence violating statistical independence and sincere voting. Thus, some supermajority rules can boost group accuracy more than majority rule while others can't. I tackle the problem of specifying supermajority rules in Chapter 7.

Research on the Condorcet Jury Theorem has mainly focused on citizens and elected representatives. Mathematicians, political scientists, and political philosophers have analysed whether the theorem gives 'substantive' or 'result-based' justifications for democracy that join its 'formal' or 'procedural' justifications. The aim has been to determine whether, alongside being fair, 'democracy is smart.' Put differently, these scholars have used the Theorem to assess whether citizens' and elected representatives' decisions made under

42 Lagerspetz 2016: 217–26.
43 Tsebelis 2002: 139–43, 149–51; Schwartzberg 2013: 92–4, 121–3; Lagerspetz 2016: 195–6, 278–83.
44 Ben-Yashar & Nitzan 1997; McGinnis & Rappaport 2008; List & Pettit 2011: 90–1. Yet Grofman et al (1983: 269), Nitzan & Paroush (1984: 259–60), and Fey (2003) suggest that supermajority rules may also boost Condorcetian accuracy when errors are symmetrical.
45 Tsebelis 2002: 139–43, 149–51; Schwartzberg 2013: 92–4, 121-3; Lagerspetz 2016: 195–6, 278–83.
46 Schwartzberg 2010.
47 Laplace [1835] 2009: 165–74; Schwartzberg 2016: 79, 87–8.

majority rule are likely better than decisions made under other political systems.[48] Other scholars reject the attempt to use the theorem to justify democracy.[49] Following Brennan, when applied to democracies, the theorem may be just 'a mathematical curiosity'[50] that 'tell[s] us little about real-world politics.'[51] The main reason for this pessimistic view is that it's doubtful that the theorem's conditions hold among citizens and elected representatives. Along with the fact that citizens and elected representatives usually face multiple options,[52] it's been questioned whether they are able and unbiased enough,[53] and whether they really vote in statistically independent ways. (As we've seen, barring information cascades,[54] research on deliberation is inconclusive.)

Against this pessimistic view, it's generally accepted that the theorem may apply in what could be called 'expert groups;'[55] meaning, the theorem may apply to relatively small groups whose members: (i) are 'experts,' in the sense that they develop mastery or skill in using some techniques, canons, or methods given by some substantive standards that other people (whom we could call 'laypeople') don't develop; and (ii) use those techniques, canons, or methods for deciding (eg, small groups of physicians performing medical diagnoses, small groups of engineers building bridges, small groups of architects designing buildings, etc.). Indeed, when shaping his theorem, Condorcet[56] mainly considered expert groups. This matters since, if constitutional courts are expert groups, Condorcet accuracy is relevant for deciding between majority rule and supermajority rules in constitutional review.

Flexibility

Flexibility means that majority rule and supermajority rules consider how humans normally behave. Specifically, these voting rules don't require total agreement for deciding, hence allowing group members to dissent. Flexibility stems from voting rules' history. Specifically, flexibility stems from from (i) the reasons for using supermajority rules in the Latin Catholic Church; (ii) Enlightenment philosophers' case *against* unanimity rule as a general voting rule; and (iii) Enlightenment philosophers' case *for* majority rule as a general voting rule.

48 Landemore 2013: 70–5, 147–56; Brennan 2016: 172–4, 179–80; Lagerspetz 2016: 301–3.
49 Landemore (2013: ch 6) is a salient dissenter. But her epistemic case for democracy is based more on the Hong-Page theorem than the Condorcet Jury Theorem.
50 2016: 181.
51 Id.
52 Elster 2013: 72–7; Lagerspetz 2016: 217–26.
53 See Converse 1990; Caplan 2008; Achen & Bartels 2016; Brennan 2016: ch 2–3, 187–95.
54 Sunstein 2006: 88–92; Farnsworth 2007: 136–9; Devine 2012: 169–71; Barry 2021: 218–9.
55 For overviews of research suggesting this, see Bang & Frith 2017: 6–7; Barry 2021: 81-3.
56 Condorcet [1785] 2014: 48–51. See also Landemore 2013: 151.

First, flexibility was arguably a key reason for the Catholic Church's adoption of the 2/3 rule in papal elections. Though the Church aimed at unanimous decisions, unanimity seldom happened, which meant that the Church's unity was regularly threatened during the Middle Ages. We also saw that church authorities progressively realised that the problem stemmed from majority rule's brittleness, and that this problem was aggravated when there was no higher authority to turn to. So, though the Church didn't abandon unanimity as an ideal, it abandoned it as a voting rule.[57]

Second, we saw that unanimity rule's brittleness was a key reason for Enlightenment philosophers' rejection of it as a general voting rule. We saw that: (i) though Enlightenment philosophers generally claimed that unanimity was necessary to establish civil societies; and (ii) though according to Enlightenment ideas, unanimity rule may have been required to ensure 'the consensus of the Enlightened;'[58] Enlightenment philosophers rejected unanimity rule due to its coercive potential. In social choice terms, Enlightenment philosophers rejected unanimity rule since it pressures group members to vote insincerely rather than revealing their true judgments.[59]

Lastly, we saw that, for Enlightenment philosophers, unlike unanimity rule, majority rule provides a better way of deciding rightly since it considers human fallibility. Put differently, majority rule considers the fact that minorities may dissent due to error, thus giving them a chance to recognise that fact.[60]

Flexibility stems from the fact that majority rule and supermajority rules don't require total agreement for deciding, hence relieving social influences and peer pressure. Since these rules don't require total agreement for deciding, they enable group members to vote sincerely by allowing them to dissent if they want to. Hence, flexibility ensures that, if unanimous decisions happen under majority rule or supermajority rules, such decisions likely stem from sincere group judgments rather than coercion. In sum, flexibility guarantees that, if unanimous decisions happen under these rules, such decisions happen due to the right reasons.

Though majority rule and supermajority rules are flexible, they aren't equally so. Comparatively speaking, since majority rule requires a lower threshold than any supermajority rule, majority rule is more flexible than any supermajority rule. And there's an inverse relation between thresholds and supermajority rules' flexibility. The higher the threshold, the less flexible a supermajority rule is and vice-versa. This happens since the higher the threshold, the more a supermajority rule approaches unanimity rule, hence boosting its potential to coerce dissenters. Conversely, the lower the threshold, the

57 Colomer & McLean 1998: 1–14; Schwartzberg 2013: ch 3; Lagerspetz 2010: 31–4.

58 Schwartzberg 2013: 75.

59 Laplace [1835] 2009: 165–74; Schwartzberg 2013: 79, 87–8.

60 Pufendorf 1703: 153–4; McLean & Hewitt 1994: 38; Rousseau 1762: 240. See also Schwartzberg 2013: 79–81.

more a supermajority rule approaches unanimity rule, hence curbing its potential to coerce dissenters.

From a Condorcetian view, flexibility matters for majority rule and supermajority rules. Flexibility matters since sincere voting is one of the Condorcet Jury Theorem's conditions, and flexibility stimulates group members to vote sincerely instead of coercing them. Yet when there's error asymmetry, Condorcet accuracy and flexibility stand against each other. When there's error asymmetry, some supermajority rules (those that aren't too close to unanimity rule) are more Condorcet accurate than majority rule,[61] but they are also less flexible. Conversely, when there's error asymmetry, majority rule is always more flexible than supermajority rules, but it's not as Condorcet accurate as them. Therefore, given error asymmetry, the trade-off between Condorcet accuracy and flexibility indicates the need to balance these two traits when choosing a voting rule.

Anonymity

Anonymity means that group members are equal in the sense that the results of a decision process don't depend on their identity. Under anonymity, the decision depends exclusively on the number of votes supporting each option: it doesn't depend on *who* votes for each option.[62] Under anonymous voting rules, 'if equal number of voters switch their [judgments] to opposite directions, the outcome does not change.'[63] To render group members' identity irrelevant for deciding, anonymity demands giving each group member just one vote. Anonymous voting rules are opposed to weighed voting rules, such as those governing shareholders' meetings (in which votes are proportional to shares) and the European Union's Council of Ministers (in which votes are proportional to population). Unlike anonymous voting rules, weighed voting rules don't treat group members equally. So, in weighed voting rules, who votes for which option matters.[64]

Majority rule and supermajority rules are anonymous. When observing voting rules' history, we can see that a key factor for using majority rule (in the Athenian *Areopagus* and the Spartan *Gerousia)* and supermajority rules (in the Catholic Church and the Italian city-states) was that both rules give each group member one vote. In these cases, giving each group member one vote symbolised that they were presumed equally able, thus reducing potential in-group conflict.[65]

61 Ben-Yashar & Nitzan 1997; McGinnis & Rappaport 2007; List & Pettit 2011: 90–1.
62 May 1952: 681.
63 Lagerspetz 2016: 34.
64 Id.
65 Colomer & McLean 1998: 1–14; Lagerspetz 2010: 31–4; Schwartzberg 2013: ch 2–3, 106-7.

Still, there's an ambiguity concerning whether supermajority rules treat group members equally. These rules give group members one vote, which shows that they treat group members equally. But these rules also allow a minority to block a majority's proposal to change a status quo,[66] which shows that they treat group members unequally. This ambiguity may be resolved by distinguishing between two traits: namely, anonymity (which I analyse here) and neutrality (which I analyse further). These traits are related, but they aren't the same. Anonymity is about treating *group members* equally; neutrality is about treating *options* equally. Anonymity is about giving each group member one vote; neutrality is about giving each option the same prior odds[67] of being chosen. Thus, while majority rule is anonymous *and* neutral, supermajority rules are anonymous but *not* neutral. Majority rule is indifferent as to who supports which option *and* as to the options' prior odds of being chosen. Conversely, supermajority rules are indifferent as to who supports which option, but they *aren't* indifferent as to their prior odds of being chosen.[68]

For example, suppose we have a five-member group, that all members are present, and that they must decide between X and Y. Suppose that the group decides by majority rule. Here anonymity and neutrality hold. This happens since each group member has one vote and since X and Y have the same prior odds of being chosen. (If three members support X, X is chosen; if three members support Y, Y is chosen.)

Now, suppose that Y is the status quo and that, unless the group chooses X by a four-to-one rule, Y is considered the group's decision. In this second case, anonymity still holds but neutrality no longer holds. This happens since each group member still has one vote, but the voting rule is stacked in favour of Y, hence giving Y higher prior odds of being chosen than X.

So, since majority rule is anonymous and neutral, majority rule treats group members equally regarding their votes and their options. Contrariwise, supermajority rules treat group members equally only regarding their votes, but

66 Tsebelis 2002: 139–43, 149–51; Schwartzberg 2013: 92–4, 121–3; Lagerspetz 2016: 195–6, 278–83.

67 These odds are 'prior' or 'prima facie' in the sense that beliefs about them are just influenced by the voting rule and the number of options—not by more data. Eg, assume that a group must choose between A and B by majority rule. If the only data one has is the voting rule, and one must gauge the odds of choosing either option, one would likely say that such odds are 50%. Yet new data may show that it's likelier that the group chooses A over B, or vice versa. Thus, one's initial beliefs on odds are 'prior' as in 'defeasible by new data.' On priors generally, see Binmore 2011: 127–36.

68 In some cases, unanimity rule and supermajority rules are neutral since these rules don't prefer any option. Eg, if in a papal conclave no candidate is supported by 2/3 of cardinals, there's no new pope. Thus, the 2/3 rule would be 'neutral' as in 'not favouring any candidate to the papacy.' Lagerspetz 2016: 35–6. See also Rivera León 2023: 6. Despite this, I assume that these voting rules are non-neutral for two reasons: first, in constitutional review, courts must decide between declaring and not declaring statutes unconstitutional; and second, until statutes are declared unconstitutional, it's usually assumed that they are constitutional.

not regarding their options.[69] Therefore, though under supermajority rules group members have one vote, ultimately, group members supporting the option favoured by supermajority rules—whoever they are—end up having more decision-making power than those supporting the other options. Yet, if under supermajority rules some group members end up having more decision-making power than others, this isn't due to their identity, but due to them favouring the options guarded by supermajority rules. This explains supermajority rules' ambiguity at treating group members equally.

Anonymity seems a relevant factor for choosing voting rules in groups in which eventual differences among members depend not only on quantitative aspects (eg, age, wealth, etc.) but also on qualitative aspects that can't be precisely measured in indisputable ways (eg, knowledge, wisdom, etc.). (Recall Pufendorf's case for majority rule,[70] and the failure of the greater and sounder part doctrine as a way of weighing votes in the Latin Catholic Church.)[71]

In groups in which eventual differences among members are quantitative and qualitative, most attempts to establish weighed voting rules will likely produce levels of in-group conflict that will risk the group's existence. Thus, in these groups, the non-viability of weighed voting rules produces a certain presumption for anonymity. This logic applies in groups whose authority highly depends on treating group members equally (eg, the Athenian *Areopagus*, the Spartan *Gerousia*, and elected representative assemblies), and in groups in which—though their authority doesn't depend on treating group members equally—it isn't viable to indisputably measure eventual qualitative differences among them (eg, conclaves and expert groups). This means that constitutional courts' voting rules should at least be anonymous since, once appointed, it doesn't seem possible to indisputably measure eventual qualitative differences among judges.

Sole Traits

There are three traits that only majority rule has. First, 'neutrality.' That is the trait by which majority rule treats options equally. Second, 'decisiveness.' This is the trait by which majority rule usually produces decisions rather than deadlocks. Finally, 'equality-signal.' This is the trait by which majority rule recognises group members' equal status. In turn, there are three traits that only supermajority rules have. First, 'non-neutrality.' This is the trait by which supermajority rules guard a status quo. Second, 'decelerator.' This is the trait by which supermajority rules delay decisions. Finally, 'agreement-signal.' This is the trait by which supermajority rules recognise an aspiration for sincere agreements among group members to ensure that their decisions are right. I

69 May 1952: 680–2; Lagerspetz 2016: 34–6.
70 1703: 153–4.
71 Colomer & McLean 1998: 6–7; Lagerspetz 2010: 32–4; Schwartzberg 2013: 55–8.

tackle majority rule's neutrality alongside supermajority rules' non-neutrality, while also tackling majority rule's decisiveness alongside supermajority rules' decelerator. I do so since supermajority rules' non-neutrality and decelerator are the opposite of majority rule's neutrality and decisiveness, respectively. Thus, treating these traits jointly instead of separately allows me to show the contrasts between them.

Majority Rule' Neutrality versus Supermajority Rules' Non-Neutrality

A sole trait of majority rule is neutrality. This trait means that, under majority rule, every option has the same prior odds of being chosen as a decision. In and of itself, majority rule doesn't favour any option. Specifically, majority rule doesn't favour any status quo or default position. Under majority rule, the deck between the options is even-handed—not stacked.[72]

For example, suppose that Weirdland's criminal code bans cannabis consumption and that Weirdland's unicameral legislature is debating decriminalisation. Call the proposal to uphold the ban 'option A' and the proposal to lift the ban 'option B.' And suppose that this legislature has 200 members, that it renders its decisions by majority rule and with all its members present, and that it's evenly split: half the legislators prefer option A while the other half prefer option B. Here, the only thing needed to tip the scales for an option is that one legislator changes their mind. If a legislator supporting option A changes their mind and supports option B, option B is chosen; if a legislator supporting option B changes their mind and supports option A, option A is chosen. So, in principle, both options' supporters have the same 50% odds of winning. Majority rule neither gives an edge to option A, nor does it give it to option B; majority rule doesn't grant any sort of favourable treatment to any option.

Conversely, supermajority rules generally favour the maintenance of a status quo or default position, the more so the higher the threshold. This happens since supermajority rules give some minority group members (those needed to reach their thresholds) the capacity to block a majority's proposal to change the status quo. Under supermajority rules, there are higher prior odds of keeping the status quo than of changing it. Under supermajority rules, the deck is stacked in favour of the status quo.[73]

Let's take again the Weirdland example but suppose that, instead of using majority rule, the legislature can only decide by a 60% rule. Suppose that a majority of legislators—meaning, 50% of legislators plus one legislator—prefer option B: a majority of legislators want to lift the cannabis consumption ban. And suppose that the rest of the legislators prefer option A: a minority of legislators want to keep the cannabis consumption ban. Here, the status quo

72 May 1952 681–2; Lagerspetz 2016: 37–8.

73 Tsebelis 2002: 139–43, 149-51; Schwartzberg 2013: 92–4, 121–3; Lagerspetz 2016: 195–6, 278–83.

is option A. That is, the cannabis consumption ban. If legislators supporting option B—that is, lifting the ban—don't reach the 60% threshold, cannabis consumption remains forbidden. In this example, we can see that there are higher prior odds of keeping the status quo than of changing it. For option B to win, legislators in the majority must convince enough legislators in the minority to change their minds to reach the 60% threshold. Contrariwise, for option A to hold, legislators in the minority must only ensure that they keep supporting it. Thus, since legislators in the minority must only stand their ground, they can block the choosing of option B. Therefore, the 60% rule boosts the odds that the cannabis consumption ban holds, hence giving an in-built edge to the status quo.

It isn't clear when a voting rule should be neutral or not. Among citizens and elected representatives, majority rule's neutrality seems a key tenet of political equality since this rule's mix of anonymity and neutrality treats group members equally at the votes level and at the options level.[74] But in these same contexts, biasing decision processes in favour of the status quo may work for guarding the rights of vulnerable minorities.[75] And in the more general context of citizens, elected representatives, *and* experts, biasing decision processes in favour of the status quo may work for generating stability, hence providing the conditions that allow groups to achieve their long-term aims.[76]

To choose between neutral or non-neutral voting rules, Condorcet's asymmetry of errors logic (seen in the previous chapter) seems quite a sound 'litmus test.'[77] According to this logic, the choice depends on comparing errors on a case-by-case basis. When there are no strong reasons for arguing that mistakenly changing the status quo is worse than mistakenly keeping it, there are no strong reasons against using neutral voting rules, and thus no strong reasons against using majority rule. Yet, when there are strong reasons for holding that mistakenly changing the status quo is worse than mistakenly keeping it, one may claim that there are strong reasons for biasing the decision process is favour of the status quo, and thus strong reasons for using supermajority rules.

We can see Condorcet's logic working in criminal juries,[78] and in List's example of medical treatment decisions.[79] In criminal juries, since mistakenly convicting the innocent is worse than mistakenly acquitting the guilty, the decision process is biased in favour of acquittal, thus justifying supermajority rules to convict. And in medical treatment decisions, it's usually accepted among physicians that, if a treatment doesn't have negative side effects, it's worse to mistakenly deny treatment to an ill patient than to mistakenly treat

74 For akin claims, see Dahl 1989: 139–41; Christiano 2008: 102–4; Waldron 2016: 264–5.
75 Christiano 2008: 289–92; Schwartzberg 2013: 141–3. See also Guinier 1995: 116–7; Kymlicka 1989: 110.
76 Schwartzberg 2013: 92–4, 123–7. See also Holmes 1995; Elster 2000.
77 1793: 14, 19; Schwartzberg 2013: 92–4.
78 1793: 14, 16–9.
79 2004: 522–5, 530. See also List & Pettit 2011: 90.

a healthy patient. Thus, in these cases, physicians generally think that the professional thing to do is to treat the patient by default unless most exams show that they are healthy. Still, many choice situations aren't as clear as that of criminal juries and medical treatment decisions. Thus, once a group decides to use an anonymous voting rule, whether that voting rule ends up being neutral or not depends on articulating sufficiently sound reasons to hold that the respective choice situation may produce asymmetric errors. This logic applies in constitutional review.

Majority Rule's Decisiveness versus Supermajority Rules' Decelerator

Along with being anonymous and neutral, majority rule is decisive. Decisiveness means that, when a group faces two options, majority rule generally ensures that one of them is chosen as a decision.[80] Under majority rule, cases of deadlock or 'no-outcome' scenarios—that is, cases in which no decision is made—rarely happen.[81] Conversely, supermajority rules may delay decisions, the more so the higher the threshold. This is a key reason why Condorcet supported supermajority rules to slow down legislative processes, which in turn he saw as boosting deliberation among group members.[82] Some examples of supermajority rules' decelerator can be seen in conclaves that took months, even years.[83] And the 1924 US Democratic Party Convention needed no fewer than 103 ballots to choose John W Davies as its presidential candidate.[84] Finally, another example in which supermajority rules delay decisions is the historical use (and for many, the historical abuse) of the 'filibuster rule' in the US Senate.[85]

Supermajority rules' decelerator stems from their non-neutrality: it stems from giving some minority group members the capacity to block a majority's decision proposal to change a status quo. Under supermajority rules, when a minority objects to a majority's proposal to change a status quo, the decision process slows down since the majority needs the support of at least some minority group members to decide. And the only ways in which the majority can get this support is by (i) deliberating, (ii) bargaining, or (iii) deliberating and bargaining;[86] all actions that can be quite time-consuming. Or at least

80 May 1952: 681–2; Lagerspetz 2016: 36-8.

81 Though majority rule is usually decisive, it isn't so when groups have even numbers of members, ties occur, and no group member changes their mind. In these cases, majority rule must be joined by tie-breaking rules. Lagerspetz 2016: 36-8.

82 Condorcet 1793: 16-7; Schwartzberg 2013: 92–4.

83 Colomer & McLean 1998: 11–2; Lagerspetz 2016: 32–4; Schwartzberg 2013: 59.

84 Lagerspetz 2016: 35–6.

85 Under the filibuster rule, unless 3/5 of US senators decide to close the debate on a bill, any senator can extend the debate indefinitely. Schwartzberg 2013: 133–4. See also Binder & Smith 1997.

86 Elster 2013: 30–6.

more time-consuming when getting the support of a supermajority of group members than when getting the support of a majority of them.

A key factor for choosing between decisive and delaying voting rules lies in the tension between speed and reflection. When deciding, timing is often everything. After all—as Elster[87] indicates—'if it didn't matter *when* a decision is made, it wouldn't matter *whether* it is made.' But for decisions to be right they must be properly thought through, which takes time. Thus, there's a tension between speed and reflection. When decisions are too quick, the may not be properly reflected on, and thus they may be wrong; when decisions are too slow, they may not solve—or not properly solve—the issues that justified them, and thus they may also be wrong.[88] Majority rule's decisiveness boosts quick decisions by generally ensuring that an option is chosen. And supermajority rules' decelerator promotes reflective decisions by boosting deliberation. Thus, whether a voting rule should be decisive or delay decisions seems to depend on a case-by-case analysis on whether specific groups should prioritise speed or reflection.

Majority Rule's Equality Signal

Majority rule's equality signal is a 'semiotic' trait: it's a trait referring to what this rule socially recognises, symbolises, or represents. This equality signal means that, unlike any other voting rule, majority rule performs a relevant social function: namely, recognising a certain equal status among group members. In the case of citizens and elected representatives, this equal status is called 'political equality.'[89] Majority rule's equality signal likely explains that this rule is intuitively appealing, thus being used in most groups without much thought.[90] And as seen is the previous chapter, this trait is a key reason underlying majority rule's adoption in pre-classical Greece's aristocratic councils.[91] As Schwartzberg claims,[92] if these councils' members hadn't been treated as equals, that would have likely produced levels of in-group conflict that would have easily turned into civil war. Finally, this equality signal is a key reason why, since the Enlightenment—and especially since Pufendorf's[93] defence—majority rule has been upheld as citizens' and elected representatives' general voting rule; often to the point where it's equated with democracy itself.[94]

87 Id 32.
88 Id 32, 44, 179–81.
89 On political equality, see Gutmann 1980; Beitz 1989; Dahl 1989: ch 7; Rawls 1999: 194–200; Christiano 2008: ch 3; Dworkin 2013: ch 18.
90 Lagerspetz 2016: 40. See also Arendt 1990: 164.
91 Lagerspetz 2010: 29, 31-4; Schwartzberg 2013: 21-2, 106-7.
92 2013: 21-2, 106-7.
93 Pufendorf 1703: 153–4. See also Pasquino 2010.
94 Eg, see Dahl 1989: 139–41; Christiano 2008: 102-4, 290; Waldron 2016: 264–5.

Majority rule's equality signal stems from mixing its neutrality and anonymity. The underlying logic is that, since majority rule treats group members equally at the votes level and at the options level, this rule recognises their equal status. In democracies, majority rule extends to elected representatives since it's assumed that the public recognition of their equal status mirrors the public recognition of citizens' equal status. So, in democracies, representative assemblies are usually considered 'institutional expressions' of political equality.[95]

There are many theories justifying group members' equal status, and that status' public recognition via majority rule. Most of these theories focus on political equality. Broadly speaking, these theories may be classified into two groups: first, what I call 'equal ability theories;' and second, what I call 'direct link theories.'

Equal ability theories—developed by Dahl,[96] Christiano,[97] Waldron,[98] and Schwartzberg,[99] among others—provide the traditional justification for group members' equal status used by the ancient Greeks and by Enlightenment philosophers. For these theories, group members' equal status is based on a presumption of equal ability, which in turn is based on some facts or values. According to equal-ability theories, some facts or values—such as personal autonomy,[100] human dignity,[101] or the inability to assess eventual qualitative differences among group members in precise and indisputable ways (put differently, the inability to indisputably determine who is wiser than whom)[102]—demand that, barring sound reasons against it, group members should be presumed equally able.

For equal ability theories, group members' alleged equal ability should be recognised since not doing so would be disrespectful. By treating group members equally at the votes level and at the options level, majority rule performs this recognition. Thus, since group members' alleged equal ability should be publicly recognised, and since majority rule performs this recognition, majority rule should be a general voting rule.[103] Put differently, group members'

95 Rawls 1999: 196-7; Christiano 2008: 104-6; Schwartzberg 2013: 117-8. I only consider 'classical' theories of democratic representation. These theories hold that representative assemblies must reflect citizens' equal status since representatives' job is to advocate for their electors' interests. I only consider these theories since they ground majority rule between elected representatives in citizens' equal status. For an alternative theory, see Ekins 2012. On representation, see Pitkin, 1972; Manin 1997; Urbinati 2008.

96 1989: ch 7.

97 2008: ch 3.

98 1999: ch 1.

99 2013: 111–6.

100 Dahl 1989: ch 6–7.

101 Christiano (2008: ch 1–3) bases majority rule on the principle of 'public equality.' That is, the principle that people must be treated as equals when pursuing their interests. In turn, public equality is based on human dignity.

102 Waldron 1999: ch 1; Schwartzberg 2013: 111–6.

103 Dahl 1989: ch 7, 139–41; Waldron 2016: ch 1; Christiano 2008: ch 3; Schwartzberg 2013: 111–6.

alleged equal ability produces a second presumption for majority rule in most kinds of groups. And especially a presumption for majority rule among citizens and elected representatives.

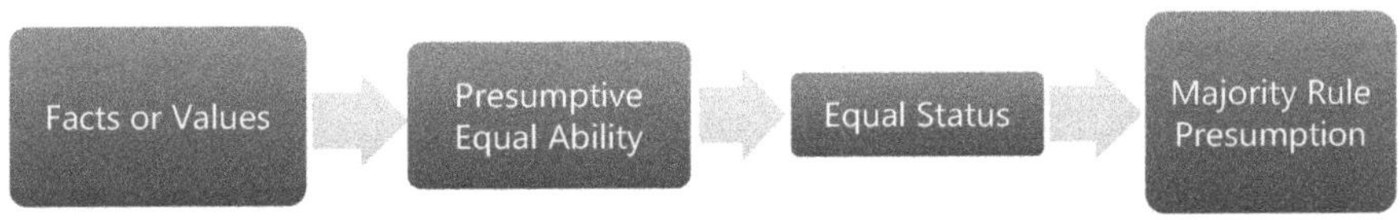

Figure 4.2 Equal ability theories

In turn, direct link theories are quite similar to equal ability theories. The difference is that, while equal ability theories base group members' equal status (and thus majority rule) on a presumption of equal ability that is in turn based on some facts or values, direct link theories skip the step of assuming equal ability, hence immediately basing such status on some facts or values. Some main direct link theories are those of Beitz,[104] Rawls,[105] and Dworkin,[106] among others. Barring the presumption of equal ability, direct link theories are akin to equal ability theories. Broadly speaking, direct link theories also hold that: (i) group members have an equal status that deserves public recognition; (ii) not performing this public recognition is disrespectful; (iii) majority rule performs this public recognition since it treats group members equally at the votes level and at the options level; and (iv) hence, majority rule should be groups' general voting rule. So, group members' equal status produces a presumption for majority rule in most kinds of groups. And particularly a presumption for majority rule among citizens and elected representatives.

Figure 4.3 Direct link theories

Majority rule's equality signal is strongly linked to anonymity and neutrality. Scholars such as Dahl,[107] Christiano,[108] and Waldron[109] suggest that these traits

104 Beitz bases group members' equal status on the idea of a social contract that no reasonable person should refuse (1989: ch 5).
105 Rawls bases group members' equal status on the need to provide citizens with a social basis for self-respect (1999: ch 4).
106 Dworkin bases group members' equal status on the moral imperative to treat citizens with equal concern and respect (2013: ch 18).
107 1989: 139–41.
108 2008: 102–4.
109 1999: 264–5.

cause majority rule's equality signal. Since majority rule treats group members equally at the votes level and at the options level—the claim goes—this rule shows respect for their equal status. Hence, it's especially majority rule's 'anonymity plus neutrality combo' that produces a presumption for majority rule in most kinds of groups; and again a presumption for majority rule among citizens and elected representatives.

Supermajority Rules' Agreement Signal

Last but not least, supermajority rules carry an agreement signal. As with majority rule's equality signal, supermajority rules' agreement signal is a semiotic trait: it's a trait referring to what a voting rule socially recognises, symbolises, or represents. In particular, supermajority rules recognise an aspiration for sincere agreements among group members to ensure that their decisions are right. Put differently, supermajority rules project a certain 'consensual ideal' towards society. The aspiration for sincere agreements seems to stem from a strong intuition: namely, that these agreements prove that such decisions are right, and therefore are authoritative. (After all, 'nine out of ten dentists prefer Colgate.') We saw in the previous chapter that, once the Church's experience showed unanimity rule's flaws, the Church developed the 2/3 rule to accommodate bad faith or moral disagreement, but without giving up on aspiring for sincere agreements. We also saw that the Italian city-states' political selection procedures aimed at producing sincere agreements, insofar as those procedures tried to ensure that chosen officials were minimally able and acceptable to the elites.[110]

The aspiration for sincere agreements appears behind many groups' attempts to decide unanimously even when unanimity isn't required. This happened during the US Supreme Court's history[111] and in recent constitutional courts; especially during their early years.[112] Further, this aspiration seems to explain why many governments, international organisations, criminal juries in Norway,[113] some European constitutional courts,[114] and the British Judicial Committee of the Privy Council (until 1967)[115] present their decisions as unanimous though they weren't really so. And Zink et al's[116] study suggests that people opposing a judicial decision are more willing to accept it if that decision is unanimous rather than divided.

110 Colomer & McLean 1998: 1–14; Lagerspetz 2010: 31–4; Schwartzberg 2013: 53–8, 67–9.
111 Corley et al 2013: ch.1.
112 The paradigm here is the German court. Kelemen 2019: 83–9.
113 Elster 2013: 31–6, 136–8.
114 Kelemen 2019: ch 2.
115 Kirby 2007: 14.
116 2009.

Lastly, some European constitutional courts (eg, France's, Italy's, Germany's, and Spain's)[117]—and France's drug approval committee,[118] among other institutions—don't generally decide by voting, but by 'non-opposition.'[119] This means that these institutions don't generally decide by *aggregating* or *counting* the opinions of each group member. Rather, they decide once *no group member opposes* the last decision proposal made inside the group. This is then considered the final decision. Put differently, even when voting is possible, many groups avoid voting and work under the assumption that silence on the last decision proposal made inside the group means consenting to it. By presuming that silence is consent, non-opposition implies (and thus projects) agreement. Hence, in our times, the aspiration for sincere agreements in decision making is alive and well.

As a factor for choosing between majority rule and supermajority rules, it seems that, in principle, supermajority rules' agreement signal is a strong point in favour of these rules in groups whose reputation highly hinges on accuracy, such as expert groups. Moreover, the Condorcet Jury Theorem partially confirms the intuition behind the aspiration for sincere agreements since the theorem proves that, in relatively small groups—and given error asymmetry—some supermajority rules boost group accuracy more than majority rule.[120] So, cases in which the agreement signal is a key factor for choosing voting rules tend to overlap with cases in which Condorcet accuracy is a key factor for choosing them as well. Thus, inasmuch as constitutional courts are expert groups, supermajority rules' agreement signal is a strong point favouring these voting rules in constitutional review.

Conclusion

From analysing voting rules' traits, I draw five conclusions. First, Condorcet accuracy seems more relevant among experts than among citizens and elected representatives. Thus, assuming that judges are experts, this means that Condorcet accuracy should be considered in deciding between majority and supermajority rules in constitutional review. Second, though flexibility is a key trait of majority rule and supermajority rules, when there's error asymmetry, there's a tension between Condorcet accuracy and flexibility. Hence, given error asymmetry, Condorcet accuracy and flexibility should be balanced when choosing voting rules in constitutional review. Third, anonymity is a key trait of majority rule and supermajority rules in groups in which it isn't viable to indubitably assess eventual qualitative differences among group members. Since constitutional courts seem to be these kinds of groups (at least

117 Ferejohn & Pasquino 2004: 1692–700; Urfalino 2014a: 333–4; Kelemen 2019: 86–9.
118 Urfalino 2014b: 182–90.
119 Urfalino 2014a. See also El-Hakim 1978; Steiner & Dorff 1980.
120 Ben-Yashar & Nitzan 1997; McGinnis and Rappaport 2008; List & Pettit 2011: 90–1.

after judges are appointed), whatever voting rule constitutional courts use to declare statutes unconstitutional, that voting rule must be anonymous.

Fourth, when choosing between neutral and non-neutral voting rules, though Condorcet's asymmetry of errors logic is a sound criterion for choosing the latter kind of voting rules, in most cases, it isn't clear whether groups face asymmetrical errors. Moreover, majority rule's equality signal produces a presumption for majority rule in most kinds of groups. Thus, to hold that constitutional courts should use supermajority rules to check the constitutionality of legislation, I must (i) undermine the majority rule presumption, and (ii) claim that, in constitutional review, there's error asymmetry, I undertake the first task in the following chapter, while undertaking the second task in Chapter 6. Lastly, supermajority rules' agreement signal is key for using supermajority rules in expert groups since those groups' reputation strongly hinges on accuracy. So, if constitutional courts are expert groups, supermajority rules' agreement signal is key for using these voting rules in constitutional review as well.

References

Achen CH & Bartels LM, *Democracy for Realists: Why Elections Do Not Produce Responsive Government* (Princeton University Press 2016) https://doi.org/10.1515/9781400882731

Anderson LR & Holt CA, 'Information Cascades in the Laboratory' (1997) 87(5) *The American Economic Review* 847 https://www.jstor.org/stable/2951328

Arendt H, *On Revolution* (Penguin 1990)

Arrow KJ, *Social Choice and Individual Values* (2nd edn, Cowles Foundation 1963)

Barry BM, *How Judges Judge: Empirical Insights into Judicial Decision-Making* (Routledge 2021) https://doi.org/10.4324/9780429023422

Banerjee AV, 'A Simple Model of Herd Behavior' (1992) 107(3) *The Quarterly Journal of Economics* 797 http://www.jstor.org/stable/2118364

Bang D & Frith CD, 'Making Better Decisions in Groups' (2017) 4 *Royal Society Open Science* http://dx.doi.org/10.1098/rsos.170193

Beitz CR, *Political Equality: An Essay in Democratic Theory* (Princeton University Press 1989) https://doi.org/10.1515/9780691221410

Ben-Yashar RC & Nitzan SI, 'The Optimal Decision-Making Rule for Fixed-Sized Committees in Dichotomous Choice Situations: The General Result' (1997) 38 *International Economic Review* 175 https://doi.org/10.2307/2527413

Bentham J, *Political Tactics* (first published 1843, James M, Blamires C and Please-Watkin C edn, Oxford University Press 1999) https://doi.org/10.1093/actrade/9780198207726.book.1

Binder SA & Smith SS, *Politics or Principle? Filibustering in the United States Senate* (Brookings Institution Press 1997)

Binmore K, *Rational Decisions* (Princeton University Press 2011) https://doi.org/10.1515/9781400833092

Bickchanandi S, Hirshleifer D, & Welch I, 'Learning from the Behaviour of Others: Conformity, Fads, and Information Cascades' (1998) 12 *Journal of Economic Perspectives* 151 https://doi.org/10.1257/jep.12.3.151

Black D, *The Theory of Committees and Elections* (Cambridge University Press 1971)

Brennan J, *Against Democracy* (Princeton University Press 2016) https://doi.org/10.1515/9781400882939

Callender S, 'Bandwagons and Momentum in Sequential Voting' (2007) 74 *The Review of Economic Studies* 653 https://doi.org/10.1111/j.1467-937X.2007.00441.x

Caplan B, *The Myth of the Rational Voter: Why Democracies Choose Bad Policies* (Princeton University Press 2008) https://doi.org/10.1515/9781400828821

Caplin A & Nalebuff B, 'On 64%-Majority Rule' (1988) 56 *Econometrica* 787 https://doi.org/10.2307/1912699

Carminker EH, 'Sincere and Strategic Voting Norms on Multimember Courts' (1999) 97 *Michigan Law Review* 2297 https://doi.org/10.2307/1290189

Christiano T, *The Constitution of Equality: Democratic Authority and its Limits* (Oxford University Press 2008) https://doi.org/10.1093/acprof:oso/9780198297475.001.0001

Coggins JS & Perali CF, '64% Majority Rule in Ducal Venice: Voting for the Doge' (1998) 97(4) *Public Choice* 709 https://doi.org/10.1023/A:1004947715017

Colomer J & McLean I, 'Electing Popes: Approval Balloting and Qualified-Majority Rule' (1998) 29 *Journal of Interdisciplinary History* 1 https://doi.org/10.1162/002219598551616

Condorcet MJA, *Essai sur l'Application de l'analyse à la probabilité des décisions rendues à la pluralité des voix* [Essay on the Application of Mathematics to the Theory of Decision-Making] (first published 1785, Cambridge University Press 2014)

——— Plan *de* Constitution *présenté a* la Convention Nationale [Constitutional Plan Presented to the National Convention] (Paris, Imprimerie Nationale 1793) https://gallica.bnf.fr/ark:/12148/bpt6k73809

Converse PE, 'Popular Representation and the Distribution of Information' in Ferejohn JA and Kuklinski JH (eds), *Information and Democratic Processes* (University of Illinois Press 1990)

Corley PC, Steigerwalt A & Ward A, *The Puzzle of Unanimity: Consensus on the United States Supreme Court* (Stanford Law Books 2013) https://doi.org/10.1515/9780804786324

Dahl RA, *Democracy and its Critics* (Yale University Press 1989)

Daughety AF & Reinganum JF, 'Stampede to Judgment: Persuasive Influence and Herding Behavior by Courts' (1999) 1(1) *American Law and Economics Review* 158 https://doi.org/10.1093/aler/1.1.158

De Vany A & Walls WD, 'Uncertainty in the Movie Industry: Does Star Power Reduce the Terror of the Box Office?' (1999) 23 *Journal of Cultural Economics* 285 https://doi.org/10.1023/A:1007608125988

Devine DJ, *Jury Decision Making: The State of the Science* (New York University Press 2012) https://doi.org/10.18574/9780814704981

Dowding K & Hees MV, 'In Praise of Manipulation' (2007) 38 *British Journal of Political Science* 1 https://doi.org/10.1017/S000712340800001X

Dworkin R, *Justice for Hedgehogs* (Harvard University Press 2013)

Ekins R, *The Nature of Legislative Intent* (Oxford University Press 2012) https://doi.org/10.1093/acprof:oso/9780199646999.001.0001

El-Hakim S, 'The Structure and Dynamics of Consensus Decision-Making' (1978) 13(1) *Man, New Series* 55 https://www.jstor.org/stable/2801065

Elster J, *Ulysses Unbound: Studies in Rationality, Precommitment, and Constraints* (Cambridge University Press 2000) https://doi.org/10.1017/CBO9780511625008

——— *Securities Against Misrule: Juries, Assemblies, Elections* (Cambridge University Press 2013) https://doi.org/10.1017/CBO9781139382762

Estlund DM, *Democratic Authority: A Philosophical Framework* (Princeton University Press 2008)

Farnsworth W, *The Legal Analyst: A Toolkit for Thinking about the Law* (University of Chicago Press 2007)

Ferejohn J & Pasquino P, 'Constitutional Adjudication: Lessons from Europe' (2004) 82 *Texas Law Review* 1671 https://heinonline.org/HOL/P?h=hein.journals/tlr82andi=1687

Fey M, 'A Note on the Condorcet Jury Theorem with Supermajority Voting Rules' (2003) 20 *Social Choice and Welfare* 27 https://doi.org/10.1007/s003550200157

Gibbard A, 'Manipulation of Voting Schemes: A General Result' (1973) 41 *Econometrica* 587 https://doi.org/10.2307/1914083

Grofman B, Owen G & Feld SL, 'Thirteen Theorems in Search for the Truth' (1983) 15 *Theory and Decision* 261 https://doi.org/10.1007/BF00125672

——— & Feld SL, 'Rousseau's General Will: A Condorcetian Perspective' (1988) 82 *American Political Science Review* 567 https://doi.org/10.2307/1957401

Guinier L, *The Tyranny of the Majority: Fundamental Fairness in Representative Democracy* (Free Press 1995)

Gutmann A, *Liberal Equality* (Cambridge University Press 1980)

Hastie R & Dawes RM, *Rational Choice in an Uncertain World* (Sage 2001)

Holmes S, *Passions and Constraint: On the Theory of Liberal Democracy* (University of Chicago Press 1995)

Hong L & Page SE, 'Groups of Diverse Problem Solvers Can Outperform Groups of High-ability Problem Solvers' (2004) 101(46) *Proceedings of the National Academy of Sciences of the United States of America* 16385 https://doi.org/10.1073/pnas.0403723101

Hung AA & Plott CR, 'Information Cascades: Replication and Extension to Majority Rule and Conformity Rewarding Institutions' (2011) 91 *The American Economic Review* 1508 https://doi.org/10.1257/aer.91.5.1508

Kahneman D, *Thinking, Fast and Slow* (Farrar, Straus and Giroux 2011)

——— Slovic P & Tversky A (eds), *Judgment Under Uncertainty: Heuristics and Biases* (Cambridge University Press 1982) https://doi.org/10.1017/CBO9780511809477

Kelemen K, *Judicial Dissent in European Constitutional Courts: A Comparative and Legal Perspective* (Routledge 2019) https://doi.org/10.4324/9781315590769

Kornhauser LA & Sager LG, 'The One and the Many: Adjudication in Collegial Courts' (1993) 81(1) *California Law Review* 1 https://doi.org/10.15779/Z38C43K

Kirby M, 'Judicial Dissent-Common Law and Civil Law Traditions' (2007) 123 *Law Quarterly Review* 379

Kymlicka W, *Liberalism, Community and Culture* (Oxford University Press 1989)

Ladha KK, 'The Condorcet Jury Theorem, Free Speech, and Correlated Votes' (1992) 36 *American Journal of Political Science* 617 https://doi.org/10.2307/2111584

Lagerspetz E, 'Wisdom and Numbers' (2010) 49(1) *Social Science Information* 29 https://doi.org/10.1177/0539018409354475

——— *Social Choice and Democratic Values* (Springer 2016) https://doi.org/10.1007/978-3-319-23261-4

Landemore H, *Democratic Reason: Politics, Collective Intelligence and the Rule of the Many* (Princeton University Press 2013)

Laplace PS, *Essai philosophique sur les probabilités* [Philosophical Essay on Probabilities] (first published 1825, Cambridge University Press 2009)

List C, 'On the Significance of the Absolute Margin' (2004) 55 *British Journal for the Philosophy of Science* 521 http://www.jstor.org/stable/3541673

——— & Pettit P, *Group Agency: The Possibility, Design, and Status of Corporate Agents* (Cambridge University Press 2011) https://doi.org./10.1093/acprof:oso/9780199591565.001.0001

Liu L, Yuan C & McLeod PL, 'Twenty-Five Years of Hidden Profiles in Group Decision Making: A Meta-Analysis' (2012) 16(1) *Personality and Social Psychology Review* 54 https://doi.org./10.1177/1088868311417243

Manin B, *The Principles of Representative Government* (Cambridge University Press 1997) https://doi.org/10.1017/CBO9780511659935

May KO, 'A Set of Independent Necessary and Sufficient Conditions for Simple Majority Decision' (1952) 20(4) *Econometrica* 680 http://www.jstor.org/stable/1907651

———The Condorcet Case for Supermajority Rules' (2008) 16 *Supreme Court Economic Review* 67 https://www.journals.uchicago.edu/doi/abs/10.1086/655880

McGinnis JO & Rappaport MB, 'Majority and Supermajority Rules: Three Views of the Capitol' (2007) 85 *Texas Law Review* 1115

McKelvey RD, 'General Conditions for Global Intransitivities in Formal Voting Models' (1979) 47(5) *Econometrica* 1085 https://doi.org/10.2307/1911951

McLean I & Hewitt F, 'Section 2: The Theory of Voting' in McLean I and Hewitt F (eds), *Condorcet: Foundations of Social Choice and Political Theory* (Edward Elgar 1994)

Miller N, 'Information, Electorates and Democracy: Some Extensions and Interpretations of the Condorcet Jury Theorem' in Groffman B and Owen G (eds), *Information Pooling and Group Decision-Making: Proceedings of the Second University of California, Irvine Conference on Political Economy* (Jai Press 1986)

Nitzan SI & Paroush J, 'Are Qualified Majority Rules Special?' (1984) 42 *Public Choice* 257 https://www.jstor.org/stable/30023741

Page SE, *The Difference: How the Power of Diversity Creates Better Groups, Firms, Schools, and Societies* (Princeton University Press 2007)

Panning WH, 'Information Pooling and Group Decision-Making in Nonexperimental Settings' in Groffman B and Owen G (eds), *Information Pooling and Group Decision-Making: Proceedings of the Second University of California, Irvine Conference on Political Economy* (Jai Press 1986)

Pasquino P, 'Samuel Pufendorf: Majority Rule (Logic, Justification and Limits) and Forms of Government' (2010) 49(1) *Social Science Information* 99 https://doi.org/10.1177/0539018409354476

Pitkin HF, *The Concept of Representation* (Revised edn, University of California Press 1972)

Pufendorf S, *Of the Law of Nature and Nations: Eight Books. Book the Seventh* (Oxford 1703)

Rawls J, *A Theory of Justice* (Revised edn, Harvard University Press 1999)

Rivera León M, 'Control and Paralysis? A Context-sensitive Anaysis of Objections to Supermajorities in Constitutional Adjudication' (2023) *International Journal of Constitutional Law* 1 https://doi.org/10.1093/icon/moad074

Rousseau JJ, *Du contrat social, ou principes du droit politique* [On the Social Contract; or, Principles of Political Right] (Leipzig, Gerard Fleischer 1762)

Saari DG, 'The Generic Existence of a Core for q-Rules' (1997) 9(2) *Economic Theory* 219 https://doi.org/10.1007/BF01213800

Satterthwaite MA, 'Strategy-Proofness and Arrow's Conditions: Existence and Correspondence Theorems for Voting Procedures and Social Welfare Functions' (1975) 10 *Journal of Economic Theory* 187

Schwartzberg M, 'The arbitrariness of supermajority rules' (2010) 49(1) *Social Science Information* 61 https://doi.org/10.1177/0539018409354474

——— *Counting the Many. The Origins and Limits of Supermajority Rule* (Cambridge University Press 2013) https://doi.org/10.1017/CBO9781139013970

Steiner J & Dorff RH, 'Decision by Interpretation. A New Concept for an Often Overlooked Decision Mode' (1980) 10(1) *British Journal of Political Science* 1 http://www.jstor.org/stable/193446

Stasser G & Titus W, 'Pooling of Unshared Information in Group Decision Making: Biased Information Sampling during Discussion' (1985) 48(6) *Journal of Personality and Social Psychology* 1467 https://doi.org/10.1037/0022-3514.48.6.1467

Sunstein CR, *Infotopia: How Many Minds Produce Knowledge* (Oxford University Press 2006)

Thompson A, 'Does Diversity Trump Ability? An Example of the Misuse of Mathematics in the Social Sciences' (2014) 61(9) *Notices of the American Mathematical Society* 1024 http://dx.doi.org/10.1090/noti1163

Tsebelis G, *Veto Players: How Political Institutions Work* (Princeton University Press 2002) https://doi.org/10.1515/9781400831456

Urbinati N, *Representative Democracy: Principles and Genealogy* (University of Chicago Press 2008) https://doi.org/10.7208/chicago/9780226842806.001.0001

Urfalino P, 'The Rule of Non-Opposition: Opening Up Decision-Making by Consensus' (2014a) 22(3) *The Journal of Political Philosophy* 320 https://doi.org/10.1111/jopp.12037

——— 'Reasons and Preferences in Medicine Evaluation Committees' in Landemore H & Elster J (eds), *Collective Wisdom: Principles and Mechanisms* (Cambridge University Press 2014b) https://doi.org/10.1017/CBO9780511846427

——— & Costa P, 'Secret-Public Voting in FDA Advisory Committees' in Elster J (ed) *Secrecy and Publicity in Votes and Debates* (Cambridge University Press 2015) https://doi.org/10.1017/CBO9781316015360

Walden E & Browne G (2002), 'Information Cascades in the Adoption of New Technology' (2002) 40 *International Conference on Information Systems 2002 Proceedings* 435 http://aisel.aisnet.org/icis2002/40

Waldron J, *Law and Disagreement* (Oxford University Press 1999) https://doi.org/10.1093/acprof:oso/9780198262138.001.0001

——— *Political Political Theory: Essays on Institutions* (Harvard University Press 2016) https://doi.org/10.4159/9780674970342

Zink JR, Spriggs II JF & Scott JT, 'The Influence of Decision Attributes on Individuals' Views of Court Opinions' (2009) 71(3) *Journal of Politics* 909 https://doi.org/10.1017/s0022381609090793

5 Against Majority Rule in Constitutional Review

In the previous chapter, I analysed majority rule's and supermajority rules' traits. We saw that Condorcet accuracy, flexibility, and anonymity are traits shared by majority rule and supermajority rules. Also, we saw that decisiveness, neutrality, and the equality signal are traits that only majority rule has. Finally, we saw that non-neutrality, decelerator, and the agreement signal are traits that apply solely to supermajority rules.

Now that we have a map of voting rules' traits, in this chapter, I develop a core case against majority rule in constitutional review. In short, I claim that majority rule's traits (separately and jointly considered) can't justify or ground this voting rule in constitutional review. These traits don't provide *conclusive* or *definitive* reasons for using majority rule to check the constitutionality of legislation; meaning, these traits don't provide strong enough reasons for using majority rule *over other voting rules*—particularly, supermajority rules—to declare statutes unconstitutional. Before starting, it's worth indicating that I don't tackle anonymity and neutrality in isolation. I don't do so since, according to many scholars, anonymity and neutrality cause majority rule's equality signal.[1] Thus, my claims on why this signal doesn't justify majority rule in constitutional review extend to anonymity and neutrality; hence making it unnecessary to tackle each of these traits.

Having made these caveats, let's proceed with the analysis.

Does Condorcet Accuracy Ground Majority Rule in Constitutional Review?

To determine whether Condorcet accuracy justifies majority rule in constitutional review, it's worth analysing the plausibility that the Condorcet Jury Theorem holds in constitutional courts in the first place. In the previous chapter, I held that the theorem's conditions seem better satisfied among experts than among citizens and elected representatives. So, the fact that—at first

1 Dahl 1989: 139–41; Christiano 2008: 102–4; Waldron 2016: 264–5. See also Lagerspetz 2016: 38.

DOI: 10.4324/9781032723952-5

sight—constitutional courts are expert groups suggests that the theorem's conditions also seem better satisfied among judges than among citizens and elected representatives. Still, constitutional courts have key features that distinguish them from other expert groups. Specifically, it's debated whether, when checking the constitutionality of statutes, judges should somehow be guided and bound by the law—or whether they should consider all sorts of factual and moral factors. This is why it matters to assess whether the Condorcet Jury Theorem holds in constitutional courts.

The Condorcet Jury Theorem in Constitutional Courts

As seen in the previous chapter, the Condorcet Jury Theorem's conditions are: (i) binary choice; (ii) ability; (iii) statistical independence; and (iv) sincere voting.[2] Let's review each of these conditions, but now with a specific focus on constitutional courts.

1. Binary Choice in Constitutional Courts

In constitutional review, it may be argued that binary choice holds since, at a basic level, judges seem to face two options: namely, to declare or not to declare statutes unconstitutional.[3] This framing of the options doesn't seem to depend much on judges' behaviour, but it's due to the nature of the choice itself.

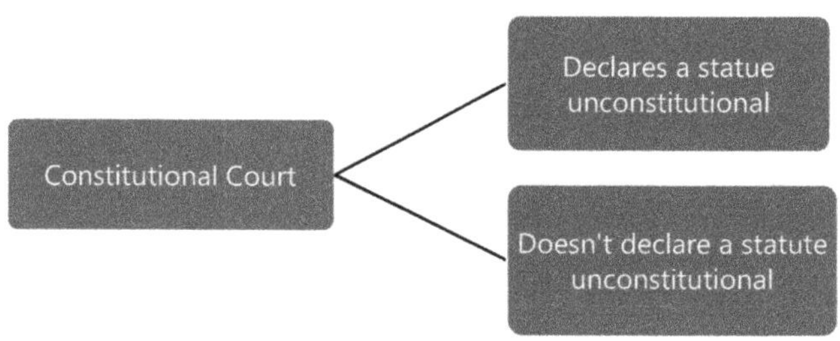

Figure 5.1 Constitutional courts' basic decision tree

Hence, a constitutional court's decision has four possible results. First, the court declares a statute unconstitutional, and that statute is unconstitutional (a 'true positive'). Second, the court declares a statute unconstitutional, and that statute isn't unconstitutional (a 'false positive'). Third, the court doesn't

2 Condorcet [1785] 2014: xxi–xxii.

3 Following Keynes (2007: ch 4), someone may argue that there's another binary choice existing *before* the choice on the constitutionality of legislation: namely, the choice on whether the provisions that judges review really are statutes. But this assessment depends on legislatures' compliance with procedural constitutional provisions. Thus, this assessment falls into the assessment on the constitutionality of legislation.

declare a statute unconstitutional, and that statute isn't unconstitutional (a 'true negative'). Finally, the court doesn't declare a statute unconstitutional, and that statute is unconstitutional (a 'false negative'). True positives and true negatives are right decisions, while false positives and false negatives are errors.

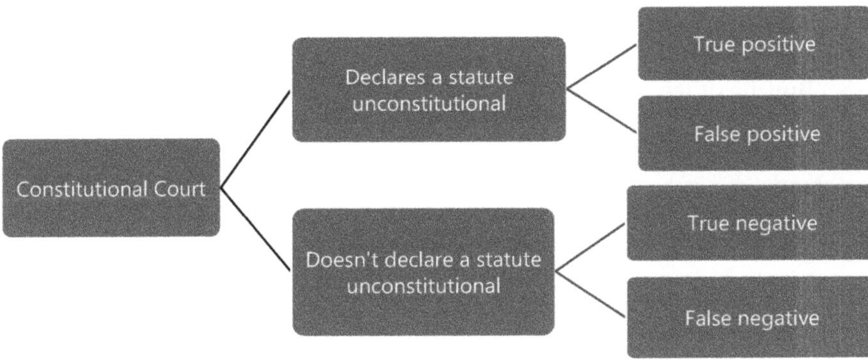

Figure 5.2 Constitutional courts' full decision tree

Still, it may be questioned whether constitutional courts face binary choices since these courts don't usually check the constitutionality of statutes in isolation, but tend to solve constitutional issues alongside other legal issues. Yet this doesn't erode the binary choice condition. When there's a constitutional issue, that issue is likely the most relevant part of the case, thus influencing how other issues are decided. So, even if a constitutional issue is decided alongside other issues, judges must first conclude whether the defied statute is or isn't constitutional to solve those other issues.

For example, suppose that Weirdland's constitutional court must decide whether to affirm or reverse a decision by the Court of Appeals applying a tax penalty to the claimant. And suppose that one of the claimant's allegations is that the statutory provision allowing Weirdland's tax officials to penalise them (call it, 'statute Z') amounts to an expropriation without compensation, thus being unconstitutional since it violates their right to private property. In this case, even if statute Z's constitutionality must be solved alongside the question of affirming or reversing the Court of Appeals' decision, to assess statute Z's application by such Court, Weirdland's constitutional court must previously conclude that statute Z is constitutional or unconstitutional. And since judging the constitutionality of statute Z is binary, the binary choice condition still holds.

2. *Ability in Constitutional Courts*

On ability, recall that this condition means that *each* group member (according to the tight interpretation)[4] or the *average* group member (according to

4 Condorcet [1785] 2014: xxi–xxii.

the loose interpretation)[5] must have above 50% odds of deciding rightly. And recall that, comparatively speaking, the ability condition seems better fulfilled by expert groups that perform 'technical reasoning.' Here, to clarify what I mean by 'technical reasoning,' it's helpful to distinguish between this type of reasoning and what could be called 'general practical reasoning.'[6]

Technical reasoning and general practical reasoning are kinds of normative reasoning: they both address what one should do to realise substantive standards.[7] But the differences between these kinds of reasoning lie in the specificity of substantive standards.[8] In short, technical reasoning is more bounded and guided than general practical reasoning. While in technical reasoning substantive standards set a canon, method, or technique for weighing the different variables, factors, or considerations—factual and moral—bearing on decisions, in general practical reasoning, no such method is available. In technical reasoning, substantive standards allow decision-makers to compare the factual and moral factors bearing on decisions: it allows them to distinguish relevant from irrelevant factors, and more relevant from less relevant factors.

In this sense, unlike general practical reasoning, in technical reasoning, substantive standards work as a filter or screening device that removes some factors from the decision process; hence binding and guiding such process. And since, in technical reasoning, substantive standards give methods for distinguishing between relevant and irrelevant factors, these standards also give criteria for assessing who shows mastery or skill in using their methods and who doesn't. Thus, unlike general practical reasoning, in technical reasoning, substantive standards determine 'expertise:' they determine who is knowledgeable or skilled in applying these standards' methods. For example, when checking if Boris is infected with Covid-19, a pulmonologist reasons technically since they use the medical method for detecting what matters in their diagnosis. It's their mastery of the medical method that allows them to recognise that Boris' flamboyant character, aesthetic preferences, or hobbies are irrelevant for determining if he has Covid-19; while his age, diet, and previous illnesses are relevant for that purpose.

It's generally accepted that, to realise the values of the rule of law—particularly impartiality and predictability—legal reasoning should generally be a technical task.[9] So, knowledge of the sources of law (that is, texts, precedents, and doctrines), and knowledge of the law's core values (eg, the ban of double jeopardy in criminal law, the avoidance of unjust enrichment in private law, the 'equality of arms' principle in procedural law, etc.), provides those who apply legal norms with methods allowing them to distinguish between

5 Grofman et al 1983: 268–70.

6 For akin distinctions, see Kumm 2007; Atria 2001: ch 8; Hübner Mendes 2015: ch 2; Urbina 2017: ch 6.

7 On practical reason generally, see Raz 1978; Audi 2005.

8 On how substantive standards may vary in their specificity, see Chang 2014: ch 1.

9 See generally Honoré 1973; MacCormick 1995; Raz 2009: 194–47; Hart 2012: 135.

relevant and irrelevant factors. Unlike general practical reasoning, legal reasoning usually assumes categories that, in MacCormick's words, 'provide a fixed starting point for deliberation.'[10] As Atria claims, '[l]egal discourse is a *formal* discourse, that is, a kind of normative discourse where participants are justified in *not* considering substantive questions that are, or may be, relevant for an all things considered decision.'[11] Put differently, as Hübner Mendes holds, '[w]hen arguing in the domain of law, something is excluded from our portmanteau of "all things considered reasons."'[12]

As in other forms of technical reasoning, in legal reasoning, '[s]ome filter reduces the number and quality of reasons available.'[13] How broad or narrow this filter must be—and thus which kinds of factors should be considered acceptable for making 'legal' decisions—is widely discussed among legal scholars. In very broad terms, positivists tend to narrow the filter while non-positivists tend to broaden the filter.[14] Yet even Dworkin—arguably a salient non-positivist—claims that, to justify the legal practice by providing its best moral interpretation, moral factors must fit with such practice.[15]

If one assumes that constitutional review is like other areas of the law—and that hence constitutional review requires technical reasoning—to assume that judges are able according to the Condorcet Jury Theorem is easy. After all, if: (i) in constitutional review, the legal method guides and binds judges; and (ii) judges are 'jurists,' in the sense that they are experts in the legal method, to claim that, in constitutional review, judges have above 50% odds of deciding according to the law is reasonable.[16] Indeed, authors such as Ely,[17] Dworkin,[18] and Rawls[19] argue along these lines by suggesting that, when checking the constitutionality of legislation, judges' legal training focuses them on some especially relevant factors. For Ely, this training focuses them on procedural fairness, and thus on ensuring political representation.[20] For Dworkin, this training focuses them on rights, and thus on principle.[21] Lastly, for Rawls, this training focuses them on text and precedents, and thus on public reasons.[22]

Still, constitutional review—specifically, constitutional review of open-ended provisions—has a feature that questions whether this activity requires technical reasoning or general practical reasoning: namely, linguistic indeterminacy. In

10 1995: 82.
11 2001: 218.
12 2015: 59.
13 Id.
14 Id 54–61.
15 Dworkin 1986. See also Dworkin 1985: ch 6; Dworkin 2013: ch 8.
16 For akin claims, see Kelsen 2015: 48, 70.
17 1980: 101–2.
18 1986: ch 2.
19 2005: 215–6, 231–40.
20 1980: 101–2.
21 1985: ch 2.
22 2005: 215–6, 231–40.

constitutional review, many of the provisions under which judges must base their decisions (particularly those recognising rights), are drafted in vague, indeterminate, or open-ended ways, using terms such as 'liberty,' 'dignity,' 'equality,' or 'fairness' that give little guidance for adjudicating cases without recurring to contestable, value-laden, moral ideas.[23] Legal indeterminacy also affects legal texts in other areas of the law.[24] But arguably not as much as it affects constitutions.

For this reason, many legal scholars and political philosophers claim—either to criticise[25] or support[26] constitutional review—that this practice doesn't require technical reasoning, but general practical reasoning. In Mattias Kumm's terms, constitutional review 'is largely an exercise of structured practical reasoning without many of the constraining features that otherwise characterise legal reasoning.'[27] For this conception, in constitutional review, judges may *not* give legal texts, doctrines, or precedents any priority or special force over competing factors. So, for this conception, it's unclear that, when constitutionally adjudicating, judges have cognitive leads over laypeople.

This account of constitutional review challenges whether ability holds in constitutional courts. If this account holds true, it seems that the only way in which one can assume that judges are able is to assume that they are moral experts. After all, a general practical decision requires decision-makers (in this case, judges) to assess all factors (including all *moral* factors) bearing on it. Yet, if constitutional review requires general practical reasoning, there wouldn't be a method for assessing judges' moral ability. Thus, under this account of constitutional review, it doesn't seem possible to hold that judges are able in the Condorcet sense. In sum, if constitutional review is general practical reasoning, and if one can't assume that judges are moral experts, how can one claim that they have above 50% odds of rightly deciding constitutional cases?

Most legal scholars don't claim that judges are moral experts. And Kumm himself has compared judges to Socrates, in the sense that they don't have any 'special knowledge on what justice requires.'[28] For Kumm, '[t]he only thing that judges can possibly claim to know is the law,'[29] and since he sees constitutional review as a task in which all factors should be allowed when deciding, claiming that judges know the law 'is much the same as saying that judges know nothing.'[30] Therefore, Yowell isn't far off the mark when arguing that

23 Ely 1980: 13–4; Dworkin 1996: 7–11; Kelsen 2015: 29–31, 60–1.
24 Hübner Mendes 2015: 74–8. On indeterminacy in law generally, see Endicott 2000.
25 Bellamy 2007: ch 1; Waldron 2016: ch 9.
26 Kumm 2007. See also Möller 2012; Cohen-Eliya & Porat 2013.
27 Kumm 2007: 162.
28 Id 163.
29 Id.
30 Id.

'[n]o one thinks that lawyers are inherently moral experts, or that they become such by donning a black robe.'[31]

Yet one may justify judges' ability even if constitutional review is general practical reasoning. Actually, one may do this using Kumm's theory.[32] For Kumm, constitutional review is justified since it institutionalises 'Socratic contestation;'[33] meaning, since it gives a framework for judges to assess whether statutes are based on public reasons. This is akin to Cohen-Eliya & Porat's claim that constitutional review is about promoting a culture of justification[34] and to Möller's claim that judges must assess whether policies are 'in the realm of the reasonable.'[35] In short, for these authors, constitutional review is about judges assessing public reasons.

Kumm claims that, though constitutional review doesn't need technical reasoning, judges have a 'special wisdom'[36] that helps them at assessing public reasons. This wisdom is based on their mastery of the proportionality test.[37] For Kumm, though in constitutional review, judges' knowledge of the law is rather unhelpful,[38] their training still gives them an edge lying 'not in what they know about theories of justice … but in the questions they know how to ask those who have, at least prima facie, a better claim of wisdom on their side.'[39] Thus, though Kumm doesn't consider judges as moral experts, he thinks that their legal expertise makes them skilful at managing the proportionality test—a test that, in his opinion, gives them enough guidance for weighing different factors when solving constitutional cases. So, under Kumm's premises, though constitutional review is general practical reasoning, legal expertise matters since it gives judges a certain mastery of the proportionality test to a degree that laypeople (meaning, non-jurists) lack. Given Kumm's claims, one may hold that, despite constitutional review being general practical reasoning, judges are more likely than laypeople at getting the constitution right since their legal expertise *indicates* their 'proportionality expertise.'

Thus, judges may be considered able even under theories that see constitutional review as general practical reasoning. Both when judges' task is seen as technical reasoning and when it's seen as general practical reasoning, one may hold that judges likely have above 50% odds of rightly deciding constitutional

31 Yowell 2018: 104.
32 I don't endorse Kumm's theory. I agree with the critiques made by Webber (2009); Urbina (2017), and Yowell (2018), among others, that this theory's account of the proportionality test doesn't give judges a precise enough method for solving constitutional cases. But my aim here isn't to support or criticise this theory. Rather, I try to show that, even accepting Kumm's theory, one may still argue that judges are able.
33 Kumm 2007: 162.
34 Cohen-Eliya & Porat 2013.
35 Möller 2012: 133.
36 Kumm 2007: 164.
37 Id 164–5.
38 Id 164.
39 Id.

cases. In the first case, judges' ability is based on their legal expertise. In the second case, judges' ability is based on their proportionality expertise, as shown by their legal expertise. So, from this point onwards, I assume that judges are able, though I don't assume that this relevance is based on their technical reasoning capacities.

But someone may wonder whether judges really are able. It may be that constitutional courts' current composition is simply contingent. The fact that constitutional courts are made of jurists may be a *fait accompli:* something that just happened, without there being much reason to it.[40]

Judges should be assumed able since, without this assumption, it's hard to justify much of constitutional review in its current form. If legal expertise isn't somehow cognitively relevant, there's little reason for doing this task the way we are familiarised with. True, one may build cases for constitutional review that aren't ability-dependent.[41] For example, following Cross[42] and Fallon[43] in the US, one may claim that, regardless of judges' ability, constitutional review should exist to check legislative excesses; that though judges may not be more able than laypeople, constitutional review boosts the chances for defying legislation, hence keeping the total amount of unconstitutional statutes lower than it would otherwise be.[44] Yet without assuming ability, it's hard to hold that constitutional review should be done by lawyers—or that these lawyers should follow procedures akin to those of a court of law.[45] Something similar may be said about the link between ability and majority rule in constitutional review. If judges are unable, the Condorcet Jury Theorem wouldn't apply to them. In turn, that would only support my argument here: that there aren't strong enough reasons for using majority rule in this task. Thus, rejecting ability would strengthen my claims.

Hence, ability seems to belong to the best arguments for constitutional review as it currently stands, including the best arguments for majority rule in this task. And since I'm not trying to build straw men, but hold that, despite constitutional review's best possible versions, there aren't strong enough reasons for using majority rule in it, I see little choice but to assume ability.

40 For an argument holding that the US Supreme Court may work better if it's made of legal experts and laypeople, see Vermeule 2007.

41 Eg, see Harel & Kahana 2010; Weinrib 2016; Hickey 2019.

42 1999.

43 2008.

44 Other scholars have argued along Cross' and Fallon's lines, but without focusing on justifying constitutional review. Roosevelt 2005: 1649, 1659–61, 1704–5; Mahoney 2005: 103, 129–31; Epstein 2014: 77–8, 98–9.

45 In principle, this claim applies to courts mixing legal experts and lay members, such as France's Constitutional Council. Without the ability assumption, it's hard to justify why, in these courts, *most* judges are still legal experts. On the Council, see Favoreu 1988.

3. Statistical Independence in Constitutional Courts

When determining if statistical independence holds among judges, it matters to assess whether this condition is hindered by deliberation, and by whether judges see how their peers vote at the time of voting.

In principle, statistical independence holds among judges even if they talk to each other. As indicated in Chapter 2, there are good reasons to assume that, in constitutional review, deliberation is cognitively sound.[46] Also, research on deliberation hasn't conclusively proved that this practice is detrimental.[47] Finally, according to some of the main interpretations of statistical independence,[48] inasmuch as there's no blind deference to others, deliberation doesn't affect statistical independence—or at least not significantly.

In turn, on whether judges see how their peers vote at the time of voting, recall that, if this is the case, sequential voting can erode statistical independence by producing information cascades.[49] Unfortunately, it's hard to establish if judges have tried to curb information cascades since: (i) procedural rules may not regulate the way in which judges vote, and (ii) judicial debates are usually secret. Thus, it isn't easy to determine whether they've adopted informal voting practices. Yet, curbing information cascades arguably is a key reason why, in some courts—eg, the Austrian, Italian,[50] Canadian,[51] Chilean,[52] and Irish[53] constitutional courts, US military courts,[54] or the District of Columbia US Court of Appeals[55]—judges vote 'in reverse order of seniority.' That is, younger judges (or those appointed earlier) vote before older judges (or those appointed later). True, voting in reverse order of seniority doesn't fully prevent judges from copying each other. But at least it prevents them from copying their presumably more influential peers.

Hence, it's plausible that statistical independence holds among judges, but only if they establish measures to curb information cascades: a thing that we don't know for sure. Still, since I want to determine if the Condorcet Jury Theorem gives strong reasons for supporting majority rule in constitutional review, I assume for the sake of argument that constitutional courts use these procedures, though it should be borne in mind that it isn't clear that this is so.

46 Kornhauser & Sager 1986: 85-6, 101–2; Hübner Mendes 2015: ch 1–2; Landemore 2013: ch 4–5.
47 Mendelberg 2002; Delli Carpini et al 2004; Ryfe 2005; Steiner 2012; Neblo 2015; Fishkin 2018; Smith & Setälä 2018.
48 Ladha 1992; 625–30; Estlund 2008: 225–26; Landemore 2013: 153–4.
49 Sunstein 2006: 88–92; Farnsworth 2007: 136–9; Devine 2012: 169–71; Barry 2021: 218–9.
50 Kelemen 2019: 43.
51 Wilson 1986: 227, 236.
52 Ch Courts Code, Art 84.
53 Barry 2021: 218.
54 Farnsworth 2007: 138.
55 Edwards 2003: 1665.

(In Chapter 7, I suggest measures that constitutional courts may use to curb information cascades.)

4. Sincere Voting in Constitutional Courts

Lastly, when determining if sincere voting holds among judges, it's worth recalling that bargaining and manipulation are pervasive in most groups.[56] Curbing bargaining and manipulation is hard, especially when these phenomena consist of logrolling, and of misrepresenting premises to advance conclusions or vice versa. Thus, any credible claim on sincere voting holding among judges is bound by the impossibility of eliminating these practices.

Despite the above, judges have incentives to *generally vote sincerely* though they may not *always* do so. Judges face a binary choice: to declare or not to declare legislation unconstitutional. This matters since one of the main phenomena that allows manipulation is having more than two options.[57] Thus, binary choice heavily binds judges' chances to manipulate the result of their court's voting process. Further, in well-functioning democracies, the judicial office is regulated in ways that bind the impact of promises or threats, hence curbing bargaining. In these democracies, the rules governing judges' office—eg, those governing appointment, compensation, tenure, interest conflicts, etc.—tend to guard judges' independence against their peers, other officials, and public opinion.[58] Thus, these rules put judges in a strong position to vote according to what they really think since these rules seek to protect them from negative repercussions.[59] Therefore, though bargaining and manipulation can't be eliminated—which means that judges can logroll, and misrepresent premises to advance conclusions or vice versa—one may still claim that sincere voting generally holds in constitutional review.

Does Condorcet Accuracy Ground Majority Rule in Constitutional Review?

Now that we've established that, given constitutional courts' current conditions—and inasmuch as information cascades are curbed—the Condorcet Jury Theorem likely holds among judges, the question is whether this fact gives conclusive reasons for using majority rule in constitutional review. To this question, the answer is no: the Condorcet Jury Theorem doesn't give conclusive reasons for using majority rule in constitutional review; it doesn't give them since, as seen in the previous chapter, supermajority rules are also Condorcet accurate, at least within some thresholds.[60] Thus, the Condorcet

56 Lagerspetz 2016: 217–26.
57 Condorcet [1785] 2014: lviii–lx, 119–20; Arrow 1963: ch 5.
58 Ferejohn & Pasquino 2004: 1677–82; Stone Sweet 2012: 824–5.
59 Urfalino argues similarly (2014: 337).
60 Condorcet 1793: 14, 16; McLean & Hewitt 1994: 35–7; List & Pettit 2011: 87–91.

Jury Theorem holding among judges doesn't suffice to exclude supermajority rules for declaring statutes unconstitutional.

When facing error asymmetry, some supermajority rules are more Condorcet accurate than majority rule.[61] So, a case for majority rule in constitutional review based on Condorcet accuracy is defeasible under that same trait. This is especially so since there are sound reasons to claim that, in strong-form constitutional review, false positives—that is, declaring statutes unconstitutional when they aren't so—are worse than false negatives, that is, not declaring statutes unconstitutional when they are so. (I develop this claim in the next chapter.) So, even if the Condorcet Jury Theorem holds in constitutional courts, the theorem doesn't conclusively ground majority rule to declare statutes unconstitutional.

Does Flexibility Ground Majority Rule in Constitutional Review?

If Condorcet accuracy doesn't conclusively ground majority rule in constitutional review, perhaps flexibility can. Recall that one of majority rule's main traits is that, since this rule doesn't require total agreement among group members for deciding, majority rule allows group members to dissent if they want to. Thus, majority rule lessens peer pressure and social influences among group members, hence reducing the incentives to coerce dissenters.[62]

Regardless of flexibility's advantages, flexibility doesn't justify majority rule in constitutional review. The Condorcet Jury Theorem may hold in constitutional courts. Thus, a voting rule's capacity to boost group accuracy is also relevant for choosing it to declare statutes unconstitutional. And when facing error asymmetry, there's a trade-off between Condorcet accuracy and flexibility. Therefore, if judges' errors at checking the constitutionality of legislation are asymmetrical, one may choose a voting rule that balances these two traits. Now, I don't intend to show here how this balance may be achieved, I just hold that it's unclear that majority rule achieves it.

Despite flexibility, a voting rule's capacity to boost group accuracy also matters in constitutional review. As we've seen thus far, despite their peculiarities, constitutional courts are expert groups in the sense that judges' legal expertise is cognitively relevant for solving constitutional cases. This happens when constitutional review is seen as technical reasoning,[63] and when it's seen as general practical reasoning.[64] Thus, if constitutional courts are expert groups—and if the Condorcet Jury Theorem likely holds in them (as it seems to be the case)—one may consider Condorcet accuracy when choosing a voting rule in

61 Ben-Yashar & Nitzan 1997; McGinnis & Rappaport 2008; List & Pettit 2011: 90–91.

62 Laplace [1835] 2009: 165–74; Schwartzberg 2013: 87–8.

63 Kelsen 2015: 48, 76.

64 Kumm 2007: 162–69.

constitutional review. Hence, flexibility isn't the only relevant factor in this choice.

Unfortunately, when facing error a-symmetry, Condorcet accuracy and flexibility stand against each other. Any increase in a voting rule's threshold (pursuant to the Condorcet Jury Theorem) increases the number of group members needed to decide. But with higher thresholds, voting rules become more rigid, thus becoming potentially more coercive towards dissenters.[65] And, as previously mentioned, in constitutional review, mistakenly declaring statutes unconstitutional may be worse than mistakenly not doing so.

Thus, given error asymmetry, one may hold that, when choosing a voting rule in constitutional review, one should balance Condorcet accuracy and flexibility. According to the Condorcet Jury Theorem, some loss in flexibility may be acceptable to boost collective accuracy. Yet this flexibility loss can't be so high as to promote coercion against dissenters, since that would void the epistemic case for requiring more people to decide in the first place. So, since one may claim that, when choosing a voting rule in constitutional review, Condorcet accuracy and flexibility should be balanced, flexibility doesn't suffice for using majority rule in this task.

Some may object that, when facing asymmetrical errors, majority rule balances Condorcet accuracy and flexibility. But it isn't clear that this happens. Majority rule may be too flexible. And some supermajority rules—those closest to majority rule—are also quite flexible while boosting group accuracy more than majority rule. Since it isn't clear that, when facing asymmetrical errors, majority rule balances Condorcet accuracy and flexibility, my claim that flexibility doesn't conclusively ground majority rule in constitutional review still holds. When considering if majority rule is flexible, and when considering if it balances Condorcet accuracy and flexibility, majority rule isn't conclusively upheld in constitutional review, one must assess other reasons.

Does Decisiveness Ground Majority Rule in Constitutional Review?

If neither majority rule's Condorcet accuracy nor its flexibility conclusively grounds majority rule in constitutional review, how about majority rule's decisiveness? Can this trait provide such ground? In principle, one may claim that decisiveness conclusively grounds majority rule in constitutional review. Or at least that it's a key trait to consider when choosing a voting rule for declaring statutes unconstitutional. By ensuring that constitutional courts decide *something* rather than getting into deadlocks, decisiveness boosts quick (and thus effective) decisions on the constitutionality of legislation, hence contributing to legal certainty. As US Supreme Court Justice Louis Brandeis argued, 'in most matters, it is most important than the applicable rule of law be settled

65 Laplace [1835] 2009: 165–74; Schwartzberg 2013: 79, 87–8.

than it be settled right.'[66] So, considering the need to quickly settle constitutional law, one may claim that decisiveness is especially conducive to that end, and that hence it gives enough reasons for favouring majority rule over other voting rules in constitutional review.

Despite the fact that, at first sight, decisiveness seems to conclusively ground majority rule in constitutional review, this trait doesn't do so since, in this task, reflection gains relevance over speed. Recall that, in the previous chapter, I claimed that (i) there's a trade-off between deciding quickly and deciding reflectively,[67] (ii) due to its decisiveness, majority rule boosts quick decisions,[68] and (iii) due to their decelerator, supermajority rules boost reflective decisions.[69] And recall that these values gain or lose relevance on a case-by-case basis. Put differently, depending on groups' peculiarities, deciding quickly may be more relevant, less relevant, or as relevant as deciding reflectively.

In constitutional review, there are sound reasons to claim that deciding reflectively gains relevance against deciding quickly. First, constitutional courts are reviewing institutions: they are institutions that check if legislatures' decisions are constitutionally sound. Following Möller, constitutional courts mustn't 'engage in the complex task of designing policies;'[70] that's legislatures' job. Instead, they must 'analyse such policies and [screen them] for possible mistakes.'[71] In Urbina's words, these courts 'must establish whether the decision of a primary decision maker is somehow deficient.'[72] So, constitutional courts can't justify their decisions on the sole fact that they must decide. Rather, they must give reasons that explain—in terms that others may understand and accept—why a statute is constitutionally flawed. Thus, these courts should base their decisions on reasons that need a high degree of rational reflection.

Second, when constitutional courts declare legislation unconstitutional, these decisions may produce gaps in the legal system that erode legal certainty.[73] After all, the issues regulated by statutes—issues that are often hard, such as assisted suicide, abortion, organ donation, sex work, campaign financing, etc.—may cease to be subject to it, hence risking people's ability to properly plan their lives. This risk may be even higher in common law polities

66 *Burnett v Coronado Oil and Gas Co* 285 US 393, 406-7 (1932).
67 Elster 2013: 32, 44, 179–81.
68 May 1952: 680, 681–2; Lagerspetz 2016: 36–8.
69 Condorcet 1793: 14, 16–7; Schwartzberg 2013: 92–4.
70 2012: 133.
71 Id 132.
72 2017: 73.
73 In many countries with Kelsenian courts, annulments only have future effects except in the case where the claim originated. Kelsen (1942: 169–99) was so worried about guarding legal certainty that he also recommended: (i) establishing deadlines for defying statutes; (ii) allowing constitutional courts to delay their decisions' effects; and (iii) allowing constitutional courts to restore the validity of statutes repealed by a defied statute. See also Ferreres Comella 2009: 24–6.

with strong-form constitutional review. In these polities, statutes are usually considered void after their *enactment* (not after they are *declared unconstitutional*). Therefore, in these polities, statute annulments may produce retroactive effects.[74] So, considering how constitutional courts' decisions may produce legal gaps—even retroactive legal gaps—one may hold that such decisions must be justified to a higher degree than other institutions' decisions. (With supermajority rules, legal gaps wouldn't happen since, if these rules' thresholds aren't met, statutes would stay constitutional.)

Third, in constitutional review, judges' reasoning skills seem a key part of their accuracy. Thus, it seems especially relevant that, when performing this task, judges' decisions are properly reflected upon.

Authors such as Dworkin,[75] Rawls,[76] and Kumm[77] remark judges' reasoning skills as ensuring their decisions' accuracy. And for Dworkin[78] and Rawls,[79] constitutional review is based on accuracy, though they differ on substantive standards. For Dworkin, the US Supreme Court is 'the forum of principle.'[80] He also holds that, due to this court's focus on principle—focus shown in the bases of its decisions—US society is more just than it would be without constitutional review.[81] Likewise, Rawls suggests that the US Supreme Court fosters basic values by exemplifying public reason, while also holding that a way in which it exemplifies such reason is by justifying its decisions according to the relevant legal texts and precedents.[82] Lastly, though Kumm's case for constitutional review isn't based on accuracy, Kumm claims that constitutional review likely improves state decisions[83] by 'forc[ing] officials into the game of having to justify [them] in terms of public reasons.'[84] Thus, since judges' reasoning skills seem highly linked to their accuracy—and thus to the justifiability of constitutional review itself (at least for Dworkin and Rawls)—one may hold that, in constitutional review, it's key to ensure that judges' decisions are properly reflected on.

Finally, constitutional review usually means that decisions made by small groups of unelected judges can trump decisions made by majorities of elected

74 To avoid these effects, constitutional courts in common law polities usually: (i) declare that their decisions don't have retroactive effects outside the respective case (eg, the US); or (ii) delay their decisions' effects to allow legislative amendments (eg, Canada since the *Manitoba* case). Yowell 2018: 159–62. See also Choudry & Roach 2003: 205, 228-9.

75 1985: ch 2.

76 2005: 215–6, 231–40.

77 2007: 153–5, 165–70.

78 1996: 8, 16–7, 23–6.

79 2005: 158–63, 215–6, 227–8, 231–40.

80 1985: ch 2.

81 1986: 356. Later, Dworkin somewhat curbed his support of this practice (2013: 385).

82 2005: 215–6, 231–40.

83 2007: 153–5, 165–70.

84 Id 168.

legislators. When judges act in this 'counter-majoritarian way' (as Bickel[85] called it), they can't argue that their authority is based on elections. Hence, beyond the quality of their claims, judges have little to hold on to—if anything at all—to ensure that their decisions are respected and followed by citizens and other officials.[86] Thus, constitutional review's counter-majoritarian nature bolsters the claim that judges' decisions on the constitutionality of legislation must stem from deep rational reflection. Therefore, when grounding their decisions, constitutional courts have a higher burden than other institutions. Particularly, due to their counter-majoritarian nature, constitutional courts have a higher justificatory burden than legislatures. So, in constitutional review, deciding reflectively gains relevance against deciding quickly. With this I'm not holding that speed is irrelevant in constitutional review. Rather, I'm holding that reflection is also a key factor to consider.

Therefore, as with Condorcet accuracy and flexibility, one may hold that, in constitutional review, judges should use a voting rule that balances speed and reflection. Thus, when declaring statutes unconstitutional, it isn't clear that deciding quickly should be preferred over deciding reflectively through majority rule. True, not using majority rule would increase constitutional courts' decision costs, particularly their time costs. But there are ways to curb these costs without giving up on balancing speed and reflection. (I tackle these ways in the next chapter.) So, when justifying majority rule in constitutional review, the need to balance speed and reflection suggests that decisiveness won't do. One must thus explore other justificatory paths.

Does the Equality Signal Ground Majority Rule in Constitutional Review?

To check whether majority rule's equality signal justifies this voting rule in constitutional review, it's worth assessing what sort of status majority rule may recognise among judges. Particularly, judges have two main equal status that majority rule may recognise: first, their political equality, that is, their equal status as citizens; and second, their equal status—or, more precisely, their *allegedly* equal status—as legal experts. Let's assess whether recognising these status justifies majority rule in constitutional review.

It's doubtful that recognising judges' political equality justifies majority rule in constitutional review. If anything, this recognition mainly justifies majority rule in elections, and when applying referenda:[87] it doesn't seem to justify majority rule among judges. In constitutional review, judges neither act as ordinary citizens, nor do they represent citizens' interests, as elected representatives do. Rather, judges act as officials that check the constitutionality

85 1962: 16–23.
86 Ferejohn & Pasquino 2004: 1680.
87 Rawls 1999: 196–7; Christiano 2008: 104–6; Schwartzberg 2013: 117–8.

of legislation. This happens when this task is seen as technical reasoning[88] and when it's seen as general practical reasoning.[89] Thus, regardless of whether judges should adjudicate by using the legal method, the claim that, to recognise their equal status as citizens, judges should declare statutes unconstitutional by majority rule isn't very convincing.

But some may hold that I hastily dismiss political equality. Some may claim that political equality should be construed broadly; meaning, that instead of applying *only* among citizens and elected representatives, it applies to *all* groups deciding by voting, including judges.[90] There's something to this objection. Yet this broad version of political equality confuses this idea with that of an equal status itself—an equal status that, in the case of judges, seems mainly based on their citizenship, or on their legal knowledge or skills. So, the claim that political equality (narrowly construed) doesn't justify majority rule in constitutional review arguably applies to this broad version. Likewise, the claim that judges' equal legal expertise doesn't justify majority rule in constitutional review—a claim I develop in what follows—applies to this broad version as well.

Following Pufendorf,[91] one may hold that, though majority rule in constitutional review can't be based on recognising judges' political equality (narrowly construed), it may still be based on recognising their equal legal expertise. One may hold that, when appointed, judges should be presumed equally able, especially since: (i) it doesn't seem possible to indubitably assess potential ability differences among them without inviting controversy; and (ii) when facing competing ability claims, there doesn't seem to be a higher authority to turn to. Judges' equal legal expertise—this 'Pufendorfian' argument may go—should be publicly recognised since not doing so would be disrespectful. By giving each judge one vote and by treating the constitutional interpretations they may prefer equally, majority rule executes this recognition. Thus, since judges' equal legal expertise should be recognised, and since majority rule executes this recognition, majority rule should be constitutional courts' general voting rule. So, majority rule should be used in constitutional review as well.

Despite this Pufendorfian argument, recognising judges' equal legal expertise doesn't justify majority rule in constitutional review. It doesn't do so since, once one examines some of the main theories justifying constitutional review—especially Ely's,[92] Dworkin's,[93] Rawls',[94] and Kumm's[95]—one con-

88 Kelsen 2015: 48, 76.
89 Kumm 2007: 161–5.
90 For akin claims, see Hills 2002: 58–69.
91 1703: 153–4.
92 1980: 101–2.
93 1985: ch 2.
94 2005: 215–6.
95 2007: 161–5.

cludes that, from different viewpoints, all of them assume that legal expertise is instrumental to group accuracy: that legal expertise serves judges' capacity for getting the constitution right. This happens when constitutional review is considered technical reasoning, and when it's considered general practical reasoning. In the first case, legal expertise matters since judges are accurate in direct proportion to their legal knowledge and skills, whether due to their focus on procedural fairness (Ely),[96] rights (Dworkin),[97] or public reasons (Rawls).[98] In the second case, legal expertise matters since it reliably indicates proportionality expertise (Kumm).[99] Hence, regardless of the sort of reasoning that constitutional review needs, one recognises judges as equally able—thus having an equal status—only if their legal expertise adds to the group's capacity for rightly interpreting the constitution. When checking the constitutionality of legislation, legal expertise is the ancillary value; group accuracy is the main value.

If legal expertise grounds judges' equal status as jurists, and if, in constitutional review, this expertise serves group accuracy, in constitutional review, realising group accuracy matters more than publicly recognising judges' equal legal expertise. Since, in this task, realising group accuracy matters more than recognising judges' equal legal expertise, and given that—within some thresholds—supermajority rules may (just may) boost group accuracy more than majority rule, one may at least claim that: (i) it isn't clear that supermajority rules disrespect judges' equal legal expertise; and (ii) even if they do so, realising group accuracy trumps recognising such status. (Note that I'm not arguing for supermajority rules in constitutional review, I do that in Chapter 6; I'm just questioning the idea that recognising judges' equal legal expertise justifies majority rule in it.)

Let's refine these claims.

If one accepts that, in constitutional review, legal expertise serves group accuracy, it isn't clear that supermajority rules disrespect judges' equal legal expertise if they boost group accuracy more than majority rule. Rather, in groups whose authority highly depends on deciding rightly—as constitutional courts are, at least according to Ely,[100] Dworkin,[101] and Rawls[102]—things seem to go backwards. Since group accuracy is the main value, any increase in accuracy, including any potential increase produced by supermajority rules, would bolster constitutional courts' reputation, thus bolstering the respect that judges get as legal experts. Put differently, the respect that judges jointly get due to boosts in accuracy would permeate to them individually.

96 1980: 101–2.
97 1985: ch 2.
98 2005: 215–6, 231–40.
99 2007: 161–5.
100 1980: 101–2.
101 1996: 8, 16–7, 23–6.
102 2005: 158–63, 215–6, 227–8, 231–40.

The Conclave is a particularly good example for this claim. This institution shows that: (i) if a group's authority highly depends on accuracy; (ii) if its members are chosen since their ability adds to group accuracy; and (iii) if the voting rule for deciding gives each member one vote, supermajority rules don't necessarily disrespect group members' equal status.

As seen in Chapter 3, in the Church, giving each cardinal one vote suffices to recognise that they are equally able. This assumption goes along the lines of my argument. Recall that the Conclave is about electing good popes—'good' as in 'according to the Holy Spirit's will.'[103] So, the Conclave is made of cardinals, who are considered spiritual experts. Since the Conclave is about choosing good popes, it's sensible to use a 2/3 rule if the Church considers that this voting rule tracks the Holy Spirit's will better than majority rule.[104] Indeed, if the Conclave usually elects good popes, that boosts the Conclave's reputation—and thus cardinals' respect as spiritual experts—since usually electing good popes proves that there are good reasons for actually having the Conclave. (For this example, it doesn't matter if the Holy Spirit really exists. As held in Chapter 2, substantive standards may be based on people's shared beliefs, such as the belief in the Holy Spirit.)

Two facts question the idea that, in groups whose authority highly depends on accuracy, non-neutral voting rules—such as supermajority rules—disrespect their members' equal status. First, before a group finds a choice situation, in principle, no group member knows which option they'll choose. Or at least not necessarily. So, if a decision is subject to supermajority rules, nobody knows beforehand whether they'll choose the option favoured by such rules. Second, though supermajority rules are non-neutral, they still give each group member one vote.[105] Hence, in principle, before the votes are counted, no group member knows beforehand whether their vote is pivotal. As Lagerspetz holds, supermajority rules 'favour *all* conservative minorities':[106] they favour anyone supporting a status quo, whoever that person is. This double uncertainty is joined by the fact that the factors affecting a voting process' result vary on a case-by-case basis. True, people may have strong intuitions about this result. But this result is still uncertain. This is likely a reason why, in the Conclave, the fact that each cardinal has one vote suffices for recognising their equal status.

Since in groups deciding by supermajority rules—particularly those whose authority highly depends on accuracy—group members neither know beforehand whether they'll choose the option favoured by these rules, nor whether

103 Papal Encyclicals Online nd. See also Apostolic Constitution *Universi Dominici Gregis* on the Vacancy of the Holy See and the Election of the Roman Pontiff.

104 Colomer & McLean 1998: 1–14; Lagerspetz 2010: 29, 31–4; Schwartzberg 2016: 53–8, 67–9.

105 May 1952: 681; Lagerspetz 2016: 34.

106 2016: 282.

their votes are pivotal, no group member has good reasons to complain that they aren't treated equally, or to complain that their status is eroded. An akin logic may apply to constitutional courts declaring statutes unconstitutional by supermajority rules. Insofar as no judge knows beforehand whether they'll choose the option favoured by the voting rule (or whether their vote is pivotal), no judge has good reason to complain that their legal expertise isn't treated as equal to their peers', or to complain that their status is eroded.

Therefore, since some supermajority rules may boost judges' accuracy more than majority rule (which means that their respect may also increase); and since under supermajority rules, no judge seems to have strong reason to complain that their status is eroded (since none of them knows beforehand how they are going to vote, nor whether their vote is pivotal); the claim that judges should constitutionally adjudicate by majority rule since not doing so would erode their equal legal expertise doesn't really fly.

Now, even if we assume that this claim does fly—meaning, even if we assume that the only voting rule that recognises judges' equal legal expertise is majority rule—since in constitutional review, legal expertise serves group accuracy, in constitutional review, boosting group accuracy matters more than recognising this expertise. We assume that judges are equally able partly[107] since they are legal experts. And legal expertise is needed since it's considered cognitively relevant; meaning, since it's considered that such expertise somehow boosts judges' ability at rightly deciding constitutional cases.[108] So, judges' legal expertise is highly (if not fully) based on its contribution to group accuracy. Thus, it doesn't seem sound to hold that judges' equal legal expertise should be respected at the expense of group accuracy. If anything, the claim goes backwards. Precisely since one assumes that, to realise group accuracy, judges are equally able, if these two values clash, realising group accuracy trumps publicly recognising judges' equal legal expertise.

For example, suppose that Weirdland's constitutional court must decide by a supermajority rule on the constitutionality of a statute criminalising the buying of sexual services. (Call it, 'the sex buying ban.') The sex buying ban is declared unconstitutional only if the supermajority threshold is met. If it isn't, the sex buying ban stays constitutional. Suppose that, after careful consideration, Judge Camille Paglia[109] concludes that the sex buying ban is unconstitutional. And suppose that, after the judges deliberate and vote, the

107 I use the word 'partly' since the other reason is that, once appointed, it doesn't seem possible to precisely and indubitably assess ability differences among judges. Note though that, if we could do so, that would give strong arguments against majority rule and in favour of granting more votes to more qualified judges.

108 Kelsen 2015: 48, 76; Kumm 2007: 161–5.

109 No offence intended against Paglia. Actually, I agree with her position on sex work. I could reverse the example and refer to 'Judge Catherine MacKinnon' checking the constitutionality of a statute *decriminalising* the buying of sexual services. On these contrasting positions on sex work, see MacKinnon 2005: ch 13; Paglia 2017: ch 10.

supermajority threshold isn't met, which means that the sex buying ban stays constitutional. Thus, the option that Judge Paglia chose wasn't chosen by the group.

In this case, if legal expertise serves group accuracy, and if some supermajority rules boost group accuracy more than majority rule, it would be untenable for Judge Paglia to hold that the voting rule disrespects her expertise, and that therefore the case should have been decided by majority rule. Even if the court's supermajority rule disrespects Judge Paglia's expertise, the proper response wouldn't be to change the voting rule.[110] After all, one assumes that Judge Paglia is as able as her peers to add to judges' capacity at rightly deciding constitutional cases. Hence, even if deciding by a supermajority rule disrespects Judge Paglia's equal legal expertise, that isn't enough to claim that, in constitutional review, majority rules should be used over other voting rules.

Lastly, the fact that some supermajority rules may boost group accuracy more than majority rule erodes a tentative claim made by Waldron. (This claim is tentative since Waldron suggests he isn't convinced by it.)[111] Waldron holds that, in the US Supreme Court, presidents appoint justices in different periods, hence reflecting inter-generational political representation. Thus, if judges don't decide constitutional cases by majority rule, that would disrespect the president that appointed them, hence also disrespecting the political equality of the US citizens that elected that president.

Waldron's claim doesn't justify majority rule in constitutional review. Regardless of how US Supreme Court justices are appointed,[112] judges aren't supposed to represent their appointers' interests, nor are they supposed to represent the interests of their appointers' electors: they are supposed to check the constitutionality of legislation by using their legal expertise (if constitutional review is technical reasoning),[113] or by using their proportionality expertise (if constitutional review is general practical reasoning).[114] As Waldron claims, 'even where judges are elected, the business of courts isn't normally conducted ... with an ethos of elections, representation, and electoral accountability.'[115] Thus, if supermajority rules may boost group accuracy more than majority rule, such voting rules may enable justices to better perform their task than with majority rule. So, despite judges' appointment procedure, there aren't conclusive reasons for using majority rule in constitutional review.

In sum, neither recognising judges' political equality, nor recognising their equal legal expertise, justifies majority rule in constitutional review. In the first case, majority rule isn't justified since judges neither act as citizens nor as their

110 My claim is based on Brennan's. Brennan 2016: ch 5.
111 Waldron 2016: 266–7.
112 Though in this book I focus on courts with appointed judges, in principle, I think this claim also applies to courts with elected judges.
113 Kelsen 2015: 48, 76.
114 Kumm 2007: 161–5.
115 Waldron 2016: 206.

elected representatives: they act as constitutional guardians. In the second case, majority rule isn't justified since (i) legal expertise serves group accuracy, and (ii) some supermajority rules may boost group accuracy more than majority rule. Thus, under two key levels of analysis, majority rule's equality signal doesn't justify this voting rule in constitutional review.

Do Majority Rule's Joint Traits Ground It in Constitutional Review?

Despite all I've argued thus far, it could be held that my analysis is incomplete. Though each of majority rule's traits may not justify this voting rule in constitutional review, they may do so as a whole. So, maybe I should assess these traits jointly, not separately.

This is a fair point. Yet my claims apply even if we assess majority rule's traits jointly. There may be two main ways in which a joint analysis of majority rule's traits may justify majority rule in constitutional review. First, these traits may intersect;[116] meaning, due to their links, these traits may produce a new trait that justifies majority rule in constitutional review. (Call it, majority rule's 'emergent' or 'rising' trait.) Second, absent a rising trait, the mere sum of majority rule's traits may justify this voting rule in constitutional review.

On the first way, there hasn't been any salient accounts in philosophy or social choice theory arguing for majority rule's rising trait. Now, this trait may exist. After all, absence of evidence isn't evidence of absence. But since there are no salient accounts claiming this trait's existence,[117] a reasonable attitude is to be agnostic about it. That is, to act as if this trait doesn't exist. Thus, one isn't bound to argue against it. On the second way, though merely adding majority rule's traits may justify this voting rule in constitutional review,[118] one may object that merely adding my claims here would question the former aggregation's justificatory force. Though it's possible that Condorcet accuracy, plus flexibility, plus decisiveness, plus the equality signal justify majority rule in constitutional review; in principle, it's equally possible that error asymmetry, plus supermajority rules' boosted group accuracy (in error asymmetry cases), plus a stronger need for group accuracy, plus a stronger need for delib-

116 I'm grateful to an anonymous reviewer of an article based on this chapter for suggesting I should use the word 'intersection.' This word is very precise for what I claim: that the ***links*** among majority rule's traits may produce an unobserved trait. Originally, I built this claim considering complex systems; especially the fact that their behaviour can't be explained by just adding their parts (Thurner et al 2018: 22–5). Still, insofar as the word 'intersection' means that discrimination experiences ***can't be reduced to the mere aggregation*** of discrimination categories (Crenshaw 1989), the word is very apt for conveying my ideas.

117 Some very complete literature reviews on majority rule can be found in Landemore 2013; Brennan 2016; Lagerspetz 2016.

118 Krishnamurthi argues along these lines when defending majority rule in judicial decision making (2020).

eration erode this justification. Hence, even if one merely adds majority rule's traits, such addition doesn't seem to justify majority rule in constitutional review.

Conclusion

None of majority rule's main traits—separately and jointly considered—seem to justify majority rule in constitutional review. On Condorcet accuracy, even if one assumes that the Condorcet Jury Theorem holds in constitutional review, Condorcet accuracy doesn't justify majority rule in this practice since: (i) some supermajority rules are also Condorcet accurate; and (ii) when errors are asymmetrical, some supermajority rules are more Condorcet accurate than majority rule. On flexibility, this trait doesn't justify majority rule in constitutional review. Though flexibility matters for choosing a voting rule, when facing error asymmetry, it's reasonable to balance flexibility and Condorcet accuracy. But it isn't clear that majority rule strikes this balance since majority rule may be too flexible. So, when checking the constitutionality of legislation, flexibility doesn't support majority rule over other voting rules.

On decisiveness, though this trait seems to justify majority rule in constitutional review, this justification fails once one considers the tension between speed and reflection, and constitutional review's peculiarities. These factors suggest the need to balance these values, a task for which majority rule seems ill-equipped. On the equality signal, this trait doesn't justify majority rule in constitutional review. Considering judges' role, it's unconvincing to claim that judges must check the constitutionality of statutes by majority rule to recognise their political equality. Also, since in constitutional review, legal expertise serves group accuracy—and since some supermajority rules may boost group accuracy more than majority rule—it's also unconvincing to claim that judges should constitutionally adjudicate by majority rule to recognise their equal legal expertise. Lastly, though a joint analysis of majority rule's traits may justify this voting rule in constitutional review, this is doubtful since: (i) there's no evidence that these traits' intersection produces a rising trait; and (ii) one may oppose a mere aggregation of majority rule's traits with a mere aggregation of the claims made here.

If this conclusion is sound—meaning, if none of majority rule's traits (separately and jointly considered) justifies this voting rule in constitutional review—there's room to claim that, in this task, there are better reasons for using supermajority rules over majority rule. Thus, the next chapter is about showing such reasons. In the next chapter, I present a core case for supermajority rules in constitutional review.

References

Arrow KJ, *Social Choice and Individual Values* (2nd edn, Cowles Foundation 1963)
Atria F, *On Law and Legal Reasoning* (Hart Publishing 2001)

Audi R, *Practical Reasoning and Ethical Decision* (Routledge 2005) https://doi.org/10.4324/9780203015681

Barry BM, *How Judges Judge: Empirical Insights into Judicial Decision-Making* (Routledge 2021) https://doi.org/10.4324/9780429023422

Bellamy R, *Political Constitutionalism: A Republican Defence of the Constitutionality of Democracy* (Cambridge University Press 2007) https://doi.org/10.1017/CBO9780511490187

Ben-Yashar RC & Nitzan SI, 'The Optimal Decision-Making Rule for Fixed-Sized Committees in Dichotomous Choice Situations: The General Result' (1997) 38 *International Economic Review* 175 https://doi.org/10.2307/2527413

Brennan J, *Against Democracy* (Princeton University Press 2016) https://doi.org/10.1515/9781400882939

Bickel A, *The Least Dangerous Branch: The Supreme Court at the Bar of Politics* (Bobbs-Merrill 1962)

Chang R, *Making Comparisons Count* (Routledge 2014)

Christiano T, *The Constitution of Equality: Democratic Authority and its Limits* (Oxford University Press 2008) https://doi.org/10.1093/acprof:oso/9780198297475.001.0001

Choudry S & Roach K, 'Putting the Past Behind Us? Prospective Judicial and Legislative Constitutional Remedies' (2003) 21 *Supreme Court Law Review* 205

Cohen-Eliya M & Porat I, *Proportionality and Constitutional Culture* (Cambridge University Press 2013) https://doi.org/10.1017/CBO9781139134996

Colomer J & McLean I, 'Electing Popes: Approval Balloting and Qualified-Majority Rule' (1998) 29 *Journal of Interdisciplinary History* 1 https://doi.org/10.1162/002219598551616

Condorcet MJA, *Essai sur l'Application de l'analyse à la probabilité des décisions rendues à la pluralité des voix* [Essay on the Application of Mathematics to the Theory of Decision-Making] (first published 1785, Cambridge University Press 2014)

——— *Plan de Constitution présenté a la Convention Nationale* [Constitutional Plan Presented to the National Convention] (Paris, Imprimerie Nationale 1793) https://gallica.bnf.fr/ark:/12148/bpt6k73809

Crenshaw K, 'Demarginalizing the Intersection of Race and Sex: A Black Feminist Critique of Antidiscrimination Doctrine, Feminist Theory and Antiracist Politics' (1989) 1 *University of Chicago Legal Forum* 139 http://chicagounbound.uchicago.edu/uclf/vol1989/iss1/8

Cross FB, 'Institutions and Enforcement of the Bill of Rights' (1999) 85 *Cornell Law Review 1529 http://scholarship.law.cornell.edu/clr/vol85/iss6/1*

Dahl RA, *Democracy and its Critics* (Yale University Press 1989)

Delli Carpini MX, Lomax Cook F & Jacobs LR, 'Public Deliberation, Discursive Participation and Citizen Engagement: A Review of the Empirical Literature' (2004) 7 *Annual Review of Political Science* 315 https://doi.org/10.1146/annurev.polisci.7.121003.091630

Devine DJ, *Jury Decision Making: The State of the Science* (New York University Press 2012) https://doi.org/10.18574/9780814704981

Dworkin R, *A Matter of Principle* (Harvard University Press 1985)

——— *Law's Empire* (Harvard University Press 1986)

——— *Freedom's Law: The Moral Reading of the American Constitution* (Harvard University Press 1996)

——— *Justice for Hedgehogs* (Harvard University Press 2013)

Edwards HT, 'The Effects of Collegiality on Judicial Decision Making' (2003) 151(5) *University of Pennsylvania Law Review 1639* https://doi.org/10.2307/3313001
Ely JH, *Democracy and Distrust: A Theory of Judicial Review* (Harvard University Press 1980)
Elster J, *Securities Against Misrule: Juries, Assemblies, Elections* (Cambridge University Press 2013) https://doi.org/10.1017/CBO9781139382762
Endicott TAO, *Vagueness in Law* (Oxford University Press 2000) https://doi.org/10.1093/acprof:oso/9780198268406.001.0001
Epstein RA, *The Classical Liberal Constitution* (Harvard University Press 2014)
Estlund DM, *Democratic Authority: A Philosophical Framework* (Princeton University Press 2008)
Fallon RH, 'The Core of an Uneasy Case for Judicial Review' (2008) 121 *Harvard Law Review* 1694 https://harvardlawreview.org/2008/05/the-core-of-an-uneasy-case-for-judicial-review/
Farnsworth W, *The Legal Analyst: A Toolkit for Thinking about the Law* (University of Chicago Press 2007)
Favoreu L, 'The Constitutional Council and Parliament in France' in Christine Landfried (ed), *Constitutional Review and Legislation* (Nomos Verlagsgesellschaft 1988)
Ferejohn J & Pasquino P, 'Constitutional Adjudication: Lessons from Europe' (2004) 82 *Texas Law Review 1671* https://heinonline.org/HOL/P?h=hein.journals/tlr82andi=1687
Ferreres Comella V, *Constitutional Courts and Democratic Values: A European Perspective* (Yale University Press 2009)
Fishkin JS, 'Deliberative Polling' in Bächtinger A, Dryzek JS, Mansbridge J, & Warren ME (eds), *The Oxford Handbook of Deliberative Democracy* (Oxford University Press 2018) https://doi.org/10.1093/oxfordhb/9780198747369.013.10
Grofman B, Owen G & Feld SL, 'Thirteen Theorems in Search for the Truth' (1983) 15 *Theory and Decision* 261 https://doi.org/10.1007/BF00125672
Harel A & Kahana T, 'The Easy Core Case for Judicial Review' (2010) 2 *Journal of Legal Analysis* 227 https://doi.org/10.1093/jla/2.1.227
Hart H, *The Concept of Law* (3rd edn, Joseph Raz & Penelope A Bulloch eds, Oxford University Press 2012)
Hickey T, 'The Republican Core of the Case for Judicial Review' (2019) 17(1) *International Journal of Constitutional Law* 288 https://doi.org/10.1093/icon/moz007
Hills R, 'Are Judges Really More Principled Than Voters?' (2002) 37 *University of San Francisco Law Review* 37
Honoré AM, 'Legal Reasoning in Rome and Today' (1973) 4 *Cambrian Law Review* 58
Hübner Mendes C, Constitutional Courts and Deliberative Democracy (Oxford University Press 2015) https://doi.org/10.1093/acprof:oso/9780199670451.001.0001
Kelemen K, *Judicial Dissent in European Constitutional Courts: A Comparative and Legal Perspective* (Routledge 2019) https://doi.org/10.4324/9781315590769
Kelsen H, 'The Nature and Development of Constitutional Adjudication' in Lars Vinx (ed), *The Guardian of the Constitution: Hans Kelsen and Carl Schmitt on the Limits of Constitutional Law (first published 1928*, Cambridge University Press 2015) https://doi.org/10.1017/CBO9781316136256

——— 'Judicial Review of Legislation: A Comparative Study of the Austrian and the American Constitution' (1942) 4 *Journal of Politics* 183 https://doi.org/10.2307/2125770

Keynes JM, *A Treatise on Probability (first published 1920*, Cosimo 2007)

Kornhauser LA & Sager LG, 'Unpacking the Court' (1986) 96(1) *Yale Law Journal* 82 https://www.jstor.org/stable/796436

Krishnamurthi G, 'For Judicial Majoritarianism' (2020) 22 *University of Pennsylvania Journal of Constitutional Law 1201* https://scholarship.law.upenn.edu/jcl/vol22/iss5/2

Kumm M, 'Institutionalising Socratic Contestation: The Rationalist Human Rights Paradigm, Legitimate Authority, and the Point of Judicial Review' (2007) 1(2) *European Journal of Legal Studies* 153 http://hdl.handle.net/1814/7708

Ladha KK, 'The Condorcet Jury Theorem, Free Speech, and Correlated Votes' (1992) 36 *American Journal of Political Science* 617 https://doi.org/10.2307/2111584

Lagerspetz E, 'Wisdom and numbers' (2010) 49(1) *Social Science Informati*on 29 https://doi.org/10.1177/0539018409354475

——— *Social Choice and Democratic Values* (Springer 2016) https://doi.org/10.1007/978-3-319-23261-4

Landemore H, *Democratic Reason: Politics, Collective Intelligence and the Rule of the Many* (Princeton University Press 2013)

Laplace PS, *Essai philosophique sur les probabilités [Philosophical Essay on Probabilities] (first published 1825*, Cambridge University Press 2009)

List C & Pettit P, *Group Agency: The Possibility, Design, and Status of Corporate Agents* (Cambridge University Press 2011) https://doi.org./10.1093/acprof:oso/9780199591565.001.0001

MacKinnon CA, *Women's Lives, Men's Laws* (Harvard University Press 2005)

Mahoney JD, 'Kelo's Legacy: Eminent Domain and the Future of Property Rights' (2005) 1 *Supreme Court Review* 103 https://www.journals.uchicago.edu/doi/10.1086/655194

May KO, 'A Set of Independent Necessary and Sufficient Conditions for Simple Majority Decision' (1952) 20(4) *Econometrica* 680 http://www.jstor.org/stable/1907651

MacCormick N, 'The Relative Heteronomy of Law' (1995) 3(1) *European Journal of Philosophy* 69 https://doi.org./10.1111/j.1468-0378.1995.tb00040.x

McGinnis JO & Rappaport MB, 'The Condorcet Case for Supermajority Rules' (2008) 16 *Supreme Court Economic Review* 67 https://www.journals.uchicago.edu/doi/abs/10.1086/655880

McLean I & Hewitt F, 'Section 2: The Theory of Voting' in McLean I and Hewitt F (eds), *Condorcet: Foundations of Social Choice and Political Theory* (Edward Elgar 1994)

Mendelberg T, 'The Deliberative Citizen: Theory and Evidence' in Delli Carpini M, Huddy L and Shapiro RY (eds), *Research in Micropolitics*, vol 6 (Elsevier Press 2002)

Möller K, *The Global Model of Constitutional Rights* (Oxford University Press 2012) https://doi.org/10.1093/acprof:oso/9780199664603.001.0001

Neblo MA, *Deliberative Democracy between Theory and Practice* (Cambridge University Press 2015) https://doi.org/10.1017/CBO9781139226592

Paglia C, *Free Women, Free Men: Sex, Gender, Feminism* (Pantheon 2017)

Papal Encyclicals Online: Church Councils, 'Third Lateran Council—1179 AD' (nd) <www.papalencyclicals.net/councils/ecum11.htm> accessed 9 June 2019

Pufendorf S, *Of the Law of Nature and Nations: Eight Books. Book the Seventh* (Oxford 1703)

Rawls J, *A Theory of Justice* (Revised edn, Harvard University Press 1999)

——— *Political Liberalism* (Expanded edn, Columbia University Press 2005)

Raz J, *Practical Reasoning* (Oxford University Press 1978)

——— *The Authority of Law: Essays on Law and Morality* (2nd edn, Oxford University Press 2009) https://doi.org/10.1093/acprof:oso/9780198253457.001.0001

Roosevelt III K, 'Constitutional Calcification: How the Law Becomes What the Court Does' (2005) 91 *Virginia Law Review 1649* https://www.jstor.org/stable/3649443

Ryfe DM, 'Does Deliberative Democracy Work?' (2005) 8 *Annual Review of Political Science* 49 https://doi.org/10.1146/annurev.polisci.8.032904.154633

Schwartzberg M, *Counting the Many. The Origins and Limits of Supermajority Rule* (Cambridge University Press 2013) https://doi.org/10.1017/CBO9781139013970

Smith G & Setälä M, 'Mini-Publics and Deliberative Democracy' in André Bächtinger, John S Dryzek, Jane Mansbridge and Mark E Warren (eds), *The Oxford Handbook of Deliberative Democracy* (Oxford University Press 2018) https://doi.org/10.1093/oxfordhb/9780198747369.013.27

Steiner J, *The Foundations of Deliberative Democracy: Empirical Research and Normative Implications* (Cambridge University Press 2012) https://doi.org/10.1017/CBO9781139057486

Stone Sweet A, 'Constitutional Courts' in Rosenfeld M and Sajó A (eds), *The Oxford Handbook of Comparative Constitutional Law* (Oxford University Press 2012) https://doi.org/10.1093/oxfordhb/9780199578610.013.0040

Sunstein CR, *Infotopia: How Many Minds Produce Knowledge* (Oxford University Press 2006)

Thurner S, Hanel R & Klimek P, *Introduction to the Theory of Complex Systems* (Oxford University Press 2018) https://doi.org/10.1093/oso/9780198821939.001.0001

Urbina FJ, *A Critique of Proportionality and Balancing* (Cambridge University Press 2017) https://doi.org/10.1017/9781316796276

Urfalino P, 'The Rule of Non-Opposition: Opening Up Decision-Making by Consensus' (2014) 22(3) *The Journal of Political Philosophy* 320 https://doi.org/10.1111/jopp.12037

Vermeule A, 'Should We Have Lay Justices?' (2007) 59(6) *Stanford Law Review 1569* http://www.jstor.org/stable/40040396

Waldron J, *Political Political Theory: Essays on Institutions* (Harvard University Press 2016) https://doi.org/10.4159/9780674970342

Webber GCN, *The Negotiable Constitution* (Cambridge University Press 2009)

Weinrib J, *Dimensions of Dignity: The Theory and Practice of Modern Constitutional Law* (Cambridge University Press 2016) https://doi.org/10.1017/CBO9781316026663

Wilson B, 'Decision-Making in the Supreme Court' (1986) 36(3) *University of Toronto Law Journal* 227 https://heinonline.org/HOL/P?h=hein.journals/utlj36andi=231

Yowell P, *Constitutional Rights and Constitutional Design: Moral and Empirical Reasoning in Judicial Review* (Hart Publishing 2018) https://doi.org/10.5040/9781509913626

6 For Supermajority Rules in Constitutional Review

After presenting the core case against majority rule in constitutional review—put differently, after arguing that there are no strong enough reasons for using majority rule to declare statutes unconstitutional—in this chapter, I present the core case for supermajority rules in this task; meaning, I present reasons that justify replacing majority rule with supermajority rules to check the constitutionality of legislation.

I divide this chapter into two sections: first, I present the core case itself, that is, the reasons for using supermajority rules in constitutional review; and second, I tackle some possible objections. As the reader will realise, the second section is longer than the first section. This is deliberate since answering possible objections arguably is the best way of showing the full strength of an argument.

The Core Case

This core case has three claims. First, supermajority rules may boost judges' accuracy more than majority rule according to the Condorcet Jury Theorem, and by promoting judicial deliberation. Second, supermajority rules may boost constitutional courts' reputation more than majority rule. Finally, supermajority rules may embody the presumption of constitutionality of legislation.

Let's refine these claims.

Supermajority Rules Boost Group Accuracy

When deciding on the constitutionality of legislation, supermajority rules may boost judges' accuracy more than majority rule. This increase may happen on Condorcetian grounds or on deliberative grounds. Supermajority rules may boost Condorcetian accuracy. That is, they may boost judges' accuracy according to the Condorcet Jury Theorem. Also, supermajority rules may boost accuracy by promoting judicial deliberation more than majority rule. I start by addressing how supermajority rules may boost Condorcetian accuracy. Next, I address how they may boost judicial deliberation.

DOI: 10.4324/9781032723952-6

1. Supermajority Rules Boost Condorcet Accuracy

According to the Condorcet Jury Theorem, in constitutional review, supermajority rules may boost judges' accuracy more than majority rule. Recall that, in Chapter 4, I held that social choice research suggests that, if groups are relatively small, and errors are asymmetrical, some supermajority rules may be more Condorcet accurate than majority rule.[1] Constitutional courts satisfy both requirements: first, constitutional courts are relatively small groups, ranging between approximately five and 15 members;[2] and second, in strong-form constitutional review, false positives (that is, declaring statutes unconstitutional when they aren't so) are worse than false negatives (that is, not declaring statutes unconstitutional when they are so). Specifically, the presumption of constitutionality of legislation, and the difficulty of rectifying false positives when compared to false negatives should influence the moral evaluation of these two kinds of errors.

When constitutional courts render false positives, they erode 'majority government;' meaning, they erode the idea of government by the majority of citizens, or by the majority of citizens' elected representatives.[3] This is recognised even by some of the main defenders of constitutional review, such as Ackerman,[4] Dworkin,[5] and Rawls.[6] And many times, the values behind majority government are constitutionally recognised, which means that—as in the case of false negatives—false positives are unconstitutional.

Thus, given reasonable disagreement, all else equal, false positives are intrinsically worse than false negatives.[7] If one assumes that, due to reasonable disagreement, hard issues must mainly be resolved by citizens themselves (or by their elected representatives), citizens' or legislatures' decisions on these issues merit some respect by courts, hence justifying statutes' presumption of constitutionality. So, all else equal, it's worse to wrongly void citizens' or legislatures' right decisions than to wrongly keep citizens' or legislatures' mistaken decisions. When constitutional courts render false positives, they erode majority government *and* trump a constitutionally acceptable decision. Following Christiano, in these cases, 'we have a double loss: a decision is made in an antiegalitarian way and is itself antiegalitarian (since it defeats a legitimate

1 Ben-Yashar & Nitzan 1997; McGinnis & Rappaport 2008; List & Pettit 2011: 90–1.

2 See generally Cappelletti 1971; Brewer-Carías 1989; Stone Sweet 2012; Kelemen 2019: 18, 23–8.

3 Another way of eroding majority government is using legislative practices only to block legislation supported by the majority of legislators present. A prime example of this is the current use of the US Senate's filibuster rule. On this rule and its practice, see Schwartzberg 2013: 133–4. See also Binder & Smith 1997.

4 1993: 60–1, 159–61, 192, 261–3.

5 1996: 8, 16–7, 23–6.

6 2005: 215–6, 231–40.

7 I am grateful to Andrew Lister for suggesting this.

democratic decision).'[8] Conversely, when constitutional courts render false negatives, though they err, they still respect majority government. When rendering false positives, constitutional courts err doubly, while when rendering false negatives, they err just once.[9] Hence, in and of themselves, false positives are worse than false negatives.

Further, false positives aren't just intrinsically worse than false negatives, they are worse than false negatives since they are likely more enduring than them. In most democracies with strong-form constitutional review, there's a key difference in institutional capacities when reacting to constitutional courts' errors. If constitutional courts render false negatives, these errors can be rectified through normal legislative procedures despite their wrongful effects. Conversely, if constitutional courts render false positives, alongside eroding majority government and trumping a constitutionally acceptable decision, these errors can often only be rectified through constitutional amendments, which are markedly harder to enact than statutes.[10] This difference between false positives and false negatives is more salient if the respective constitution has unamendable provisions.[11]

The difficulty of rectifying false positives vis-à-vis false negatives is usually remarked upon by judges and legal scholars. In his dissent in *Burnett v Coronado Oil and Gas Co,* US Supreme Court Justice Brandeis held that—though 'in most matters it is more important that the applicable rule of law be settled than it be settled right'[12]—in constitutional cases, a court shouldn't be bound by precedent since, if the court wrongly declares a statute unconstitutional, 'correction through legislative action is practically impossible.'[13] Likewise, Ely recognises that, when judges declare statutes unconstitutional, they do so in ways that aren't 'subject to "correction" by the ordinary lawmaking process.'[14] Further, Yowell argues that in most polities, judges' decisions declaring statutes unconstitutional can only be reversed by constitutional amendments, or by the judges deciding to make jurisprudential turns.[15] Finally, anti-constitutional review scholars, such as Bellamy[16] and Waldron,[17] have also indicated the difficulty to amend false positives to base their claims.

8 2008: 280.
9 Id 280–1.
10 *Burnett v Coronado Oil and Gas Co,* 285 US 393, 406 (1932); Ely 1980: 4–5, 45; Yowell 2018: 139–45.
11 On unamendable constitutional provisions—and on the doctrine of 'unconstitutional constitutional amendments' generally—see Barak 2011; Roznai 2017; Albert & Oder 2018.
12 *Burnett v Coronado Oil and Gas Co,* 285 US 393, 406 (1932).
13 Id 406–7. See also *Seminole Tribe v Florida,* 517 US 44, 63 (1996).
14 Ely 1980: 4–5, 45.
15 Yowell 2018: 140–3.
16 2007: 98.
17 2016: 232–3.

As Yowell[18] holds, in principle, false positives aren't only *procedurally* harder to rectify than false negatives, they are also *substantively* harder to rectify than false negatives; especially when constitutional amendments aim at open-ended provisions. Generally speaking, it's unlikely that these amendments are drafted in a language that's 'sufficiently general'[19] to be included in a constitution, and 'specific enough to overturn the particular result of a case.'[20] Constitutional amendments need broad political support. To get this support, these amendments likely have to be as open-ended as the provisions they replace. Yet if this happens, these amendments are probably going to be ineffective. That is, they aren't likely to rectify the false positives justifying their formulation.[21] Thus, even if amendments aimed at open-ended provisions satisfy all procedural rules, the odds that they'll rectify the false positives justifying their drafting are low.

Therefore, considering 'the circumstances of politics,'[22] these amendments seem trapped between a rock and a hard place. If open-ended, these amendments are probably ineffective; if specific, these amendments are unlikely to be enacted. Something similar may be said about other possible drafts of these amendments, such as drafts 'specify[ing] that certain constitutional provisions cannot be used as grounds for nullifying legislation,'[23] or drafts that try 'to delineate the permissible scope or level of scrutiny for [constitutional] review.'[24]

True, judges may change their decisions. And procedures such as section 33 of Canada's Charter of Rights and Freedoms allow legislatures to rectify false positives through normal legislative procedures, without amending the constitution. But it's unlikely that these procedures become regular ways of tackling false positives, at least for the time being. Due to aspirations for certainty, absent special cases, judges may be reticent to change their decisions. Further, procedures like section 33 are rare in most democracies,[25] and their use may carry strong political costs.[26] In sum, ceteris paribus, false positives aren't only intrinsically worse than false negatives, their effects are also likely more enduring than false negatives' effects. Thus, constitutional courts should mainly focus on avoiding false positives; especially considering how group

18 Yowell 2018: 139–45.
19 Id 142.
20 Id.
21 Id 141–3.
22 Waldron 1999: 102.
23 Yowell 2018: 142.
24 Id.
25 Waldron 2016: 200–1.
26 Kahana 2001; Weinrib 2016: 163–4.

accuracy influences constitutional courts' authority, at least according to some of constitutional review's main defenders.[27]

This logic is akin to the logic behind criminal juries' institutional design. Since convicting the innocent is worse than acquitting the guilty, criminal juries are built in ways that mainly avoid convicting the innocent.[28] Likewise, since false positives are worse than false negatives, constitutional courts should be built in ways that mainly avoid false positives as well.

These claims don't depend on comparing constitutional courts and legislatures. So, these claims don't depend on constitutional courts and legislatures having 'symmetrical' odds of erring, as Dworkin held.[29] I've neither held that constitutional courts' errors are worse than legislatures' errors, nor have I held that constitutional courts are more likely to err than legislatures; I only hold that, when comparing constitutional courts' errors—not constitutional courts' and legislatures' errors—false positives are worse than false negatives. It's just from this premise that I hold that constitutional courts should mainly focus on avoiding false positives.

If false positives are worse than false negatives, according to the Condorcet Jury Theorem, supermajority rules may boost judges' accuracy indirectly. That it, they may boost their accuracy by making it harder for courts to render the worst kinds of decisions (in this case, false positives). This stems from supermajority rules' non-neutrality,[30] since these rules may be used to guard statutes' alleged constitutionality as a worthy status quo against false positives. And as I hold in the next sub-section, supermajority rules bind bargaining more than majority rule.[31] By doing so, supermajority rules may boost sincere voting more than majority rule, hence boosting the odds that the Condorcet Jury Theorem holds in constitutional courts. Thus, supermajority rules may produce positive feedback loops that favour Condorcet accuracy in constitutional review.

Still, there's a worry that, in constitutional review, focusing on avoiding false positives via supermajority rules may produce excessive false negatives. I tackle this worry in the final section.

27 Ely 1980: 101–2; Dworkin 1996: 8, 16–7, 23–6; Rawls 2005: 158–63, 215–6, 227–8, 231–40.
28 Condorcet 1793: 14, 16–9; List & Pettit 2011: 90–1.
29 1996: 32–3.
30 Tsebelis 2002: 139–43, 149–51; Schwartzberg 2013: 92–4, 121–3; Lagerspetz 2016: 195–6, 278–83.
31 Tsebelis 2002: 139–43, 149–51; Gersen & Vermeule 2007: 718–20; Lagerspetz 2016: 195–6, 278–83.

2. Supermajority Rules Boost Judicial Deliberation

Alongside boosting judges' accuracy on Condorcetian grounds, supermajority rules may boost their accuracy on deliberative grounds; meaning, they may promote judicial deliberation more than majority rule.

Deliberation may aid judges' accuracy by curbing their cognitive biases. Specifically, insofar as judges differ in their constitutional interpretations, deliberation may provide a check against group polarisation and confirmation bias.[32] In tasks in which rational justification is key—such as constitutional review—regularly subjecting one's opinions to peer-contestation should, in principle, reduce the odds the one blindly upholds such opinions, or that one ignores challenging data. So, inasmuch as deliberation curbs judges' cognitive biases, supermajority rules may boost their accuracy by encouraging this practice among themselves to a larger extent than majority rule.

There isn't much empirical research assessing voting rules' influence on deliberation.[33] Many experiments involving mini-publics require a supermajority rule to decide,[34] but little attention has been paid to whether the rule itself stimulates group members to deliberate.[35] Still, research in Belgium by Caluwaerts[36]—and by Caluwaerts & Deschouwer[37]—on mini publics show that 'imposing supermajority or unanimity rule in deliberative settings fosters high-quality deliberation.'[38] These mini publics were made of Flemings and Walloons discussing vexed issues. Specifically, in Caluwaerts & Deschouwer's[39] study, mini-publics were compared using majority rule as the control condition, and supermajority rules and unanimity rule as the treatment conditions. Caluwaerts & Deschouwer[40] found that supermajority rules and unanimity rules are 'significantly related to deliberative quality, even after controlling for potentially confounding variables.'[41] But these effects greatly diminish if group members are divided along language lines. And this research didn't assess the effects of peer pressure and social influences among group members, which may skew the experiment's results.

32 Landemore 2013: 122, 136–42; Mercier & Sperber 2017: ch 12, 15, 17.

33 For overviews of judicial decision making studies, see Barry 2021. For overviews of jury decision making studies, see Saks 1997; Vidmar & Hans 2007; Devine 2012. For overviews of studies on mini publics, see Fishkin 2009; Mendelberg 2002; Delli Carpini et al 2004; Ryfe 2005; Steiner 2012; Neblo 2015; Fishkin 2018; Smith & Setälä 2018.

34 Participedia nd.

35 Carson & Schecter 2017.

36 2012.

37 2014: 427, 433–4, 442–7.

38 O'Flynn & Caluwaerts 2018: 749.

39 2014.

40 In this research, deliberative performance was measured using a 'Discourse Quality Index' ('DQI'). Id 436–38.

41 Id 442.

Yet, though more empirical research is needed, considering supermajority rules' traits, one can at least claim that supermajority rules may boost judicial deliberation more than majority rule due to their decelerator.[42] Compared to majority rule, under supermajority rules, judges for declaring a statute unconstitutional need the support of a higher number of peers to do so. Thus, under supermajority rules, a sceptical judge whose support is needed may block a declaration of unconstitutionality, hence slowing down the decision process. So, under supermajority rules, judges for declaring a statute unconstitutional have a stronger incentive to deliberate with their more sceptical peers than under majority rule. After all, a majority of these judges likely need the support of their more sceptical peers to reach the supermajority threshold, thus having to try to convince them with arguments.

Now, it could be argued that judges for declaring a statute unconstitutional may manipulate or bargain rather than deliberate. Yet recall that, due to binary choice, in constitutional review, manipulation is limited.[43] And in well-functioning democracies, the rules guarding judicial independence bind bargaining.[44] Further, though bargaining can't be eliminated, social choice research suggests that supermajority rules bind bargaining more than majority rule.[45] Due to their non-neutrality,[46] under supermajority rules, each judge needs the support of more of their peers than they would need under majority rule to declare legislation unconstitutional. Thus, each judge's vote has less bargaining power than it would have under majority rule. This prevents judges from bargaining to the same extent than they would under majority rule. Hence, for declaring statutes unconstitutional, supermajority rules give judges little choice but to deliberate with their peers.

Some may object though that, under supermajority rules, judges sceptical of declaring statutes unconstitutional may still bargain, for they could block a declaration of unconstitutionality. But this already happens under majority rule. Bargaining's potential is higher under majority rule than under supermajority rules. Under majority rule, *all* judges may bargain to a high degree. Conversely, under supermajority rules, the only judges that may bargain as much as they could under majority rule are those sceptical of declaring statutes unconstitutional.[47] Therefore, ceteris paribus, supermajority rules are better than majority rule for curbing bargaining.

Moreover, though supermajority rules are non-neutral, they are still anonymous: they are indifferent to judges' identity. Supermajority rules favour *any*

42 Condorcet 1793: 14, 16–9; Schwartzberg 2013: 92–4.
43 Condorcet [1785] 2014: lviii–lx, 119–20; Arrow 1963: ch 5.
44 Ferejohn & Pasquino 2004: 1677–82; Stone Sweet 2012: 824–5.
45 Tsebelis 2002: 139–43, 149–51; Gersen & Vermeule 2007: 718–20; Lagerspetz 2016: 195–6, 278–83.
46 Tsebelis 2002: 139–43, 149–51; Schwartzberg 2013: 92–4, 121–3; Lagerspetz 2016: 195–6, 278–83.
47 Gersen & Vermeule 2007: 718–20.

judge wanting to keep statutes constitutional, *whoever* that judge is. Under supermajority rules, any judge sceptical of declaring statutes unconstitutional may block such declaration. And the same judges may not always want to keep legislation constitutional. Even if one assumes—as the so-called 'attitudinal model' holds[48]—that judges have stable policy ideas that they want to realise through their decisions, it's unlikely that they'll do so by blocking all declarations of unconstitutionality. For example, even if a judge is 'conservative'—in the sense that they prefer traditional values on social issues and free market policies on economic issues—it's unlikely that they'll promote their ideas by guarding the constitutionality of every statute they review. Instead, it's likelier that they'll want to keep the constitutionality of legislation criminalising cannabis consumption, while wanting to declare unconstitutional statutes nationalising investment banks. This seems to have occurred in the US Supreme Court.[49] Since the 1980s, 'no judge has stood out for a willingness or unwillingness to strike down laws.'[50]

Once we consider the variety of issues that constitutional courts regularly review, the same judges may not always be sceptical of declaring statutes unconstitutional. Thus, they may not always want to block declarations of unconstitutionality. Further, judges usually engage in long-term interactions. These facts should foster cooperation between them—and thus openness to peers' arguments—rather than obstructionism.[51] Actually, studies suggest that despite their ideological differences, judges already tend to compromise when possible.[52] Therefore, there are grounds to claim that supermajority rules may boost this cooperative attitude, thus boosting deliberation as well.

Supermajority Rules Boost Constitutional Courts' Reputation

Supermajority rules signal agreement: they socially express the aspiration for sincere agreements to ensure that decisions are right. We saw that the Latin Catholic Church and the Italian city-states tapped into supermajority rules' agreement-signal to justify their decisions.[53] And we saw that the intuition behind this signal—that is, the intuition that sincere agreements on decisions give evidence that such decisions are right, and thus are authoritative—explains why many contemporary groups show their decisions as unanimous though they aren't necessarily so.[54] Considering supermajority rules' capacity

48 Segal & Spaeth 2002: ch 3.

49 Epstein & Martin 2012.

50 Baum 2019: 139.

51 For akin claims on representative assemblies, see Landemore 2013: 156. See also Axelrod 2006.

52 Baum 2019: 139–42; Barry 2021: 219–20.

53 Colomer & McLean 1998: 1–14; Lagerspetz 2010: 31-4; Schwartzberg 2013: 53–8, 67–9.

54 Eg, see Ferejohn & Pasquino 2004: 1692–700; Corley et al 2013: ch 1; Elster 2013: 31–6, 136–8.

to signal agreement, these rules may boost constitutional courts' reputation.[55] Declarations of unconstitutionality issued by a supermajority of judges may be seen as more authoritative than if issued by a majority of them.[56] This perception may work on citizens for and against these declarations.

On citizens upholding declarations of unconstitutionality made by a supermajority of judges, these citizens may intuit that these decisions' supermajoritarian nature somehow proves their rightness. Supermajority rules' agreement-signal not only makes intuitive sense, it makes analytical sense. Given that: (i) a constitutional court is made of jurists; (ii) due to their different moral views, these jurists may differ in their constitutional interpretations; (iii) despite these differences, they widely agree that statute 'Y' is unconstitutional; and (iv) this wide agreement doesn't stem from bargaining or coercion, it seems clear that this agreement is strong evidence that statute Y actually is unconstitutional. Or at least it gives stronger evidence that this judgment is right than an akin majority decision.

In turn, on citizens opposing declarations of unconstitutionality made by a supermajority of judges, it's also likely that to them, these decisions are more authoritative (and thus more reputable) than majority decisions. This is because these citizens may at least be told that, among jurists, the supermajority rule needed to declare statutes unconstitutional ensures that all reasonable efforts are made to reach right decisions in good faith. This guarantee seems especially strong in cases involving open-ended provisions since, in these cases, supermajority decisions likely require agreements between judges holding different moral views. If there are doubts as to whether judges were coerced, it may be argued that, though they could publicly dissent, they chose not to. If these doubts persist, it may also be argued that, if judges hadn't made a supermajority decision, due to the presumption of constitutionality of legislation, the defied statute's validity would have been confirmed; thus relieving any pressures to agree based on concerns about producing legal uncertainty.

True, judges may not reach supermajority decisions. But that wouldn't necessarily erode constitutional courts' reputation—or it wouldn't erode it more than majority rule. Currently, many constitutional courts declare statutes unconstitutional through majority decisions that can mirror the ideological conflicts present in their societies. (Arguably, the paradigm here is the US Supreme Court.)[57] Thus, these decisions may erode constitutional courts' reputation since citizens against them may see these courts not as impartial institutions, but as political weapons. Conversely, though under supermajority

55 Shugerman 2002: 893, 932–42; Doerfler & Moyn 2021: 1734, 1736–7.

56 Zink et al 2009.

57 It's been held that, in this court, the number of 'five-to-four' decisions has increased in the last decades. Epstein et al 2001; Henderson 2007. For statistics on the US court, see Epstein et al 2021. And empirical studies suggest that the justices generally vote according to their political ideology. Segal & Spaeth 2002; Sunstein et al 2006; Baum 2019: 130–6.

rules, judges may issue 'majority declarations of unconstitutionality'—that is, they may issue majority opinions holding that legislation is unconstitutional (note that I use the word 'opinions,' not 'decisions')—those opinions won't generate legal effects, hence curbing their impact on opposing citizens.

What about citizens upholding majority declarations of unconstitutionality that would like these opinions to void defied legislation? Well, in these cases, these citizens can at least be told that it's still possible to change or repeal this legislation through the regular tools available in a democracy: they can at least be told that, if their views gain enough political support, they can change or repeal this legislation through normal legislative procedures. And these citizens can be told that, if the court had declared statutes ***they liked*** unconstitutional through majority decisions, they wouldn't be able to use these tools to reinstate them, but would probably need constitutional amendments. Thus, these citizens can be told that the supermajority rule hinders the odds that this unwelcome scenario occurs.

Actually, under supermajority rules, majority declarations of unconstitutionality may boost constitutional courts' reputation. Under supermajority rules, these majority opinions may be seen as recognitions that the issues behind constitutional cases—especially hard cases—are issues in which people reasonably disagree. Thus, given the presumption of constitutionality of legislation, constitutional courts should generally respect such statutes, which is what would happen absent a supermajority decision. In sum, under supermajority rules, majority declarations of unconstitutionality may boost constitutional courts' reputation inasmuch as they are seen as respectful of legislatures' task[58] when facing factual and moral complexity.[59]

Supermajority Rules Embody the Presumption of Constitutionality of Legislation

Last but not least, there isn't much basis for using neutral voting rules in constitutional review. If, due to reasonable disagreement, statutes must be presumed constitutional, and if false positives are generally worse than false negatives, there isn't much basis against shaping constitutional courts' voting rules in ways that usually keep statutes' constitutionality, hence preventing false positives. In short, neutrality doesn't seem an advantage for choosing a voting rule in constitutional review.

58 Shugerman 2002: 895, 901–6; Gersen & Vermeule 2007: 679–82; Doerfler & Moyn 2021: 1734, 1736–7.

59 In South Korea, Joon Seok Hong suggests that majority declarations of unconstitutionality boosted the constitutional court's influence over the legislature, since these decisions were seen as indications that the defied statute should be reformed (2019: 203–11).

Conversely, due to their non-neutrality,[60] supermajority rules may guard the presumption of constitutionality of legislation, thus preventing false positives. Put differently, supermajority rules may 'institutionally recognise' statutes' alleged constitutionality.[61] This is akin to what happens in criminal juries. In juries, unanimity rule guards a worthy status quo (the presumption of innocence) by allowing some juries to block proposals to change it. Likewise, in constitutional review, supermajority rules may hinder the odds that statutes are declared unconstitutional unless it's sound to do so, hence also decreasing false positives' odds.

Crucially though, unlike unanimity rule, supermajority rules allow judges to dissent while simultaneously deciding.[62] So, though supermajority rules are non-neutral, they don't generate a risk of coercing dissenters as high as unanimity rule's.[63] Also, since supermajority rules are indeterminate—that is, since they are a gamut, range, or spectrum of voting rules between majority rule and unanimity rule[64]—supermajority rules allow constitution drafters, legislators, and policy-makers generally the capacity to address coercion risks by calibrating them downwards.[65] In other words, if policy-makers want to curb coercion against dissenters, supermajority rules allow them to do so by choosing rules closer to majority rule than rules farther from it.

Yet it's been argued that, by guarding statutes' alleged constitutionality, supermajority rules are somehow 'unfair' towards parties defying it.[66] I tackle this objection in the next section.

Possible Objections

Now that I've shown the core case, it's worth tackling some possible objections against it. I tackle thirteen objections. First, the objection that supermajority rules may produce excessive false negatives. Second, the objection that supermajority rules may be unfair towards claimants. Third, the objection that the Condorcet Jury Theorem doesn't hold in constitutional review. Fourth, the objection that judges don't face binary choices. Fifth, the objection that supermajority rules may overprotect statutes' alleged constitutionality—or that they may stimulate judges to stop applying restrictive review standards. Sixth, the objection that supermajority rules boost interpretive decisions. Seventh, the objection that—as in Poland—supermajority rules may be used to nullify

60 Tsebelis 2002: 139–43, 149–51; Schwartzberg 2013: 92–4, 121–3; Lagerspetz 2016: 195–6, 278–83.

61 Gersen & Vermeule 2007; Seok Hong 2019: 193.

62 Laplace [1825] 2009: 165–74; Schwartzberg 2013: 79, 87–8.

63 On this risk in US criminal juries, see Saks 1997: 39–41; Vidmar & Hans 2007: 1444; Devine 2012: 152–3, 158–61; Schwartzberg 2013: 95–7.

64 Schwartzberg 2010.

65 Gersen & Vermeule 2007: 687, 696, 700–04.

66 Krishnamurthi 2020: 1218–21, 1244.

a constitutional review system. Eighth, the objection that, under supermajority rules, constitutional courts wouldn't have made decisions one judges as right. Ninth, the objection that, on Condorcetian grounds, one should increase courts' size rather than using supermajority rules. Tenth, the objection that my argument doesn't apply to easy cases. Eleventh, the objection that supermajority rules would heavily increase courts' decision costs. Twelfth, the objection that supermajority rules would produce coordination issues. Lastly, the objection that supermajority rules should also apply to constitutional review of executive action and judicial decisions.

As the reader can see, these objections aren't necessarily inter-connected. Thus, the reader may partly or fully skip my answers to them depending on their interests.

Excessive False Negatives

Some may object that focusing on avoiding false positives may produce excessive false negatives. If a constitutional court focuses on avoiding false positives, too many statutes that should have been declared unconstitutional may be saved. In criminal juries, the focus on not convicting the innocent produces more acquittals that would otherwise be produced. When one focuses on avoiding some errors over others, the frequency of the overlooked error may surge.[67] Hence, the worry that focusing on false positives may generate excessive false negatives is sound.

The little empirical research on courts that constitutionally adjudicate using supermajority rules doesn't suggest that focusing on avoiding false positives produces excessive false negatives. According to Tiede & Ponce,[68] the Peruvian court's declarations of unconstitutionality rates are akin to those of other courts adjudicating by majority rule. And Seok Hong[69] claims that the South Korean court has declared thousands of statutes unconstitutional. Further, Rivera León's[70] study suggests that supermajority rules haven't prevented the Mexican court from declaring statutes unconstitutional. According to Rivera León's quantitative analysis, among 137 cases in which the supermajority threshold wasn't reached—and thus the defied statutes stayed constitutional—in only 10.1% of the cases this result was influenced by the supermajority rule itself,[71] while in the remaining 89.9% of the cases, this result 'would most likely have been the same with or without the supermajority requirement if Justices had voted in a similar fashion.'[72]

67 Condorcet 1793: 14, 16–9; List & Pettit 2011: 90–1.
68 Tiede & Ponce 2014: 149–51, 156–8.
69 2019: 183, 193–4.
70 2023: 18–24.
71 Id 22.
72 Id.

Still, even if focusing on avoiding false positives produces excessive false negatives, constitutional courts should do so. The worry that focusing on avoiding false positives may produce excessive false negatives depends on intuitively or mathematically gauging probabilities. But in hard cases, this assessment is uncertain. In hard cases, reasonable disagreement impairs the identification of false positives and false negatives, hence impairing their probability assessment; in hard cases, reasonable disagreement permeates, percolates, or trickles down to probability assessments. For example, 'pro-life' people consider statutes decriminalising abortion constitutional while 'pro-choice' people consider them constitutional. If constitutional courts declare such statutes unconstitutional, pro-life people will consider these decisions right while pro-choice people will consider them wrong. Something similar happens in other cases. These disagreements may not suffice to eliminate constitutional review. But they suffice to erode the idea that, in hard cases, we can surely identify and probabilistically assess constitutional courts' errors.

In these cases—cases in which, due to informational bounds, it's very hard or impossible to gauge probabilities—one may use at least two methods for deciding under uncertainty: first, one may use the 'equal assignment rule' (or 'equal assignment');[73] and second, one may use what could be called 'the survival heuristic.'[74] In constitutional review, both methods uphold supermajority rules. But equal assignment requires mathematically gauging probabilities while the survival heuristic doesn't. There are other methods for deciding under uncertainty (eg, 'cost-benefit analysis,' 'maximin,' and 'satisficing').[75] Yet unlike equal assignment and the survival heuristic, many of these methods depend more on judges' intuitions about probabilities, hence being more vulnerable to reasonable disagreement.

1. Equal Assignment

According to equal assignment, when results are uncertain—but one knows that some results are worse than others—the most rational way to decide is to (i) assume that all results are equally likely, and (ii) bias the decision process to avoid the worst error. For example, if we don't know anything about coronaviruses—hence being unable to model Covid-19's behaviour—one may assume that the odds of getting and not getting Covid-19 are equal. So, since getting Covid-19 is worse than not getting it, one should self-quarantine rather than behave as usual. Likewise, if in a criminal trial the accused's culpability is uncertain, one may assume that their odds of being guilty or not guilty are

73 This method—developed by Bernoulli and Laplace—is also called 'the principle of indifference,' 'the principle of insufficient reason,' and 'the principle of non-sufficient reason.' Hacking 1971; Laplace [1825] 1902: 6–7. See also Keynes 2007: ch 4.

74 'Heuristics' are mental shortcuts that we use for deciding. Kahneman et al 1982; Gigerenzer et al 1999. On the survival heuristic, see Taleb 2018: 24–6, ch 19, 246–52.

75 Vermeule 2006: 168–71.

equal. Thus, since convicting the innocent is worse than acquitting the guilty, one should acquit the accused.

In constitutional review, equal assignment means that, since it's very hard to identify (and thus gauge the odds of) false positives and false negatives, one should assume that they are equally likely. Hence, these odds shouldn't be a key factor for deciding which errors should be avoided, and therefore they should not be a key factor for designing constitutional courts' voting rules.

Conversely, we can reasonably claim that false positives are worse than false negatives, both intrinsically and due to their higher durability. And we can reasonably claim so even if we can't precisely identify constitutional courts' decisions as false positives or false negatives. Thus, since when facing uncertainty, false positives' and false negatives' odds should be considered equal, and since false positives are worse than false negatives, this latter factor should matter more than probabilities for assessing which kinds of errors constitutional courts should avoid. Therefore, this latter factor should also matter more than probabilities for designing constitutional courts' voting rules, hence supporting supermajority rules.

Some may object that equal assignment assumes that decision makers know the whole range of options, and thus the whole range of possible results. But this isn't necessarily true. In many cases, options have a disjunction problem. That is, they can be split into more options.[76] This is challenging since, if binary options are split into multiple options, cycles may occur. (As seen in Chapter 4, possible cycles are one of manipulation's main causes.)[77] And the number of options that group members face influences their odds assignment, thus influencing their decision.[78] Thus, when options can be split into more options, a group member—or another individual or group—may manipulate the decision by manipulating the number of options shown to the group. Yet there are situations in which the nature of the choice doesn't allow disjunctions, in which case the odds assignment is fixed. This happens in constitutional review. Ultimately, in constitutional review, judges face binary choices: to declare or not to declare statutes unconstitutional. Hence, when checking the constitutionality of legislation, judges don't seem vulnerable to disjunctions.

2. *The Survival Heuristic*

Second, along with using equal assignment, one may use the survival heuristic—a heuristic not vulnerable to the disjunction objection—to support supermajority rules in constitutional review. According to this heuristic, from an adaptative, ecological, or evolutionary viewpoint, if one can't mathematically gauge the odds of some results, the most rational way of deciding is doing so

76 Keynes 2007: ch 4; Estlund 2008: 228–30.
77 Condorcet [1785] 2014: lviii–lx, 119–20; Arrow 1963: ch 5.
78 Keynes 2007: ch 4; Estlund 2008: 228–30; Lagerspetz 2016: 306.

in ways that ensure survival. After all, without survival, other aims can't be pursued.[79] Thus, taking the previous example, if one can't gauge the odds of getting Covid-19, one should still self-quarantine since getting Covid-19 is more life-threatening than not getting it.

In constitutional review, this means that, under uncertainty, one should design a system that can survive long-term despite erring repeatedly. So, one should design a system that generally avoids the errors that more likely threaten its existence. All else equal, false positives are worse than false negatives, both intrinsically[80] and due to their higher durability.[81] Thus, false positives pose a higher threat to a constitutional review system's survival than false negatives. Hence, even if constitutional courts may produce excessive false negatives, the fact that false positives are worse than false negatives matters more when designing these courts' voting rules, thus supporting supermajority rules. Therefore, despite the risk that supermajority rules may produce excessive false negatives in constitutional review, constitutional courts should still use these voting rules.

Now, some may argue that equal assignment and the survival heuristic are irrational ways of deciding. On equal assignment, it doesn't follow from uncertainty that different results are equally likely: some results may be more likely than others.[82] As Vermeule holds, equal assignment may be 'akin to try to pick the larger of two numbers by choosing the one with the larger digit in the second decimal place, even if one knows nothing about the digit in the first decimal place.'[83] And on equal assignment and the survival heuristic, it may also happen that there's a result as bad (or worse) than the result considered worst and that one hasn't accounted for. For example, if the result of a prolonged quarantine is that it will hamper one's immune system by depriving it of necessary stressors,[84] one may die of Covid-19 or of other diseases anyway.

The problem with these objections though is that they don't give decision makers reasonable alternative criteria to decide under very limited information.[85] Sure, decisions made under equal assignment and the survival heuristic aren't perfectly rational. Yet if the main data one has refers to the particularly harmful effects of a result, while one has little or no information about probabilities or about other results, it's hard making sensible decisions without somehow relying on equal assignment or the survival heuristic.

79 Taleb 2018: 24–6, ch 19, 246–52.
80 Christiano 2008: ch 7.
81 *Burnett v Coronado Oil and Gas Co,* 285 US 393, 406 (1932); *Seminole Tribe v Florida,* 517 US 44, 63 (1996); Ely 1980: 4–5, 45; Yowell 2018: 139–45.
82 Elster 1989: 32–6; Vermeule 2006: 174.
83 Vermeule 2006: 174.
84 On things that need stressors to survive and improve, see Taleb 2012.
85 Elster (1989: 135) and Vermeule (2006: 174–5) argue similarly.

3. Offsetting Measures

Due to reasonable disagreement, it doesn't seem feasible to surely gauge false positives' and false negatives' probabilities. And given that some constitutional courts' decisions are errors—even if we can't tell which ones are so—there are solid grounds to assume that false positives are worse than false negatives. So, in these circumstances, the most reasonable stance to take when designing a constitutional review system is that such system focuses on avoiding false positives. And since supermajority rules may do this, constitutional courts should use them for declaring statutes unconstitutional.

Still, if the reader isn't fully convinced by this claim—or the reader is almost fully convinced, but thinks I should dwell further on the risk of producing excessive false negatives—it's worth indicating that, when zooming out from our analysis of voting rules and taking more of a 'big picture' institutional approach, there are many offsetting measures that one may apply to curb excessive false negatives. These measures may be applied in constitutional courts, legislatures, or both. In constitutional courts, though this core case assumes that all other institutional variables stay equal, once we relax this assumption, the risk of producing excessive false negatives may be tackled by changing rules other than the voting rule (eg, those governing amicus curiae, evidence, interventions, hearings, standing, etc.)[86] And this risk may be mitigated by calibrating supermajority rules downwards. The closer a supermajority rule is to majority rule, the lower the risk of producing excessive false negatives.[87] So, a simple way of curbing this risk is choosing the supermajority rule that's closest to majority rule.

In turn, legislatures may be made more sensitive to rights—hence pre-emptively addressing false negatives—by changing their electoral and procedural rules. For example, legislators elected by proportional representation may be more sensitive to rights than legislators elected by plurality rule.[88] Something similar may be said about legislators elected by gender or racial quotas versus legislators not elected through these quotas.[89] Finally, legislatures may be made more sensitive to rights if their bills are reviewed by specialised rights commissions[90] than if they aren't subject to such review. In sum, even if voting rules in constitutional review are changed from majority rule to supermajority rules, there's vast room for institutional tinkering to offset potential excessive false negatives. Thus, though the worry that supermajority rules may produce

86 On different ways of designing constitutional courts, see Hübner Mendes 2015: ch 6; Yowell 2018: 151–62.

87 Gersen & Vermeule 2007: 687, 696, 700–4.

88 On different voting rules for electing legislators, see Lagerspetz 2016: ch 3.

89 On differences between legislatures, see Sartori 1997: ch 5–7; Carey 2008; Fish & Kroenig 2009; Lijphart 2012: ch 11; McCormick et al 2022: ch 9.

90 Here I mainly consider the UK Parliament's Joint Committee on Human Rights (Hunt et al 2015) and the Finnish Parliament's Committee for Constitutional Law (Husa 2000).

excessive false negatives is fair, it isn't enough to preclude using these voting rules in constitutional review.

Unfairness towards Claimants

In a recent article defending majority rule in judicial decisions, Guha Krishnamurthi[91] argued that, due to its neutrality, majority rule ensures 'representational fairness;'[92] meaning, it ensures that, all else equal, courts don't privilege one party (or set of parties) over another. He also argued that, in principle, this fairness should be shown in the way judicial procedures are built.[93] For Krishnamurthi, this neutrality justifies majority rule in judicial decisions. Thus, in his view, supermajority rules may be 'unfair' towards claimants. That is, towards parties defying a statute's constitutionality.

It seems that, when Krishnamurthi refers to representational fairness between parties, he's referring to giving parties *equal prior odds* of winning the case. Hence, in a case in which party A defies statute C's constitutionality while party B supports it, by giving each party a prior 50% odds of getting or not getting a declaration of unconstitutionality, respectively, majority rule would be representationally fair. This seems clear considering that, in the US context, Krishnamurthi holds that supermajority rules would 'systematically benefit one set of parties by requiring the other set of parties [to] obtain a supermajority to obtain a favorable judgment;'[94] an asymmetry that may be seen as 'impeding a party's right to judicial review.'[95]

It isn't clear that representational fairness demands giving parties equal prior odds of winning. And even if this is generally the case, it isn't clear that it applies in constitutional review. Though one may hold that judicial procedures should generally be representationally fair (in Krishnamurthi's sense), in specific contexts, there may be other competing values that justify preferring some judicial results over others; hence giving more prior odds of winning to the parties supporting such results via voting rules. In criminal procedures, this value is the presumption of innocence—a presumption that justifies generally preferring acquittals over convictions, thus giving more prior odds of winning to defendants over prosecutors through unanimity rule. In turn, in constitutional review, this value arguably is the presumption of constitutionality of legislation—a presumption that justifies generally preferring false negatives over false positives, thus giving more prior odds of winning to defendants over claimants through supermajority rules.

91 2020: 1218–21, 1244.
92 When referring to parties, Krishnamurthi (2020: 1218–21, 1244) also calls this trait 'party neutrality.'
93 Id 1218–9.
94 Id 1244.
95 Id.

Now, I'm not arguing that statutes' alleged constitutionality should have the same level of protection as the presumption of innocence. And I agree with Krishnamurthi that, for constitutional review to be meaningful, its procedures should give claimants a good chance of winning. (This is a reason why, in the following chapter, I suggest choosing the supermajority rule that's closest to majority rule.) But a good chance of winning isn't the same as equiprobability. Thus, despite Krishnamurthi's claims, there are still grounds to guard the presumption of constitutionality of legislation through supermajority rules.

Inapplicability of the Condorcet Jury Theorem

It could be objected that the Condorcet Jury Theorem doesn't hold in constitutional courts, in which case, my Condorcetian claims for using supermajority rules in constitutional review wouldn't apply.

There's some empirical evidence suggesting that the theorem applies to small groups.[96] Thus, we may infer that something similar happens among judges. But if the Condorcet Jury Theorem doesn't apply to constitutional courts, that wouldn't just erode the core case for supermajority rules in constitutional review: it would also erode some of the main grounds for having all kinds of collegiate courts, including constitutional courts. A main reason for issuing judicial rulings by collegiate courts rather than by a judge is that 'two heads are better than one:' that having more than one judge cognitively adds something to a ruling's accuracy. And arguably, the main explanation for why this happens is the Condorcet Jury Theorem,[97] either in its original form or some variant of it. Thus, if this theorem doesn't hold in collegiate courts, there seems to be little point in having them in the first place. In sum, as it happens between ability and constitutional review theories, the Condorcet Jury Theorem seems somehow to belong to the best versions of the case for collegiate courts, including the best versions of the case for constitutional courts.

Still, if the theorem doesn't hold in constitutional courts, that would only bolster this core case insofar as some constitutional courts' decisions are errors and false positives are worse than false negatives. I've argued that constitutional courts should mainly avoid false positives in an optimistic scenario: I've argued that they should mainly avoid false positives under conditions that boost the odds that they'll decide more rightly than wrongly. Thus, if these conditions don't hold, considering that these institutions would be more

96 For overviews of this research, see Bang & Frith 2017; Barry 2021: 81–3.

97 Another explanation for this 'wisdom of crowds' effect may be the Hong-Page theorem. This theorem states that, if group members are sufficiently competent, cognitively diverse groups outperform homogeneous groups. Hong & Page 2004; Page 2007. Yet it's doubtful that the Hong-Page theorem applies to constitutional courts since these courts are mainly made of legal experts, and the theorem's mathematical rigour has been questioned by Thompson (2014). For an argument claiming that the US Supreme Court should have lay justices, see Vermeule 2007.

error-prone, there would be more grounds to claim that constitutional courts should mainly avoid false positives.

An akin objection may be that the Condorcet Jury Theorem mainly applies to factual judgments—not value judgments:[98] that though the theorem may apply to things such as assessing the evidence for or against someone's claims, it wouldn't apply when assessing if the conclusions garnered from that evidence are 'good' or 'bad.' Or, in our case, constitutionally acceptable or not.[99] Thus, since in constitutional review, courts mainly render value judgments, the theorem wouldn't apply to them.

Though it's generally useful to distinguish between factual and value judgments, many times these judgments are entangled.[100] Adjectives such as 'brave,' 'cruel,' 'generous,' 'noble,' or 'strong' include both judgments,[101] and many value judgments need a factual basis that one considers right. For example, one must consider the evidence indicating that intra-state economic inequalities have risen as factually right for claiming that such rise is morally wrong.[102] Likewise, for judges to hold that certain statutes are unconstitutional on some grounds, they must rely on the evidence proving that these statutes produce the effects they consider unconstitutional. Since in practice factual and value judgments are entangled, to assume that—all else equal—the conditions boosting a group's factual accuracy also boost a group's normative accuracy is sensible. And considering the factual assessments regularly involved in constitutional review, the words 'constitutional' or 'unconstitutional' seem the sort of words that include both kinds of judgments.

In any case, in group decision making, there's usually little practical choice but to assume that the conditions boosting factual accuracy also boost normative accuracy. Regardless of the bases of normative accuracy—meaning, regardless of whether one thinks normative accuracy is based on universal values, or on fact-based agreements—in groups, a main test for checking whether claims are normatively accurate is arguably by counting heads:[103] by seeing how many people agree to them in conditions favouring rational reflection.[104]

98 I'm grateful to David Dyzenhaus for raising this objection.

99 Here I'm considering 'value judgments' as a synonym for 'moral judgments' and 'constitutionality judgments.' I clarify this since there are other judgments (eg, aesthetic judgments) that are usually considered value judgments as well. Ortega y Gasset 1964: 315–22; Putnam 2002: 18–9.

100 It's also questionable that there's anything 'essential' or 'metaphysical' behind the distinction. Putnam 2002: ch 1–2.

101 Id 24–5, 34–43.

102 For akin examples, see Harari 2016: ch 5.

103 According to Putnam 2002: 19–20, Hume actually thought this.

104 Another test could be to ask a higher authority to settle the issue. As seen in Chapter 3, the Catholic Church tried to do this by developing the 'greater and sounder part' doctrine. But in many cases, this higher authority doesn't exist, or one can't indisputably establish it.

Multiple Choice

Until now, I've assumed that judges face binary choices: they either declare or not declare statutes unconstitutional. What if I am wrong though? What if judges face more than two options? Wouldn't this erode the application of the Condorcet Jury Theorem, and thus this core case?[105]

It's worth noting that List & Goodin[106] claim that, in small groups facing multiple options, the theorem's results hold if group members are able. But even if this isn't the case[107]—and if one accepts that manipulation should be bound—multiple options provide a stronger case for supermajority rules than for majority rule. As social choice research shows, when there are multiple options, cycles may occur.[108] Hence, if constitutional courts face more than two options, depending on the respective court's dynamics,[109] the judge leading the court—or the judge drafting its decision[110]—may engage in manipulation: they may mould the voting process' results by framing the options for deciding in ways that favour their preferred option. Put differently, possible cycles may give too much power to some judges over the options shown to their peers.

There are at least two reasons for binding manipulation in constitutional courts. First, there's legal certainty. In principle, legal certainty demands that judges' constitutional interpretations should be as transitive as possible. This transitivity demand is arguably behind the idea of 'treating like cases alike.' After all, it's only by keeping at least some stability in one's opinions that one can make relatively uniform—and hence, predictable—decisions. Thus, all else equal, in constitutional review, manipulation is undesirable since, by enabling some judges to erode transitivity by tinkering with the options shown to their peers, manipulation hinders the odds that they make relatively uniform decisions vis-à-vis cases in which manipulation is bound. Second, on Condorcet accuracy grounds, manipulation curbs ability by allowing a disjunction of options. That is, by allowing options to be split into more options.[111] As Estlund claims, ability is affected by the number of options shown to the group: the more options shown to the group, the more ability decreases.[112] Hence, if one wants to boost Condorcetian accuracy, one should bind manipulation.

105 I am grateful to Paul Yowell and Jacob Weinrib for raising this objection.

106 2001.

107 Estlund (2008: 15–6, 223–5) and Lagerspetz (2016: 306) have criticised List & Goodin's results.

108 Condorcet [1785] 2014: lviii–lx, 119–20; Arrow 1963: ch 5.

109 For differences between the decision processes of many constitutional courts in Europe, North America, and South America, see Wilson 1986; Ferrer Mac-Gregor 2009; Ferejohn & Pasquino 2004; Pasquino 2015; Kelemen 2019: ch 2; Baum 2019: ch 4.

110 Kelemen 2019: 39–44.

111 Keynes 2007: ch 4; Estlund 2008: 228–30; Lagerspetz 2016: 306.

112 2008: 15–6, 223–5.

As mentioned in Chapter 4, due to their non-neutrality,[113] supermajority rules tackle possible cycles—hence binding manipulation—more than majority rule.[114] Under majority rule, one can manipulate for and against the presumption of constitutionality of legislation. Contrariwise, under supermajority rules, the chances of manipulating against the presumption of constitutionality of legislation are bounded, while the chances of manipulating for this presumption stay constant. Considering that, on legal certainty and Condorcet accuracy grounds, manipulation should be bound, even with multiple options, there's a stronger case for supermajority rules than for majority rule in constitutional review. By deciding by majority rule, currently, constitutional courts are more vulnerable to manipulation than they would be under supermajority rules.

Overprotection or Adaptation

Another objection that could be held against this core case is that judges[115] and scholars[116] have already developed doctrines based on false negatives being worse than false positives. Thus, if one applies supermajority rules in constitutional review without changing those doctrines, one may overprotect statutes' alleged constitutionality. Or judges may adapt to supermajority rules by not applying these doctrines anymore.[117]

This claim is sound. Broadly speaking, there are 'deferential' or 'restrictive' constitutional doctrines applied by judges. But I'm sceptical of whether they suffice for two reasons. First, it's quite debated what these doctrines imply in constitutional review, and thus if judges really follow them.[118] Due to these debates, the way in which these doctrines are applied mainly depends on each judge's opinion. Hence, by themselves, these doctrines don't seem fully reliable for guarding statutes' alleged constitutionality.

Second, despite deferential doctrines, the extensive use of the proportionality test in most constitutional courts erodes these doctrines' application.[119] Many courts seem to use a version of the proportionality test that follows

113 Tsebelis 2002: 139–43, 149–51; Schwartzberg 2013: 92–4, 121–3; Lagerspetz 2016: 195–6, 278–83.
114 Caplin & Nalebuff 1988; Saari 1997; Colomer & McLean 1998; Tsebelis 2002: 139–43, 149--51; Lagerspetz 2016: 195–6, 278–83.
115 Eg, see *Burnett v Coronado Oil and Gas Co*, 285 US 393, 406 (1932); *Seminole Tribe v Florida*, 517 US 44, 63 (1996).
116 Eg, see Thayer 1893; King 2008.
117 I'm grateful to Benjamin Ewing and an anonymous reviewer of an article based on this research for raising this objection.
118 Among other issues, one can see the depths of these debates by browsing the literature on the proportionality test. Eg, see Aleinikoff 1987; Alexy 2002; Beatty 2005; Kumm 2007; Tsakyrakis 2009; Webber 2009; Barak 2012; Möller 2012; Urbina 2017.
119 On how the proportionality test has spread worldwide, see Barak 2012; Möller 2012.

Kumm's theory.[120] Under this version, judges may ignore deferential doctrines if they think other factors outweigh them. And they can do so even if the respective factors aren't 'legal;' meaning, they can do this even if these factors aren't based on legal texts or precedents. So, if most constitutional courts actually apply the proportionality test *à la* Kumm—and there are good reasons to claim so—deferential doctrines may no longer suffice to guard statutes' alleged constitutionality.

Finally, it may happen that judges adapt to supermajority rules in constitutional review by no longer applying deferential standards. But more evidence is required to fully know so. Currently, we just don't know.

Interpretation Booster

It can be held against this core case that, in constitutional review, supermajority rules would boost interpretive decisions—decisions that may meddle with legislatures' tasks as much as annulments or disapplications. Put differently, the worry here is that, once supermajority rules in constitutional review are established, judges may try to 'game the system' by issuing decisions that propose strained interpretations of defied statutes to avoid constitutional problems.[121]

There's little evidence that this has happened in courts using supermajority rules in constitutional review. As previously mentioned, the South Korean constitutional court has declared thousands of statutes unconstitutional.[122] Further, the Peruvian court seems to declare statutes unconstitutional with the same frequency as other courts using majority rule.[123] Moreover, the Mexican court's supermajority rule doesn't seem to much affect judges' decisions on whether to declare defied statutes unconstitutional.[124] And Shugerman also argues along these authors' lines when referring to interviews conducted with the judges of the Nebraskan and North Dakotan supreme courts.[125]

But even if supermajority rules boost interpretive decisions—and assuming that these decisions meddle with legislatures' tasks as much as annulments and disapplications—it's easier to rectify interpretive decisions' effects than to rectify annulments' and disapplications' effects. Interpretive decisions' effects can be tackled through normal legislative means; something that can't happen with annulments and disapplications. Thus, even if constitutional courts issue more interpretive decisions under supermajority rules, these voting rules are still preferable to majority rule.

120 Yowell 2018: 30–5. For a description of the theory, see Kumm 2007.
121 I'm grateful to Benjamin Ewing for raising this objection.
122 Seok Hong 2019: 183, 193–4.
123 Tiede & Ponce 2014: 149–51, 156–8.
124 Rivera León 2023: 18–24.
125 2002: 955–6.

Poland

Though this core case doesn't apply to Poland, it's worth referring to the Polish case; particularly since the Polish Government tried to nullify Poland's constitutional review system by changing the Constitutional Tribunal's voting rule from majority rule to a 2/3 rule.[126]

First, the Polish Government didn't change the Tribunal's voting rule since the respective statute was voided.[127] And the attempt to change the Tribunal's voting rule belonged to a wider set of policies aimed at nullifying the Tribunal, the most relevant of which wasn't changing the voting rule, but replacing the judges with people faithful to the Government. Once the Government's plan succeeded, the Government ditched its attempts at changing the Tribunal's voting rule.[128] Thus, since one can't see supermajority rules' effects in the Constitutional Tribunal, nor can one see these effects in isolation, one can't hold that supermajority rules per se nullify Poland's constitutional review system. That may happen, but we can't surely know so.

Second, though supermajority rules in constitutional review may be used to erode a democracy, the same happens with almost *any* other policies that well-functioning democracies usually undertake. Democratic erosion stems from the joint effect of policies that, when seen in isolation, from a non-context sensitive viewpoint (what Sadurski calls 'the Martian's test')[129] don't cause alarm.[130] Supermajority rules may erode a democracy as much as any standard policy applied in well-functioning contexts. For example, corruption sanctions may be used for purging one's adversaries;[131] checks and balances may be used for guarding a dictatorship's policies;[132] emergency measures may be used for limiting fair political competition;[133] electoral reforms may be used for artificially boosting one's support;[134] and unicameral legislatures may be used for

126 Sadurski 2019: 90–5.

127 K 47/15 of 9 March 2016 of the Constitutional Tribunal. I'm grateful to Piotr Mikuli for helping me solve my doubts on this decision.

128 Sadurski 2019: 61–70, 79.

129 In Sadurski's words: 'would an intelligent and … well-informed Martian, having for herself all the information culled only from the structures of government, and knowing none of the practice, discern the non-democratic character of the regime? Probably not' (2019: 7).

130 Zakaria 1997; Tushnet 2004; Landau 2013; Levitsky & Ziblatt 2018; Ginsburg & Huq 2019; Sadurski 2019: ch 1, 7.

131 Eg, former Brazilian judge Sergio Moro was accused of doing this while directing the 'car wash' investigations. After the investigations, Moro became President Bolsonaro's justice minister. Leahy & Schipani 2018.

132 This happened in Chile. Couso 2011: 393, 405–14; Huneeus 2007: ch 12.

133 This happened in Weimar Germany and, more recently, in Turkey. Vinx 2015; Levitsky & Ziblatt 2018: 96.

134 This happened in Chile as well. Couso 2011: 405–14.

stifling deliberation.[135] In sum, many policies—regardless of how justifiable or well-designed—may be used for eroding a democracy.

Unfortunately, most cases of democratic erosion that have happened during this century[136] suggest that Benjamin Franklin was right: democracies exist only if their citizens can keep them.[137] This is a reason why, through history, many political leaders and philosophers have remarked civic education's key relevance.[138] Democracies' last line of defence doesn't lie in their policies or institutions, but in their citizens' hearts and minds, as shown in their behaviour. As Learned Hand held, when a democracy 'dies there, no constitution, no law, no court can save it; no constitution, no law, no court can even do much to help.'[139]

Despite their differences, if in a democracy, most citizens (and thus most officials) don't comply with basic social norms—norms that, broadly speaking, involve 'mutual toleration'[140] and 'forebearance,'[141] especially when using political power—that democracy will likely erode, and there's little that policies or institutions can do about it.[142] In Linz & Stepan's words, for democracies to thrive, 'even in the face of severe political and economic crises,'[143] their practices must become 'deeply internalized in social, institutional, and ... psychological life.'[144] If not, that democracy has little survival odds. Good institutions are necessary but insufficient for the proper functioning of a democracy. As Thayer held, 'under no system can the power of courts save a people from ruin; our chief protection lies elsewhere.'[145]

Yet the fact that policies or institutions can be abused doesn't mean that they shouldn't be used to achieve worthy goals, or that one can't recommend them if based on proper conditions. Just as corruption sanctions' potential for abuse don't exclude them in all cases, supermajority rules' potential for

135 Jeremy Waldron questions New Zealand's unicameralism on these grounds. Waldron 2016: 9, 73.

136 For an overview of these cases, see Mounk 2018; Levitsky & Ziblatt 2018; Ginsburg & Huq 2019; Sadurski 2019. See also Applebaum 2020.

137 A lady allegedly asked Benjamin Franklin (cited in McHenry 1906) whether the US Constitutional Convention had agreed on a republic or a monarchy. 'A republic' Franklin replied, 'if you can keep it.'

138 For an overview of some of these leaders and philosophers, see Mounk 2018: 245–6. More recently, Lukianoff & Haidt (2018: 250–1), and Nussbaum (2018: ch 7), have claimed that US students should work or undertake a compulsory 'civic service' before going to tertiary education.

139 Hand, cited in Dworkin 1996: 342.

140 Levitsky & Ziblatt 2018: 102–6.

141 For Levitsky & Ziblatt, 'forbearance' means avoiding actions that, while respecting the letter of the law, violate its spirit (2018: 106-11). The opposite of forebearance is 'constitutional hardball' (Tushnet 2004).

142 Mounk (2018: ch 9) and Sadurski (2019: 182–7) have argued similarly.

143 Linz & Stepan 1996: 15.

144 Id 16.

145 Thayer 1893: 30.

abuse don't exclude them in all cases either. Thus, the fact that the Polish Government tried to use supermajority rules to nullify the Constitutional Tribunal only proves that, under bad conditions, supermajority rules may be used for bad purposes; little else. So, despite the Polish case, supermajority rules' potential for abuse doesn't exclude them in constitutional review.

Now, some may claim that supermajority rules in constitutional review are more likely to erode a democracy than these other measures, and that therefore they are a riskier policy.[146] But there's too little evidence to claim this for sure. As it happens with false positives' and false negatives' odds, in this case, we face uncertainty. And in this context, to assume that supermajority rules in constitutional review are as likely as other policies to erode a democracy seems more robust than to intuitively claim that supermajority rules are likelier to erode it.

Counter-Facts

Another objection against supermajority rules in constitutional review may be the 'counter-factual objection.' That is, the objection that some declarations of unconstitutionality that one considers right may not have occurred under supermajority rules.[147] For example, some may object that, if the US Supreme Court had decided *Obergefell v Hodges*[148] under supermajority rules, same-sex marriages wouldn't have been recognised in the US; or that if the Supreme Court of Canada had decided *Sauvé v Canada (Chief Electoral Officer)*[149] under supermajority rules, Canadian prisoners wouldn't have their right to vote recognised; etc.

This objection has merit: ceteris paribus, under supermajority rules, some statutes likely wouldn't have been declared unconstitutional. But this objection focuses on the trees rather than the forest: it focuses on salient cases rather than on constitutional review systems as a whole. Yet constitutional review systems are—for lack of a better word—'systems:'[150] they are 'a set of connected things or devices that operate together.'[151] Hence, when assessing constitutional review systems, one shouldn't cherry-pick and only consider 'good' decisions. Instead, one should treat constitutional review systems as 'wholesale' packages and consider (i) the salient decisions one likes, (ii) the salient decisions one dislikes, and (iii) non-salient decisions. The same system

146 I'm grateful to Jacob Weinrib for raising this objection.

147 Vermeule (2006: 280–2) answers a similar objection using *Brown v Board of Education of Topeka*, 347 US 483 (1954). My argument is based on Vermeule's, but I don't use *Brown* as an example since that case was unanimously decided.

148 *Obergefell v Hodges*, 576 US __ (2015).

149 *Sauvé v Canada (Chief Electoral Officer)*, [2002] 3 SCR 519.

150 Vermeule 2006: 280–2.

151 Cambridge Dictionary nd.

producing *Obergefell* by a five-to-four decision produces *Citizens United*[152](or *District of Columbia v Heller)*[153] by five-to-four decisions; the same system producing *Sauvé* by a bare majority of Canadian Supreme Court justices produces *Chaoulli v Quebec*[154] by another bare majority of Canadian Supreme Court justices. Thus, on constitutional review systems (and institutions generally), one can't have one's cake and eat it too. Following Vermeule, one can't have all the annulments that one likes and none of the annulments that one dislikes.[155]

Ultimately, the counterfactual objection seems a product of the 'availability bias.' That is, our intuitive tendency to only pay attention to salient, noticeable, or vivid facts, and then assume that such facts are frequent.[156] In this case, the availability bias means that we focus on past decisions 'A,' 'B,' or 'C' that we consider right, and then assume that the constitutional review system that made those decisions usually produces akin results. Thus, once an institutional change is proposed (in this case, a change in the voting rule), and the vivid information suggests that, if that change had occurred beforehand, past decisions A, B, or C may not have happened, we tend to see the respective change as producing an overall loss when that may not be the case. The question isn't whether 'good' past decisions would have been made under supermajority rules; the question is whether, with these voting rules, constitutional courts make more right than wrong decisions. Or at least make fewer very wrong decisions. Due to what I've claimed in this chapter, there are good reasons for holding that supermajority rules may produce this effect in constitutional review. Thus, supermajority rules still seem better than majority rule for declaring statutes unconstitutional.

Additionally, under majority rule, the respective court may have decided its past hard cases backwards. The counterfactual objection applies to very controversial decisions that one considers right. Actually, it's *because* these decisions were controversial that they were decided by a bare majority of judges. This means that, though these decisions turned out the way one likes, it's likely that they could have turned out otherwise. What if in *Obergefell* the US Supreme Court had decided not to declare statutory bans on same-sex

152 In this case, the US Supreme Court ruled that the bounds on independent expenditures (a form of campaign spending) put by the Bipartisan Campaign Reform Act of 2002 are unconstitutional on free speech grounds. *Citizens United v Federal Elections Commission,* 558 US 310 (2010).

153 In this case, the US Supreme Court voided the District of Columbia's limits on gun sales and ownership. A majority of justices held that such limits violated the US Constitution's second amendment. *District of Columbia v Heller,* 554 US 570 (2008).

154 In this case, the Supreme Court of Canada voided Quebec's ban of private medical insurance. A majority of justices held that such a ban violated the Quebec Charter of Human Rights and Freedoms. *Chaoulli v Quebec,* [2005] 1 SCR 791.

155 Vermeule 2006: 281.

156 This bias is also called 'availability heuristic' and 'salience bias.' Kahneman et al 1982; Kahneman 2011.

marriage unconstitutional, arguing that US states have a valid interest in fostering traditional marriage?[157] What if in *Sauvé* the Canadian Supreme Court had decided that, under the Canadian Charter of Rights and Freedoms, denying prisoners the vote is an acceptable policy choice that the Canadian Parliament could make?[158] Insofar as judges decide by majority rule, the outcome of cases such as *Obergefell* and *Sauvé* boils down to convincing a single judge of the merits of one's case. Hence, though past judicial decisions issued by majority rule seem inevitable in hindsight, they were far from sure.[159]

Further, the counter-factual objection suggests that judicial decisions are the only way to produce the results one likes. But since one doesn't know what would have happened in different circumstances, one can't claim that the same results wouldn't have been accomplished by other means. True, insofar as the factors influencing judges' behaviour stay constant, neither *Obergefell* nor *Sauvé* would have been decided similarly under supermajority rules. Yet this tells us nothing on the matter of how other actors—eg, other officials, international organisations, citizens themselves, etc.—may have responded to these decisions. Thus, chances are that, through other chains of events, we may have had the same results. When guessing about the past (or the future) we just don't know. We may hold that it's likely that some event would have happened (or will happen), but likelihood isn't certainty.

Finally, due to reasonable disagreement, in hard cases, intuitions and claims about the quality of constitutional courts' decisions go against each other. The counterfactual objection may be raised by people upholding *Obergefell* (or *Sauvé*) and by people upholding *Citizens United* (or *Chaoulli*). Of course, if one upholds *Obergefell* (or *Sauvé*) and is against *Citizens United* (or *Chaoulli*), one may claim that the former decisions were 'actually right' while the latter decisions were 'actually wrong.' But the claim can be turned around, and there's little in the cases themselves for solving the dispute. Thus, our assessment of voting rules in constitutional review shouldn't rely on specific cases. Rather, focusing on these rules themselves is more reliable.[160] Supermajority

157 This is part of what Chief Justice Roberts argued in his dissenting opinion. *Obergefell v Hodges,* 576 US __ (2015).

158 *Sauvé v Canada (Chief Electoral Officer),* [2002] 3 SCR 519.

159 When checking past events, one should be aware of 'hindsight bias' (also called 'creeping determinism' or 'knew-it-all-along effect'). This bias is the human mind's tendency to see past events as predictable and inevitable though they weren't so. Hindsight bias is a cognitive error since there's always a possibility that things could have turned out differently. Hindsight bias is partially influenced by the availability bias. Kahneman et al 1982; Kahneman 2011.

160 Another reliable action is using statistics. As Steven Pinker argues: '[w]hen a debate devolves into sliding definitions, cherry-picked examples, and ad hoc excuses, it's time to call in the statistics' (2012: 281). Yet, as in the case of gauging probabilities, in constitutional review, the main issue with statistics is that reasonable disagreement may affect their interpretation. Put differently, people will likely reasonably disagree on whether the measured information suggests that a constitutional court's voting rule should be reformed. Eg, suppose a statistic

rules' traits give sound reasons for holding that, under them, constitutional courts will tend to rightly decide constitutional cases. Or at least they will tend not to decide them terribly wrongly. Therefore, despite this objection, supermajority rules should be used in constitutional review.

Increasing Courts' Size

Some may hold that, to get the Condorcet Jury Theorem's benefits, one may increase constitutional courts' size instead of using supermajority rules. Under the theorem, one way of boosting group accuracy is by adding new competent members.[161] Thus, insofar as all[162] (or most)[163] new members are competent, the larger a group becomes, the likelier it's that its decisions are right.

Yet there are three problems with increasing size. First, under the theorem, what mostly matters is neither group size nor the proportion of the majority to group size: what mostly matters is absolute margin size.[164] Thus, even if a constitutional court becomes larger, its absolute margins—that is, the differences produced in each decision between majorities and minorities—may stay constant, which means that size increases may not report much cognitive gains.

Second, even if we assume that by increasing size we can boost Condorcet accuracy, it's likely that this increase would have to be significant. But a significant size increase may curb judicial deliberation, thus curbing deliberation's cognitive benefits.[165] Following Hessick & Jordan, constitutional courts may have to become so large that they may 'inhibit the productive exchange of information through deliberation, thus undercutting the informational benefits of a larger size.'[166] Hence, when boosting group accuracy on Condorcet accuracy *and* deliberative grounds, changing a constitutional court's voting rule seems safer than increasing size.

Finally, even if we increase a constitutional court's size on Condorcet accuracy grounds, there's still error asymmetry: false positives would still be worse than false negatives. So, if one must choose between: (i) applying a supermajority rule among judges (a policy that may boost group accuracy *and* avoid false positives); and (ii) increasing constitutional courts' size (a policy that may only boost accuracy), the former policy seems better than the latter.

---

showing that, in constitutional court X, 50% of decisions are declarations of unconstitutionality. What does that tell us about X's voting rule? That depends on factors lying outside the statistic, such as each case's facts, the moral views of the statistic's interpreters, etc.

161 Condorcet [1785] 2014: xxi–xxii.

162 Id.

163 Recall here the difference between the tight and loose versions of the ability condition. Grofman et al 1983: 268–9; Estlund 2008: 225; Landemore 2013: 73; Lagerspetz 2016: 307.

164 McLean & Hewitt 1994: 35–7; List & Pettit 2011: 91.

165 Hessick & Jordan 2009: 645, 649, 695–8; Hübner Mendes 2015: 151–2. Elster (2013: 219–20) has also analysed this trade-off in constituent assemblies.

166 2009: 649.

Easy Cases

It could be claimed that this argument for supermajority rules in constitutional review mainly applies to hard cases. That is, cases involving open-ended constitutional provisions, such as those recognising basic rights. Yet this argument may not apply to easy cases. That is, cases based on clear constitutional provisions.[167] Many of this book's claims depend on reasonable disagreement; an arguably prevalent phenomenon in hard cases, but not in easy cases. Therefore, some may argue that, when checking the constitutionality of legislation under clear constitutional provisions, judges should decide by majority rule.

Still, though the argument for supermajority rules in constitutional review is stronger for hard cases, it also applies to easy cases. There may be cases that, though seemingly easy, may actually be hard. In these cases, due to the reasons set out thus far, supermajority rules seem better suited than majority rule for resolving them. Also, in actually easy cases, there's practically unanimous agreement in the literature that constitutional review is a technical task.[168] Thus, it shouldn't be hard for judges to sincerely agree on how to interpret clear provisions, especially considering that they are jurists. For example, judges may reasonably disagree on whether religious freedom is compatible with state-imposed vaccinations, or with state-imposed limits on religious dress. But if the constitution's timelines are based on the Gregorian calendar, they shouldn't reasonably disagree on whether a president (or prime minister) is 35 years old or older.

Costs

Some may argue that supermajority rules in constitutional review would heavily increase judges' decision costs—meaning, their costs involved at deciding—thus offsetting many of the advantages claimed thus far. But this isn't clear. Following Buchannan & Tullock,[169] there's arguably a trade-off between decision costs and external costs. Thus, though judges may currently decide with relative ease, they may be imposing—or, in economic terms, 'externalising'—other costs to the rest of society. As Gersen & Vermeule claim, judges may be 'exporting … costs to other actors in the legal system, simplifying their own task while creating net systemic harms.'[170] For example, due to their false positives—and along with producing sunk costs—judges may be imposing opportunity costs, such as the bargaining costs that other officials must incur to repair them. And judges may be imposing information costs. That

167 On easy cases generally, see Schauer 1985; Vermeule 2006: 270–2.

168 Eg, see Kelsen 2015: 29–31, 48, 60–1, 76; Ely 1980: 13; Dworkin 1996: 7–11; Kumm 2007: 156–7.

169 1999: ch 7–15. See also McGinnis & Rappaport 2007: 1122–5; Gersen & Vermeule 2007: 716–8.

170 2007: 716–8.

is, they may be increasing the costs that other officials and citizens must incur to know their main doctrines. Once these costs are considered, it isn't clear that increasing judges' decision costs is bad. Actually, it could be claimed that judges' decision costs should increase so that they internalise the other costs that they currently impose on others.[171]

Further, even assuming that judges' decision costs increase under supermajority rules (and that this increase is bad), there are at least two ways of curbing that increase. First, there's the presumption of constitutionality of legislation. Due to this presumption, if the respective supermajority threshold isn't reached, the defied statute stays constitutional. Thus, this presumption curbs decision costs by preventing situations in which no decision is made. Second, supermajority rules and decision costs are directly linked. The higher the supermajority threshold, the higher judges' decision costs, and vice versa.[172] Hence, if one wants to curb judges' decision costs, one may do so by choosing the supermajority rules closer to majority rule rather than the supermajority rules farther from it. Therefore, potential increases in judges' decision costs don't seem forceful enough to exclude supermajority rules in constitutional review.

Coordination Issues

If supermajority rules are used in constitutional review, some may wonder about the exact effects of majoritarian declarations of unconstitutionality. Put differently, what happens when a majority—but not a supermajority—of the constitutional court holds that a statute is unconstitutional? This matters especially when lower courts also consider said statute unconstitutional.

As it's been done in the Czech Republic,[173] Peru,[174] and South Korea,[175] this issue can be addressed by determining—either via constitutional or statutory provisions, or via judicial interpretation—that if the supermajority threshold for declaring the defied statute unconstitutional isn't reached, the decision declaring it constitutional is drafted by the minority of the court. This solution implies voiding any decisions made by lower courts declaring the defied statute unconstitutional. Another way of clarifying the effects of majoritarian declarations of unconstitutionality is through constitutional or statutory provisions reaffirming the presumption of constitutionality of legislation. These provisions may state that, if the supermajority threshold isn't reached, it'll be assumed that the defied statute stays constitutional, which means that any decision by lower courts declaring it unconstitutional should be considered

171 Id 716–8.
172 Buchanan & Tullock 1999: ch 7–15.
173 Kosar & Vyhnánek 2020: ch 4.
174 Peru CC Law, art 5.
175 Eg, see Constitutional Court of Korea 2021: 77–84.

void. This resembles what happens in Germany when there are ties inside the Federal Constitutional Court's panels.[176]

Additionally, on the precedential value of decisions in which judges don't reach the supermajority threshold, considering statutes' alleged constitutionality—and this chapter's logic that false positives are worse than false negatives—constitutional courts should be bound by their previous decisions not declaring statutes unconstitutional even if this happened just because the supermajority threshold wasn't reached. Yet, if the respective court wants to reverse these precedents, it should only do so by the same supermajority rule needed to declare the defied statute unconstitutional.

Executive and Judicial Decisions

Last but not least, some may wonder why this core case for supermajority rules only applies to constitutional review of legislation and not to constitutional review of non-statutory sources of law, such as executive and judicial decisions. I support supermajority rules in these kinds of constitutional review, but my case for these voting rules doesn't seem to apply as strongly in these contexts as it does in the constitutional review of legislation context.

Recall that, in constitutional review of legislation, false positives are worse than false negatives since: (i) they are harder to rectify than false negatives; and (ii) alongside trumping constitutionally acceptable decisions, they erode majority government, hence being intrinsically worse than false negatives. The first claim is applicable to constitutional review of executive or judicial decisions. So, based on this claim, I favour using supermajority rules to declare these decisions unconstitutional. If a constitutional court mistakenly declares executive or judicial decisions unconstitutional, it's likely that these errors can only be rectified via constitutional amendments.

Yet it's hard to claim that mistakenly declaring executive or judicial decisions unconstitutional erodes majority government. So, in constitutional review of these decisions, it's also hard to claim that false positives are intrinsically worse than false negatives. On constitutional review of executive decisions, it may be argued that mistakenly declaring unconstitutional decisions made by heads of government or cabinet members erodes majority government. After all, these officials are part of the legislative majority (in parliamentary regimes), or are appointed by a directly elected president to act on their behalf (in presidential regimes).[177] But the picture becomes murkier considering that the main task of some executive institutions made of appointed officials—particularly

176 Kelemen 2019: 30–5. Though, in Germany, only the Constitutional Court can review the constitutionality of federal legislation. Kommers & Miller 2012: 3–4.

177 This argument also applies to semi-presidential regimes. In these regimes, cabinet members must be appointed (or supported) by presidents and legislatures. On the differences between presidential, parliamentary, and semi-presidential regimes, see Lijphart 1992; McCormick et al 2022: 188–201.

institutions having some degree of legal or constitutional autonomy from governments, such as central banks or electoral commissions—may not be to enact public policies based on most citizens' or most legislators' preferences.

In turn, on constitutional review of judicial decisions, it's hard to claim that false positives erode majority government since judges' task isn't to 'govern,' in the sense that their task doesn't involve representing citizens' interests. Rather, judges' task is to apply the law to solve the conflicts shown to them. This task doesn't change even if judges are elected, as happens in many US states.[178] Thus, though I support supermajority rules for declaring executive and judicial decisions unconstitutional, the case for doing so seems weaker than the case for supermajority rules in constitutional review of legislation.

Conclusion

There are sound reasons for holding that constitutional courts should use supermajority rules in constitutional review. These voting rules likely outperform majority rule on accuracy grounds, agreement-signalling grounds, and presumption of constitutionality grounds. Moreover, none of the possible objections analysed here provide definitive reasons against these voting rules for declaring statutes unconstitutional.

It's one thing to claim though that supermajority rules should be used in constitutional review; it's quite another to turn this claim into specific policies. Once we accept that supermajority rules should be used for declaring statutes unconstitutional, how should we apply these voting rules? I partially address this question in the final chapter.

References

Ackerman BA, *We the People, vol 1: Foundations* (Harvard University Press 1993)

Albert R & Emrah Oder B (eds), *An Unamendable Constitution? Unamendability in Constitutional Democracies* (Springer 2018)

Aleinikoff A, 'Constitutional Law in the Age of Balancing' (1987) 96 *Yale Law Journal* 943 https://doi.org/10.2307/796529

Alexy R, *A Theory of Constitutional Rights (Julian Rivers* tr, Oxford University Press 2002)

Applebaum A, *Twilight of Democracy: The Seductive Lure of Authoritarianism* (Doubleday 2020)

Arrow KJ, *Social Choice and Individual Values* (2nd edn, Cowles Foundation 1963)

Axelrod R, *The Evolution of Cooperation* (Revised edn, Basic Books 2006)

Bang D & Frith CD, 'Making better decisions in groups' (2017) 4 *Royal Society Open Science* http://dx.doi.org/10.1098/rsos.170193

Barak A, 'Unconstitutional Constitutional Amendments' (2011) 44 *Israel Law Review* 321 https://doi.org/10.1017/S0021223700018082

178 Waldron 2016: 127.

——— *Proportionality: Constitutional Rights and their Limitations* (Cambridge University Press 2012) https://doi.org/10.1017/CBO9781139035293

Barry BM, *How Judges Judge: Empirical Insights into Judicial Decision-Making* (Routledge 2021) https://doi.org/10.4324/9780429023422

Baum L, *The Supreme Court* (13th edn, CQ Press 2019)

Beatty DM, *The Ultimate Rule of Law* (Oxford University Press 2005) https://doi.org/10.1093/acprof:oso/9780199269808.001.0001

Bellamy R, *Political Constitutionalism: A Republican Defence of the Constitutionality of Democracy* (Cambridge University Press 2007) https://doi.org/10.1017/CBO9780511490187

Ben-Yashar RC & Nitzan SI, 'The Optimal Decision-Making Rule for Fixed-Sized Committees in Dichotomous Choice Situations: The General Result' (1997) 38 *International Economic Review* 175 https://doi.org/10.2307/2527413

Binder SA & Smith SS, *Politics or Principle? Filibustering in the United States Senate* (Brookings Institution Press 1997)

Brewer-Carías AR, *Judicial Review in Comparative Law* (Cambridge University Press 1989)

Buchanan J & Tullock G, *The Calculus of Consent: Logical Foundations of Constitutional Democracy* (Liberty Fund 1999) http://oll.libertyfund.org/title/1063

Caluwaerts D, *Confrontation and Deliberation: Deliberative Democracy in Divided Belgium* (Peter Lang 2012)

——— & Deschouwer K, 'Building Bridges Across Political Divides: Experiments on Deliberative Democracy in Deeply Divided Belgium' (2014) 6(3) *European Political Science Review* 427 https://doi.org/10.1017/S1755773913000179

Cambridge Dictionary, 'System' <https://dictionary.cambridge.org/es/diccionario/ingles/system> accessed 10 January 2019

Cappelletti M, *Judicial Review in the Contemporary World* (Bobbs-Merrill 1971)

Caplin A & Nalebuff B, 'On 64%-Majority Rule' (1988) 56 *Econometrica* 787 https://doi.org/10.2307/1912699

Carey JM, 'Legislative Organization' in Binder SA, Rhodes R and Rockman BA (eds), *The Oxford Handbook of Political Institutions* (Oxford University Press 2008) https://doi.org/10.1093/oxfordhb/9780199548460.001.0001

Carson L & Schecter D, 'The Role of Voting in Citizens' Juries' (Research and Development Note, newDemocracy Foundation, 08 March 2017) <https://www.newdemocracy.com.au/research-and-development-notes/> accessed 04 April 2021

Christiano T, *The Constitution of Equality: Democratic Authority and its Limits* (Oxford University Press 2008) https://doi.org/10.1093/acprof:oso/9780198297475.001.0001

Colomer J & McLean I, 'Electing Popes: Approval Balloting and Qualified-Majority Rule' (1998) 29 *Journal of Interdisciplinary History* 1 https://doi.org/10.1162/002219598551616

Condorcet MJA, *Essai sur l'Application de l'analyse à la probabilité des décisions rendues à la pluralité des voix* [Essay on the Application of Mathematics to the Theory of Decision-Making] (first published 1785, Cambridge University Press 2014)

——— *Plan de Constitution présenté a la Convention Nationale* [Constitutional Plan Presented to the National Convention] (Paris, Imprimerie Nationale 1793) https://gallica.bnf.fr/ark:/12148/bpt6k73809

Constitutional Court of Korea, 'Constitutional Court Decisions' (Constitutional Court of Korea 2021) https://library.ccourt.go.kr/en/#/about/pub/case

Corley PC, Steigerwalt A & Ward A, *The Puzzle of Unanimity: Consensus on the United States Supreme Court* (Stanford Law Books 2013) https://doi.org/10.1515/9780804786324

Couso J, 'Trying Democracy in the Shadow on an Authoritarian Legality: Chile's Transition to Democracy and Pinochet's Constitution of 1980' (2011) 29 *Wisconsin International Law Journal* 393

Delli Carpini MX, Lomax Cook F & Jacobs LR, 'Public Deliberation, Discursive Participation and Citizen Engagement: A Review of the Empirical Literature' (2004) 7 *Annual Review of Political Science* 315 https://doi.org/10.1146/annurev.polisci.7.121003.091630

Devine DJ, *Jury Decision Making: The State of the Science* (New York University Press 2012) https://doi.org/10.18574/9780814704981

Doerfler RD & Moyn SM, 'Democratizing the Supreme Court' (2021) 109 *California Law Review* 1703 https://www.californialawreview.org/print/democratizing-the-supreme-court

Dworkin R, *Freedom's Law: The Moral Reading of the American Constitution* (Harvard University Press 1996)

Ely JH, *Democracy and Distrust: A Theory of Judicial Review* (Harvard University Press 1980)

Elster J, *Solomonic Judgments: Studies in the Limitations of Rationality* (Cambridge University Press 1989)

——— *Securities Against Misrule: Juries, Assemblies, Elections* (Cambridge University Press 2013) https://doi.org/10.1017/CBO9781139382762

Epstein L, Segal JA & Spaeth HJ, 'The Norm of Consensus in the US Supreme Court' (2001) 45 *American Journal of Political Science* 362 https://doi.org/10.2307/2669346

——— & Martin AD, 'Is the Roberts Court Especially Activist? A Study of Invalidating (and Upholding) Federal, State, and Local Laws' (2012) 61 *Emory Law Journal* 737 https://scholarlycommons.law.emory.edu/elj/vol61/iss4/3

——— Segal JA, Spaeth HJ, & Walker TG, *The Supreme Court Compendium: Two Centuries of Data, Decisions, and Developments* (7th edn, CQ Press 2021)

Estlund DM, *Democratic Authority: A Philosophical Framework* (Princeton University Press 2008)

Ferejohn J & Pasquino P, 'Constitutional Adjudication: Lessons from Europe' (2004) 82 *Texas Law Review 1671* https://heinonline.org/HOL/P?h=hein.journals/tlr82andi=1687

Ferrer Mac-Gregor E (coord.) *Crónica de Tribunales Constitucionales en Iberoamérica [Chronicle of Constitutional Courts in Iberian America] (UNAM Marcial Pons* 2009)

Fish MS & Kroenig M, *The Handbook of National Legislatures: A Global Survey* (Cambridge University Press 2009)

Fishkin JS, *When the People Speak: Deliberative Democracy and Public Consultation* (Oxford University Press 2009) https://doi.org/10.1093/acprof:osobl/9780199604432.001.0001

——— 'Deliberative Polling' in Bächtinger A, Dryzek JS, Mansbridge J, & Warren ME (eds), *The Oxford Handbook of Deliberative Democracy* (Oxford University Press 2018) https://doi.org/10.1093/oxfordhb/9780198747369.013.10

Gersen J & Vermeule A, 'Chevron as a Voting Rule' (2007) 116 *Yale Law Journal* 676 https://doi.org/10.2307/20455738

Gigerenzer G, Todd PM and The ABC Research Group, *Simple Heuristics that Make Us Smart* (Oxford University Press 1999)

Ginsburg T & Huq AZ, *How to Save a Constitutional Democracy* (University of Chicago Press 2019)

Grofman B, Owen G & Feld SL, 'Thirteen Theorems in Search for the Truth' (1983) 15 *Theory and Decision* 261 https://doi.org/10.1007/BF00125672

Hacking I, 'Jacques Bernoulli's Art of Conjecturing' (1971) 22(3) *British Journal for the Philosophy of Science* 209

Harari YN, *Homo Deus: A Brief History of Tomorrow* (Signal 2016)

Henderson MT, 'From Seriatim to Consensus and Back Again: A Theory of Dissent' (2007) 7 *Supreme Court Review* 283

Hessick A & Jordan S, 'Setting the Size of the Supreme Court' (2009) 41 *Arizona State Law Journal* 645 https://scholarship.law.slu.edu/faculty/185/

Hong L & Page SE, 'Groups of diverse problem solvers can outperform groups of high-ability problem solvers' (2004) 101(46) *Proceedings of the National Academy of Sciences of the United States of America* 16385 https://doi.org/10.1073/pnas.0403723101

Hübner Mendes C, *Constitutional Courts and Deliberative Democracy* (Oxford University Press 2015) https://doi.org/10.1093/acprof:oso/9780199670451.001.0001

Huneeus C, *The Pinochet Regime (Lake Sagaris tr*, Lynne Rienner 2007)

Hunt M, Hooper HJ & Yowell P (eds), *Parliaments and Human Rights: Redressing the Democratic Deficit* (Hart Publishing 2015) https://doi.org/10.5040/9781474201704

Husa J, 'Guarding the Constitutionality of Laws in Nordic Countries: A Comparative Perspective' (2000) 48(3) *American Journal of Comparative Law* 345 https://doi.org/10.2307/840859

Kahana T, 'The Notwithstanding Mechanism and Public Discussion: Lessons from the Ignored Practice of Section 33 of the Charter' (2001) 44(3) *Canadian Public Administration/Administration Publique du Canada* 255 https://doi.org/10.1111/j.1754-7121.2001.tb00891.x

Kahneman D, *Thinking, Fast and Slow* (Farrar, Straus and Giroux 2011)

——— Slovic P & Tversky A (eds), *Judgment Under Uncertainty: Heuristics and Biases* (Cambridge University Press 1982) https://doi.org/10.1017/CBO9780511809477

Kelemen K, *Judicial Dissent in European Constitutional Courts: A Comparative and Legal Perspective* (Routledge 2019) https://doi.org/10.4324/9781315590769

Kelsen H 'The Nature and Development of Constitutional Adjudication' in Lars Vinx (ed), *The Guardian of the Constitution: Hans Kelsen and Carl Schmitt on the Limits of Constitutional Law (first published 1928*, Cambridge University Press 2015) https://doi.org/10.1017/CBO9781316136256

Keynes JM, *A Treatise on Probability (first published 1920*, Cosimo 2007)

King JA, 'Institutional Approaches to Judicial Restraint' (2008) 28 *Oxford Journal of Legal Studies* 409 https://doi.org/10.1093/ojls/gqn020

Kommers DP & Miller RA, *The Constitutional Jurisprudence of the Federal Republic of Germany* (3rd edn, Duke University Press 2012)

Kosar D & Vyhnánek L, 'The Constitutional Court of Czechia' in von Bogdandy A, Huber P, & Grabenwarter C (eds), *The Max Planck Handbooks in European Public Law, vol 3: Constitutional Adjudication: Institutions* (Oxford University Press 2020)

Krishnamurthi G, 'For Judicial Majoritarianism' (2020) 22 *University of Pennsylvania Journal of Constitutional Law 1201* https://scholarship.law.upenn.edu/jcl/vol22/iss5/2

Kumm M, 'Institutionalising Socratic Contestation: The Rationalist Human Rights Paradigm, Legitimate Authority, and the Point of Judicial Review' (2007) 1(2) *European Journal of Legal Studies* 153 http://hdl.handle.net/1814/7708

Lagerspetz E, 'Wisdom and numbers' (2010) 49(1) *Social Science Information* 29 https://doi.org/10.1177/0539018409354475

——— *Social Choice and Democratic Values* (Springer 2016) https://doi.org/10.1007/978-3-319-23261-4

Landau D, 'Abusive Constitutionalism' (2013) 47 *University of California, Davis Law Review* 189 https://ir.law.fsu.edu/articles/555

Landemore H, *Democratic Reason: Politics, Collective Intelligence and the Rule of the Many* (Princeton University Press 2013)

Laplace PS, *Essai philosophique sur les probabilités [Philosophical Essay on Probabilities] (first published 1825*, Cambridge University Press 2009)

——— *A Philosophical Essay on Probabilities* (first published 1825, Frederick Wilson Truscott & Frederick Lincoln Emory tr, Chapman and Hall 1902) https://bayes.wustl.edu/Manual/laplace_A_philosophical_essay_on_probabilities.pdf

Leahy J & Schipani A, 'Bolsonaro Appoints Judge who Helped Jail Lula as Justice Minister' *Financial Times* (London, 1 November 2018) https://www.ft.com/content/9e134242-dded-11e8-8f50-cbae5495d92b

Levitsky S & Ziblatt D, *How Democracies Die* (Crown 2018)

Lijphart A (ed), *Parliamentary Versus Presidential Government* (Oxford University Press 1992)

——— *Patterns of Democracy: Government Forms and Performance in Thirty-Six Countries* (2nd edn, Yale University Press 2012)

Linz JJ & Stepan A, 'Towards Consolidated Democracies' (1996) 7 *Journal of Democracy* 14 https://doi.org/10.1353/jod.1996.0031

List C & Pettit P, *Group Agency: The Possibility, Design, and Status of Corporate Agents* (Cambridge University Press 2011) https://doi.org./10.1093/acprof:oso/9780199591565.001.0001

——— & Goodin RE, 'Epistemic Democracy: Generalising the Condorcet Jury Theorem' (2001) 9 *Journal of Political Philosophy* 277 https://doi.org/10.1111/1467-9760.00128

Lukianoff G & Haidt J, *The Coddling of the American Mind: How Good Intentions and Bad Ideas are Setting Up a Generation for Failure* (Penguin 2018)

McCormick J, Hague R, & Harrop M, *Comparative Government and Politics: An Introduction* (12th edn, Bloomsbury 2022)

McGinnis JO & Rappaport MB, 'Majority and Supermajority Rules: Three Views of the Capitol' (2007) 85 *Texas Law Review* 1115

——— 'The Condorcet Case for Supermajority Rules' (2008) 16 *Supreme Court Economic Review* 67 https://www.journals.uchicago.edu/doi/abs/10.1086/655880

McHenry J, 'Papers of Dr James McHenry on the Federal Convention of 1787' (1906) 11 *The American History Review* 595 https://doi.org/10.2307/1836024

McLean I & Hewitt F, 'Section 2: The Theory of Voting' in McLean I and Hewitt F (eds), *Condorcet: Foundations of Social Choice and Political Theory* (Edward Elgar 1994)

Mendelberg T, 'The Deliberative Citizen: Theory and Evidence' in Delli Carpini M, Huddy L and Shapiro RY (eds), *Research in Micropolitics*, vol 6 (Elsevier Press 2002)

Mercier H & Sperber D, *The Enigma of Reason* (Harvard University Press 2017)

Möller K, *The Global Model of Constitutional Rights* (Oxford University Press 2012) https://doi.org/10.1093/acprof:oso/9780199664603.001.0001

Mounk Y, *The People vs Democracy: Why Our Freedom is in Danger and How to Save It* (Harvard University Press 2018)

Neblo MA, *Deliberative Democracy between Theory and Practice* (Cambridge University Press 2015) https://doi.org/10.1017/CBO9781139226592

Nussbaum MC, *The Monarchy of Fear: A Philosopher Looks at Our Political Crisis* (Simon and Schuster 2018)

O'Flynn I & Caluwaerts D, 'Deliberation in Deeply Divided Societies' in André Bächtinger, John S Dryzek, Jane Mansbridge and Mark E Warren (eds), *The Oxford Handbook of Deliberative Democracy* (Oxford University Press 2018) https://doi.org/10.1093/oxfordhb/9780198747369.013.51

Ortega y Gasset J, '¿Qué son los valores? Introducción a una estimativa' [What are Values? Introduction to an Estimation] in Ortega y Gasset J, *Obras Completas de José Ortega y Gasset [The Complete Works of José Ortega y Gasset]*, vol 6 (first published 1923, 6th edn, Revista de Occidente 1964)

Page SE, *The Difference: How the Power of Diversity Creates Better Groups, Firms, Schools, and Societies* (Princeton University Press 2007)

Participedia, 'Method: Citizen's Jury' (Participedia) <https://participedia.net/method/155> accessed 04 April 2022

Pasquino P, 'E Pluribus Unum: Disclosed and Undisclosed Votes in Constitutional/Supreme Courts' in Elster J (ed), *Secrecy and Publicity in Votes and Debates* (Cambridge University Press 2015) https://doi.org/10.1017/CBO9781316015360

Pinker S, *The Better Angels of Our Nature: Why Violence Has Declined* (Reprint edn, Penguin 2012)

Putnam H, *The Collapse of the Fact/Value Dichotomy and Other Essays Including the Rosenthal Lectures* (Harvard University Press 2002)

Rawls J, *Political Liberalism (Expanded edn*, Columbia University Press 2005)

Rivera León M, 'Control and paralysis? A context-sensitive anaysis of objections to supermajorities in constitutional adjudication' (2023) *International Journal of Constitutional Law* 1 https://doi.org/10.1093/icon/moad074

Roznai Y, *Unconstitutional Constitutional Amendments: The Limits of Amendment Powers* (Oxford University Press 2017)

Ryfe DM, 'Does Deliberative Democracy Work?' (2005) 8 *Annual Review of Political Science* 49 https://doi.org/10.1146/annurev.polisci.8.032904.154633

Saari DG, 'The Generic Existence of a Core for q-Rules' (1997) 9(2) *Economic Theory* 219 https://doi.org/10.1007/BF01213800

Sadurski W, *Poland's Constitutional Breakdown* (Oxford University Press 2019) https://doi.org/10.1093/oso/9780198840503.001.0001

Saks MJ, 'What Do Jury Expertiments Tell Us about How Juries (Should) Make Decisions' (1997) 6 *Southern California Interdisciplinary Law Journal* 1

Sartori G, *Comparative Constitutional Engineering: An Inquiry into Structures, Incentives, and Outcomes* (2nd edn, New York University Press 1997)

Schauer F, 'Easy Cases' (1985) 58 *Southern California Law Review* 399
Schwartzberg M, 'The arbitrariness of supermajority rules' (2010) 49(1) *Social Science Information* 61 https://doi.org/10.1177/0539018409354474
——— *Counting the Many.* The Origins and Limits of Supermajority Rule (Cambridge University Press 2013) https://doi.org/10.1017/CBO9781139013970
Segal JA & Spaeth HJ, *The Supreme Court and the Attitudinal Model Revisited* (Cambridge University Press 2002) https://doi.org/10.1017/CBO9780511615696
Seok Hong J, 'Signalling the Turn: The Supermajority Requirement and Judicial Power on the Constitutional Court of South Korea' (2019) 67 *American Journal of Comparative Law* 177 https://doi.org/10.1093/ajcl/avz008
Shugerman JH, 'A Six-Three Rule: Reviving Consensus and Deference on the Supreme Court' (2002) 37 *Georgia Law Review 893 https://heinonline.org/HOL/P?h=hein.journals/geolr37andi=915*
Smith G & Setälä M, 'Mini-Publics and Deliberative Democracy' in André Bächtinger, John S Dryzek, Jane Mansbridge and Mark E Warren (eds), *The Oxford Handbook of Deliberative Democracy* (Oxford University Press 2018) https://doi.org/10.1093/oxfordhb/9780198747369.013.27
Steiner J, *The Foundations of Deliberative Democracy: Empirical Research and Normative Implications* (Cambridge University Press 2012) https://doi.org/10.1017/CBO9781139057486
Stone Sweet A, 'Constitutional Courts' in Rosenfeld M and Sajó A (eds), *The Oxford Handbook of Comparative Constitutional Law* (Oxford University Press 2012) https://doi.org/10.1093/oxfordhb/9780199578610.013.0040
Sunstein CR, Schkade D, Ellman LM & Sawicki A, *Are Judges Political? An Empirical Analysis of the Federal Judiciary* (Brookings Institution Press 2006)
Taleb NN, *Antifragile: Things that Gain from Disorder* (2019 Box Set edn, Random House 2012)
——— *Skin in the Game: Hidden Asymmetries in Daily Life* (2019 Box Set edn, Random House 2018)
Tiede LB & Ponce AF, 'Evaluating Theories of Decision-making on the Peruvian Constitutional Tribunal' (2014) 6(2) *Journal of Politics in Latin America* 139 https://doi.org/10.1177/1866802X1400600205
Thayer JB, *The Origin and Scope of the American Doctrine of Constitutional Law* (Little, Brown, and Company 1893) https://openlibrary.org/books/OL23449489M/The_Origin_and_Scope_of_the_American_Doctrine_of_Constitutional_Law
Thompson A, 'Does Diversity Trump Ability? An Example of the Misuse of Mathematics in the Social Sciences' (2014) 61(9) *Notices of the American Mathematical Society 1024* http://dx.doi.org/10.1090/noti1163
Tsakyrakis S, 'Proportionality: An Assault on Human Rights?' (2009) 7(3) *International Journal of Constitutional Law* 468 https://doi.org/10.1093/icon/mop011
Tsebelis G, *Veto Players: How Political Institutions Work* (Princeton University Press 2002) https://doi.org/10.1515/9781400831456
Tushnet M, 'Constitutional Hardball' (2004) 37 *John Marshall Law Review* 523 http://repository.jmls.edu/lawreview/vol37/iss2/7
Urbina FJ, *A Critique of Proportionality and Balancing* (Cambridge University Press 2017) https://doi.org/10.1017/9781316796276
Vermeule A, *Judging Under Uncertainty: An Institutional Theory of Legal Interpretation* (Harvard University Press 2006)

——— 'Should We Have Lay Justices?' (2007) 59(6) *Stanford Law Review 1569* http://www.jstor.org/stable/40040396
Vidmar N & Hans VP, *American Juries: The Verdict* (Prometheus Books 2007)
Vinx L, 'Introduction' in Vinx L (ed), *The Guardian of the Constitution: Hans Kelsen and Carl Schmitt on the Limits of Constitutional Law* (Cambridge University Press 2015) https://doi.org/10.1017/CBO9781316136256
Waldron J, *Law and Disagreement* (Oxford University Press 1999) https://doi.org/10.1093/acprof:oso/9780198262138.001.0001
——— *Political Political Theory: Essays on Institutions* (Harvard University Press 2016) https://doi.org/10.4159/9780674970342
Webber GCN, *The Negotiable Constitution* (Cambridge University Press 2009)
Weinrib J, *Dimensions of Dignity: The Theory and Practice of Modern Constitutional Law* (Cambridge University Press 2016) https://doi.org/10.1017/CBO9781316026663
Wilson B, 'Decision-Making in the Supreme Court' (1986) 36(3) *University of Toronto Law Journal* 227 https://heinonline.org/HOL/P?h=hein.journals/utlj36andi=231
Yowell P, *Constitutional Rights and Constitutional Design: Moral and Empirical Reasoning in Judicial Review* (Hart Publishing 2018) https://doi.org/10.5040/9781509913626
Zakaria F, 'The Rise of Illiberal Democracy' (1997) 76 *Foreign Affairs* 22 https://doi.org/10.2307/20048274
Zink JR, Spriggs II JF & Scott JT, 'The Influence of Decision Attributes on Individuals' Views of Court Opinions' (2009) 71(3) *Journal of Politics* 909 https://doi.org/10.1017/s0022381609090793

7 Practical Issues

Now that I've argued that constitutional courts should use supermajority rules for declaring legislation unconstitutional, in this chapter, I tackle some of the main issues that one faces when applying these voting rules in the real world. Specifically, I focus on three issues. First, considering that supermajority rules are indeterminate—that is, that they are a range of voting rules[1]—how should one choose a supermajority rule? I claim that, between the judges present, one should choose the supermajority rule that's closest to majority rule. I focus on this issue since, once it's decided that a group's voting rule should be a supermajority rule, specifying the supermajority rule is unavoidable.

Second, once a supermajority rule is chosen, how should one design the voting protocol, that is, the particular way in which judges vote? I claim that, provided a formal separation between debating and voting: (i) at the time of voting, judges' votes should be secret; and (ii) at the time of counting the votes, judges' votes should be public, in the sense that their peers, other officials, and citizens generally should be able to link the votes with specific judges. I focus on this issue since the voting protocol's design can influence whether coercion against dissenters and information cascades—phenomena that can severely affect judges' accuracy—occur between them.

Lastly, since judges debate and vote, how should one mix these practices? I claim that one should use a procedure of 'debating-voting'. Put differently, one should use a procedure in which, after receiving the parties' claims, a judge prepares a decision proposal to be debated by all the judges in face to face meetings. During these meetings, judges should try to decide unanimously by non-opposition; meaning, they should try to agree on a common decision proposal that no judge opposes, without having to count each judge's opinion on it. Yet, if such unanimous agreement isn't possible, the judges should vote. I focus on this issue since the way in which deliberation and voting are mixed influences whether judges benefit from these practices' accuracy boosting traits.

1 Schwartzberg 2010.

DOI: 10.4324/9781032723952-7

In short, I argue for the following decision procedure: imagine a court of, say, eleven judges. And imagine that this court needs a quorum of seven judges for deciding, and that this quorum is met. Once the judges are presented with the parties' claims, a judge is tasked with writing a decision proposal. Later, the judges meet face to face to debate the proposal and try to unanimously agree on it by non-opposition. Depending on the court's time-constraints, if the court can't reach such an agreement, the judges vote. In this case, the judges use paper ballots in which they must indicate their names (or in which their names are indicated) alongside their judgments. While writing the decision proposal, the judge in charge of drafting it may discuss it with their peers before the face to face meetings.

If the judges vote to declare a statute unconstitutional, the votes favouring this declaration must reach the supermajority threshold that's closest to majority rule. Since seven judges are present, this threshold is five judges. Still, if nine or eleven judges were present, this threshold would be six or seven judges, respectively. If the supermajority threshold isn't reached, defied statutes stay constitutional.[2] The judges would be allowed to publish separate opinions. The rest of this court's decision procedures may be akin to those already existing in constitutional courts.

I insist on applying the supermajority rule among judges present rather than among all judges to avoid cases in which—since not everyone is present—a very small minority can block a declaration of unconstitutionality. For example, in the South Korean court, Seok Hong claims that, if there are only seven judges present, 'two justices prevail over five justices who rule a law unconstitutional.'[3] This may happen since this court has nine judges and the supermajority rule—in this case, a six-to-three rule—applies between them all. Thus, to prevent these situations, supermajority rules should be applied among judges present, not among all judges.

Moreover, it's worth recalling that, despite the seemingly universal nature of this chapter's claims, they are hypotheses. Thus, they may not work in every cultural context, including courts that in principle fit within this book's scope. There may be factors that I haven't considered—and that, at this level of analysis, I can't consider—that may curb (or even trump) the positive effects of the practices I argue for here. Still, it's worth arguing for these practices since this can at least open one's mind to new possibilities of organising (and hopefully improving) judicial decision procedures.

Let's tackle each of the issues on implementing supermajority rules in constitutional review.

2 As mentioned in Chapter 2, if the court has an even number of judges present, we may eliminate the presiding judge's casting vote. Thus, if there are ties, defied statutes stay constitutional.
3 2019: 200.

Choosing the Supermajority Rule

Before arguing why, among judges present, one should choose the supermajority rule that's closest to majority rule, it's worth noting that there doesn't seem to be much research on specifying supermajority rules. In political philosophy, Schwartzberg's[4] research is key. And in social choice theory, research by Nitzan & Paroush,[5] and Caplin & Nalebuff,[6] stand out. I mainly consider Schwartzberg's research. Conversely, I don't consider Nitzan & Paroush's research, nor do I consider Caplin & Nalebuff's research, since this research has assumptions that I've rejected in constitutional review. (In Nitzan & Paroush's research, the assumption that errors are symmetrical,[7] and in Caplin & Nalebuff's research, the assumption that options are multiple.)[8]

I claim that, in constitutional review, judges should use the supermajority rule that's closest to majority rule since: (i) this supermajority rule minimises coercion against dissenters, false negatives, and decision costs; and (ii) supermajority rules' indeterminacy suggest caution.

Let's refine these claims.

Need to Minimise Coercion, False Negatives, and Decision Costs

I've suggested that unanimity rule may coerce dissenters. This happens not only due to potential peer pressure, but also since, to avoid such pressure, dissenters may behave in conformist ways; hence censoring themselves and deferring to their peers instead of voting sincerely. According to mathematical[9] and empirical research,[10] unanimity rule's potentially coercive effects seem severe. Further, I've held that supermajority rules may be more or less flexible depending on their closeness to unanimity rule. Though supermajority rules allow group members to decide while simultaneously dissenting, the closer to unanimity rule a supermajority rule is, the more inflexible a supermajority rule becomes, hence having a higher potential to coerce dissenters. Conversely, the farther from unanimity rule a supermajority rule is—put differently, the closer to majority rule a supermajority rule is—the more flexible a supermajority rule becomes, hence having a lower potential to coerce dissenters.[11]

Moreover, recall that, though I've held in the previous chapter that false positives (that is, declaring statutes unconstitutional when they aren't so) are worse than false negatives (that is, not declaring statutes unconstitutional

4 2010. See also Schwartzberg 2013.
5 1984.
6 1988.
7 1984: 260.
8 1988.
9 Laplace [1825] 2009: 165–74; Schwartzberg 2013: 87–8.
10 Saks 1997: 39–41; Vidmar & Hans 2007: 142–4; Devine 2012: 152–3, 158–61; Schwartzberg 2013: 95–7.
11 Laplace [1825] 2009: 165–74; Schwartzberg 2013: 87–8.

when they are so), I also held that the worry that supermajority rules may produce excessive false negatives is fair. And though I rejected the claim that, in constitutional review, parties should have equal prior odds of winning, I also held that claimants should at least have a good chance of doing so. Finally, in the previous chapter, I held that supermajority rules may boost constitutional courts' decision costs. Yet I also claimed that there's a directly proportional link between constitutional courts' decision costs and how high or low a supermajority threshold is.[12] Thus, increases in these costs may be tackled by calibrating supermajority rules downward.

In these circumstances, the most appropriate action is to choose the supermajority rule that's closest to majority rule. This supermajority rule produces at least[13] an absolute margin of three in groups with odd members present. For example, in a nine-judges court in which all judges are present, the supermajority rule that's closest to majority rule is a six-to-three rule. Thus, this voting rule produces at least an absolute margin of three since six minus three equals three.

When compared against other voting rules, this supermajority rule minimises the risk of coercion against dissenters by giving judges the most chances of dissenting. Further, the supermajority rule that's closest to majority rule minimises the risk of producing excessive false negatives and gives claimants a better chance of winning than other voting rules, though without renouncing the premise that false positives are worse than false negatives. Thus, within a framework in which constitutional courts' voting rules should be biased against false positives, in principle, the supermajority rule that's closest to majority rule tackles the risk of producing excessive false negatives and enables claimants to win in the most satisfactory way. Lastly, the supermajority rule that's closest to majority rule reduces the most constitutional courts' decision costs vis-à-vis other supermajority rules.[14] After all, reaching agreements between 50% of the judges present plus two judges present is easier than reaching agreements between 50% of the judges present plus three judges present, 50% of the judges present plus four judges present, etc. So, when reducing decision costs while benefitting from supermajority rules, choosing the supermajority rule that's closest to majority rule seems one's safest bet.

Indeterminacy Suggests Caution

My second argument for choosing the supermajority rule that's closest to majority rule among judges present is based on philosopher Melissa Schwartzberg's analysis of supermajority rules in constitutional amendment

12 Buchanan & Tullock 1999: ch 7–15.

13 I use the qualification 'at least' since, depending on the case, the absolute margin may be higher than that produced by the supermajority rule.

14 Id.

procedures.[15] In short, Schwartzberg holds that specifying supermajority rules is problematic due to these rules' indeterminacy. Thus, this research suggests that, when deciding to use supermajority rules, one should tread carefully.

Schwartzberg claims that supermajority rules' indeterminacy is a main hurdle for justifying them in constitutional amendment procedures. Though there may be good reasons for using supermajority rules *generally*, these reasons aren't conclusive for using *specific* supermajority rules. Put differently, if constitution drafters or legislators choose a supermajority rule for amending the constitution, the reasons behind that choice aren't strong enough for supporting it over other supermajority rules.[16] For example, if constitution drafters or legislators choose a 2/3 rule to keep constitutional stability, that aim can also be accomplished by a 4/7 rule, a 3/5 rule, or a 3/4 rule. Thus, the need for constitutional stability can't justify a 2/3 rule over its alternatives. Due to supermajority rules' indeterminacy—Schwartzberg claims—one may randomly choose a supermajority rule. When one can't choose between two or more options in justified ways (either since the options are indeterminate, immensurable,[17] or on a par),[18] random selection seems a good way of choosing.[19]

But if one randomly chooses a supermajority rule, one may have to justify that choice to people dissatisfied with the existing constitutional arrangement. This may be especially challenging if the constitution entrenches distributive inequalities that can't be easily solved *due to* the supermajority rule.[20] As Schwartzberg holds, when supermajority rules' indeterminacy 'intersects with highly salient distributive inequalities and, most critically, with the self-correcting nature of the [constitution],'[21] the impossibility of justifying a supermajority rule's choice—or, put differently, the impossibility of definitively answering the question: '[w]hy is *this* the threshold rather than another?'[22]—is 'especially grave.'[23] Thus, Schwartzberg is sceptical of using random selection for specifying supermajority rules in constitutional amendment procedures. For Schwartzberg, '[t]o the extent that we want our constitutional norms, especially those with considerable distributive implications ... to be supported by reasons, randomization will be a poor strategy.'[24]

15 2010.
16 Id.
17 On immensurability, see De Sousa 1974; Sinnott-Armstrong 1985; Griffin 1988: ch 5; Chang 1997; Berlin 2002; Raz 2009: ch 13.
18 On parity, see Chang 2014. See also Caviedes 2017.
19 For arguments in favour of random decision making in different contexts, see Duxbury 1999; Goodwin 2005; Stone 2011a; Stone 2011b.
20 2010: 71–6.
21 Id 71.
22 Id 74.
23 Id 71.
24 Id 79.

Schwartzberg's claims can't be immediately transplanted to supermajority rules in constitutional review. After all, using supermajority rules to guard the constitutionality of legislation isn't the same as using them to curb constitutional changes. Actually, by guarding statutes' alleged constitutionality, supermajority rules give legislatures more space for interpreting the constitution—including interpreting the constitution in ways beneficial to those that initially stood to lose from it. And even if Schwartzberg's claims carry over to supermajority rules in constitutional review, these rules' indeterminacy problem would be curbed since constitutional courts are relatively small groups. So, the amount of supermajority rules available for constitutional courts is lower than the amount of supermajority rules available for constitutional assemblies and legislatures.

True, justifying a choice between supermajority rules may be especially hard in assemblies of 100 or more people. But this problem doesn't seem severe in groups of five members, seven members, nine members, 11 members, 13 members, or 15 members (constitutional courts' usual sizes).[25] In these groups, options are more limited, and thus more determinate. For example, in a nine-judges court with all its members present, one would only have to randomly choose between three supermajority rules: six-to-three, seven-to-two, and eight-to-one; in an 11-judge court with all its members present, one would only have to randomly choose between four supermajority rules: seven-to-four, eight-to-three, nine-to-two, and ten-to-one, etc.

Yet, Schwartzberg's research suggests that choosing the most appropriate supermajority rule is challenging and involves significant discretion. In constitutional amendment procedures, the challenges stem from the lack of justification to those hurt by existing constitutional arrangements. In constitutional review, the challenges stem from the need to balance: (i) having a neutral voting rule that boosts judges' accuracy; and (ii) having a voting rule that's flexible, doesn't produce excessive false negatives, gives claimants a good chance of winning, and doesn't excessively increase decision costs. Thus, Schwartzberg's thoughts suggest caution—caution that, in turn, suggests choosing the supermajority rule that's closest to majority rule.

Shaping the Voting Protocol

Alongside specifying the supermajority rule, a second challenge one must tackle is shaping the voting protocol. That is, shaping the specific methods by which judges cast their votes on the constitutionality of legislation.[26] Voting protocols usually address issues such as the object of the vote (should group members vote on decisions? Or on the reasons behind those decisions?); the

25 Stone Sweet 2012; Kelemen 2019: 18, 23–8.

26 For overviews of the challenges involved in shaping voting protocols—and decision procedures generally—see Bentham [1843] 1999; Elster 2013; Elster 2015; Lagerspetz 2016.

supporting medium of the vote (should group members use paper ballots? Pebbles? Shells? Coloured balls? Electronic machines? Or just their hands or mouths to vote?); the way in which judgments are expressed in a vote (should group members express just one judgment? Or rather rank judgments?); etc.

I analyse two issues that the voting protocol should address: first, whether votes should be secret or public; and second, once it's assumed that judges' votes should be public, how to avoid 'public sequential voting.' That is, how to avoid judges voting publicly and one after the other. I focus on these issues since the way in which they are regulated can boost or hinder coercion against dissenters and information cascades, hence also boosting or hindering judges' accuracy.

Secret versus Public Voting

To understand why judges should vote secretly or publicly, we must assess the strengths and flaws of these voting methods. Secret voting' s main strength is that it produces 'maximally autonomous judgments;'[27] meaning, secret voting ensures that group members' opinions aren't due to coercion. This happens since, under secret voting, the only person knowing which voter expressed which opinion is the one casting the respective vote; unless voters willingly reveal that information—or the voting process is somehow tampered with.[28] Still, in groups that must justify their decisions, secret voting may hinder accountability by allowing group members to vote according to preferences rather than judgments. Since, under secret voting, group members don't have to publicly explain how they vote, they may vote according to their purely subjective inclinations rather than trying to rationally ground their vote.[29] In sum, they may vote according to Juvenal's adage, 'thus I will, thus I command, my will stands for the reason'[30] rather than as officials that must explain their decisions to others.

Conversely, public voting's main strength is its capacity to produce '*maximally responsible judgments.*'[31] Under public voting, group members vote 'under the eyes and control of others.'[32] So, public voting allows group members to link some opinions to their peers, hence making them accountable. But since, under public voting, each voter can see their peers' opinions, public voting can produce coercion against dissenters. And when group members vote sequentially—that is, when group members vote one after the other—public voting may produce information cascades since, by knowing how their peers

27 Vermeule 2015: 223.
28 Bentham [1843] 1999: 145–9; Elster 2013: 128–38, 232; Manin 2015: 209–14.
29 Bentham [1843] 1999: 144–5; Elster 2013: 232. This is why Brennan & Pettit (1990) argue against secret voting for choosing officials. For a critique, see Manin 2015.
30 *Sic volo, sic jubeo, sic pro ratione voluntas.* Juvenal, cited in Pasquino 2015: 198.
31 Vermeule 2015: 223.
32 Manin 2015: 211.

voted, group members may be tempted to just copy them for any number of reasons (eg, sloth; insecurity about their own judgments; excessive agreeableness; wanting to be part of 'the winners' rather than 'the losers;' wanting to appear as a team player rather than as a contrarian, rebel, or troublemaker; etc.).[33] Therefore, by producing information cascades, public voting may erode statistical independence, and thus Condorcet accuracy.

Given that constitutional courts' decisions must be grounded in judgments, it isn't convenient to apply secret voting in them. Since judges must make rationally defensible decisions, the chance of linking specific votes to specific judges ensures that they'll try to explain their votes to others.[34]

Yet secret voting has a key virtue that should be considered when shaping the supermajority protocol: the fact that, *at the time of voting*, nobody but the voters themselves knows the content of their votes. This curbs coercion against dissenters and information cascades; two desirable effects considering that one of deliberation's goals is that judges reach sincere agreements, and that information cascades erode their statistical independence. Thus, given that judges' votes should be public, one should try to produce some of secret voting's salutary effects against coercion against dissenters and information cascades, while simultaneously producing public voting's accountability effects. I address how to produce these effects in what follows.

Avoiding Public Sequential Voting

Sequential voting can stimulate information cascades. In most forms of sequential voting (forms that could be called 'public sequential voting'), group members can see how their peers vote at the time of voting, thus being able to just copy them. For this same reason, public sequential voting seems ripe with chances for coercion, particularly if group members dissent with their peers.

Now, a constitutional court may not have distinct, formally defined stages in which judges debate and vote. Instead, these activities may be somewhat entangled. For example, in the Brazilian,[35] Canadian,[36] US[37] and UK[38] courts, judges state their opinions and justify them at around the same time, without there being a full separation between these two acts. As suggested in Chapter 5, in these kinds of courts, rather than avoiding public sequential voting, judges may curb information cascades by voting in 'reverse order of seniority;'[39] meaning, younger judges (or those appointed earlier) vote—and

33 Sunstein 2006: 88–92; Farnsworth 2007: 136–9; Devine 2012: 169–71; Barry 2021: 218–9.
34 Pasquino 2015: 199–200.
35 do Vale 2017: 174–97.
36 Songer et al 2012: 87–93
37 Baum 2019: 116–7.
38 Paterson 2013: 84–91.
39 For examples of courts whose judges vote this way, see Wilson 1986: 236; Edwards 2003: 1665; Farnsworth 2007: 138; Paterson 2013: 84–5; do Vale 2017: 174–6; Kelemen 2019: 43; Barry 2021: 218.

justify their votes—before older judges (or those appointed later). Still, though this procedure prevents judges from seeing how their presumably more influential peers vote, it doesn't prevent them from seeing how their *other* peers vote. Thus, though this procedure curbs information cascades, this procedure doesn't seem as effective as avoiding public sequential voting altogether, which requires a formal separation between debating and voting.

If this separation between debating and voting is applied, there are at least three options to public sequential voting that keep group members' accountability. First, one may use public simultaneous voting; meaning, voting methods in which group members vote at the same time, while watching how their peers vote. Second, one may use a voting procedure that, following Elster[40]—and for lack of a better term—one may call 'secret-public voting.' This option keeps sequentiality, but eliminates publicity at the time of voting. Third, one may establish voting procedures that avoid sequentiality *and* eliminate publicity at the time of voting. Let's assess these options.

One may apply public simultaneous voting. Public simultaneous voting requires group members to vote at the same time, while also allowing each group member to see how their peers vote. Hence, public simultaneous voting avoids simultaneity while keeping publicity at the time of voting. Some typical forms of public simultaneous voting are hand raising and electronic voting. These voting methods 'avoid' rather than 'eliminate' simultaneity since, though they incentivise group members to vote at the same time, they can't ensure that they do so. After all, though group members are supposed to vote simultaneously, a group member can always raise a hand (or press a button) after another. As Bentham holds, in public simultaneous voting, 'if two men agreed to play the parts of master and slave … [the slave] may wait to observe the part taken by the master's voice or hand, so that his may take the same.'[41]

An institution currently using public simultaneous voting to avoid information cascades is the US Federal Drug Administration ('FDA').[42] Specifically, the FDA uses public simultaneous voting in its advisory committees. Advisory Committees are expert groups in charge of checking whether new drugs are safe to be sold. According to Urfalino & Costa,[43] initially, advisory committee members voted orally and sequentially. But due to mounting fears that, under oral sequential voting, 'first voters would influence later [voters]'[44]—something that was seen as benefitting large drug companies—in 2007, oral sequential voting was gradually replaced by electronic voting. For Urfalino & Costa,[45] since the 2007 reform, there's been a sharp decrease in unanimous

40 Elster 2013: 128–9.
41 Bentham [1843] 1999: 107.
42 Urfalino & Costa 2015.
43 Id.
44 Id 170.
45 Id 179–81.

votes in the FDA's advisory committees. This suggests that public simultaneous voting has reduced instances of coercion against dissenters and information cascades.

Further, one may tackle coercion against dissenters and information cascades by using secret-public voting. This voting method—suggested for legislatures by Jeremy Bentham[46]—keeps sequentiality but eliminates publicity at the time of voting. Under secret-public voting, group members must cast their votes in ways akin to those applicable in secret voting; meaning, they must use paper ballots (or other supporting media), ballot boxes, and other devices that ensure that, at the time of voting, votes are unseen by all group members except the one that votes. (This is secret-public voting's secret stage.) Unlike secret voting though, under secret-public voting, group members' names are indicated in their ballots—or group members must indicate them. Thus, when counting the votes, all group members know how their peers voted.[47]

Since under secret-public voting, at the time of voting, no group member can see how their peers vote, this method curbs the odds that group members are coerced, along with curbing information cascades. Following Elster, secret-public voting reduces 'irrational conformism'[48] and forces group members 'to take their task seriously.'[49] Secret-public voting also keeps accountability when counting the votes since, at this stage, group members can see how their peers voted. In Bentham's words, 'it is only the will of the seducer that is concealed, for the moment, from the knowledge of the voter—not the conduct of the voter that is concealed, at the long run, from the knowledge of the public.'[50] Moreover, secret-public voting may be applied without using advanced technology. For example, a form of secret-public voting was used in Dominican monasteries during the 13th century.[51] Secret-public voting can be applied using the same analogue devices generally used in secret voting (eg, paper ballots, ballot boxes, and pens or pencils), while it can also be implemented through electronic machines. Thus, when tackling public sequential voting's problems at a reasonable cost while keeping accountability, secret-public voting seems quite effective.

Finally, one may tackle coercion against dissenters and information cascades by using voting procedures that avoid sequentiality and eliminate publicity at the time of voting. For example, this may happen under electronic voting systems in which each voting machine has a cover, and in which the vote's

46 [1843] 1999: 106–7.
47 Bentham [1843] 1999: 106–7; Elster 2013: 128–9.
48 2013: 129
49 Id 129.
50 Bentham [1843] 1999: 107.
51 Gaudemet et al 1979: 322–4. See also Pasquino 2015: 166. More recently, secret-public voting was used in the first session of the Chilean Constitutional Convention to choose its president and vice-president. Biblioteca del Congreso Nacional de Chile nd.

results—joined by a breakdown of the way in which each group member voted—is shown only after everyone votes.

Given a separation between debating and voting, among the voting methods analysed here, secret-public voting seems the best one for addressing coercion against dissenters and information cascades; particularly since applying this method doesn't require advanced technology, hence being a low-cost solution. What seems clear is that coercion against dissenters and information cascades aren't boosted by sequentiality itself—they are boosted when sequentiality is joined by publicity at the time of voting. The problem isn't that group members vote one after the other—the problem is that they can see how their peers voted before they vote. Thus, when curbing coercion against dissenters and information cascades, one should mainly focus on eliminating ex ante publicity, not on avoiding sequentiality. Even with the best technology, trying to ensure that group members vote at the exact same time (even when some of them don't want to) doesn't seem very effective. And insofar as no group member knows how their peers voted at the time of voting, the fact that group members vote sequentially doesn't seem very relevant; especially since no group member has the necessary data to pressure a peer or just copy them.

Mixing Debating and Voting

To solve cases, judges debate and vote. Thus, mixing these practices in ways that boost group accuracy matters when applying a supermajority rule in constitutional review. One can picture at least four ways of mixing debating and voting in constitutional courts. Some of these procedures are currently used by these courts, while others are just hypothetical. First, after the parties present their claims, the judges immediately meet face to face, vote on a decision, justify their votes, and task one of their peers to put the decision in writing. During the decision writing stage, the judges may still debate the case and change their vote, but in this procedure, judges vote relatively early in the decision process. Currently, this procedure is used in the Canadian,[52] US,[53] and UK[54] supreme courts.[55] We may call this procedure 'voting-debating.'

Second, after the parties present their claims, a judge (usually called the 'reporter' or 'reporting' judge)[56] may be tasked with writing a decision proposal to be later debated by all the judges in face to face meetings. During the writing stage, to gain as much support as possible before the meetings, the reporter judge may discuss the decision proposal with their peers. In the meetings, if no judge objects to the latest version of the decision proposal,

52 Songer at al 2012: 87–93.
53 Baum 2019: 116–9.
54 Paterson 2013: 83–94.
55 In practice though, in these courts, there's no clear distinction between debating and voting.
56 This judge is called *rapporteur* in French (Cohen 2014: 963–80), *ponente* in Spanish (do Vale 2017: ch 1), and *Berichterstatter* in German (Kelemen 2019: ch 2).

the case is decided by non-opposition. Put differently, the latest version of the decision proposal becomes the court's decision. Conversely, if in the meetings a judge objects to this proposal, the case is decided by voting. Since in this procedure, judges vote relatively late in the process (if they vote at all), we may call this procedure 'debating-voting.' This procedure is currently used in many Continental European constitutional courts.[57]

Third, one may imagine a procedure in which, after the parties present their claims, the judges immediately meet face to face, vote on a decision, and justify their votes. Later in that meeting (or in subsequent meetings), the judges debate the case, try to decide it unanimously by non-opposition, and if such unanimity can't be reached, they take a final vote. After this final vote, a judge is tasked with writing the decision. During this writing stage, judges may still debate the case and change their votes. We may call this procedure 'voting-debating-voting.'

Lastly, one may imagine a procedure in which the voting-debating-voting process is repeated several times before the judges take a final vote. The rest of this procedure—which somehow resembles the Conclave[58]—is akin to voting-debating-voting. We may call this procedure 'iterative voting-debating-voting.'

Let's assess how these procedures mix debating and voting.

Voting-Debating

On voting-debating, this procedure can immediately give judges data on their peers' initial opinions. This matters for two reasons. First, having to reveal one's initial opinions boosts the disclosure of privately held data if that data grounds such opinions.[59] This curbs a main problem that many debating groups face: namely, 'the common knowledge problem.' That is, the problem that groups usually focus on data that all (or most) group members share rather than on data that only one group member holds.[60] In constitutional review, since all judges have the same evidence, it's unlikely that they hold key private data on the case's facts.[61] But judges may hold key private data on legal reasons, and they may also hold key private data on moral reasons.

Second, knowing their peers' initial opinions may infuse judges with 'a stiff dose of epistemic humility.'[62] Specifically, knowing how one's peers voted may constitute evidence that one should change one's views—or at least seriously

57 Cohen 2014: 963–80; Ferejohn & Pasquino 2004: 1692–6; Urfalino 2014: 333–7; do Vale 2017: ch 1; Kelemen 2019: 86–9.
58 Apostolic Constitution *Universi Dominici Gregis* on the Vacancy of the Holy See and the Election of the Roman Pontiff.
59 Sunstein 2006: 208–10; Vermeule 2015: 222–5.
60 Sunstein 2006; Liu et al 2012; Barry 2021: 88.
61 On how shared evidence influences group accuracy, see List & Pettit 2011: 101–2.
62 Posner & Vermeule 2016: 163.

consider their claims.[63] This humility seems necessary in constitutional courts, especially since: (i) all judges are able (according to theories that see constitutional review as technical reasoning, and to theories that see this activity as general practical reasoning); and (ii) that ability is presumably equal. The closer the absolute margin between judicial majorities and minorities, the stronger the case for judicial epistemic humility.

Despite these advantages, in voting-debating, judges may treat cases as decided, thus only discussing the premises upholding their already arrived at conclusions—and little else. Put differently, in voting-debating, judges may not be open to change their views, which means that their *initial* opinions may become their *final* opinions. Considering that the US Supreme Court uses voting-debating, this problem of treating cases as decided may already be happening in that court. Though it isn't clear whether this is due to voting-debating, there's evidence suggesting that, when meeting face to face, US Supreme Court justices tend to just check if they agree on a decision instead of deliberating.[64]

Actually, according to psychological research[65]—and to Carson's,[66] and Carson & Schecter's[67] experience in organising mini publics—voting too early can be 'the death knell of consensus.'[68] This happens since, by publicly sharing their judgments, people somehow entrench them,[69] thus 'shut[ing] down exploration, open-mindedness, and critical thinking.'[70] For Carson & Schecter,[71] just choosing a side anchors people's initial judgments, thus curbing their willingness to accept feedback and change their opinion even when presented with new data. In sum, voting too early boosts a 'rush to judgment,'[72] strengthening the idea that, when the voting rule's threshold is reached, 'the subject is closed … and we can stop talking.'[73] Conversely, Carson & Schecter hold that, even when it appears that support for a possible decision is evenly split, 'common ground (leading to 90%–100% support) is often achievable if people are left to explore possibilities.'[74]

Similar results can be seen in jury decision making studies. Some of these studies suggest that the earlier jurors vote, the likelier it is that most of them stick to their initial judgments, though it isn't fully clear that this rigidity

63 Id 163–6, 175–82.
64 Gastil 2008: 142–5; Baum 2019: 116–9
65 For overviews of this research, see Oskamp & Schultz 2005: 250; MacCoun 2006: 116–7.
66 2017.
67 2017.
68 Carson 2017: 2.
69 Rosenbaum & Zimmerman 1959; Jellison & Mills 1969; Kiesler & Munson 1975; Pallak et al 1980; Bohm 1990.
70 Carson & Schecter 2017: 1.
71 Id 1.
72 Id.
73 Id.
74 Id.

is caused by the timing of the votes. According to Vidmar & Hans[75]—and Devine,[76] among others—in juries in which votes are taken before debating the case,[77] most jurors seldom change their minds. Rather, these jurors tend to behave as 'advocates for particular verdicts'[78] seeking to 'align themselves with those who are on the same side and talk about the evidence that supports the verdict.'[79]

From a deliberative viewpoint, the fact that voting-deliberation may lead judges to treat cases as decided is problematic. After all, one of deliberation's core values is openness to changing one's judgments. Thus, though voting-debating may contribute to revealing data and stimulating epistemic humility, this procedure seems to carry a high inbuilt risk of hindering deliberation. So, this first procedure should generally be rejected in constitutional courts.

Debating-Voting

In the case of the second procedure (that is, debating-voting), this procedure's strengths and flaws seem the exact opposite of voting-deliberation. Voting after the case has been debated gives judges some assurances that a decision hasn't already been made, and that, therefore, their claims will be seriously considered by their peers. Put differently, voting after the case has been debated makes it more likely that judges deliberate,[80] thus making it more likely that they reach a sincere agreement. After debating the case, judges may decide by non-opposition, hence unanimously agreeing on a decision without needing to vote. But if judges don't take an initial vote, they may not feel encouraged to reveal key data that they may privately hold. And there's the risk that—oblivious to their peers' initial opinions—some judges try to dominate the conversation rather than trying to listen to such opinions, or the reasons behind them.

Still, in constitutional courts, the risk that debating-voting stimulates the common knowledge problem may be overblown. According to available evidence, the common knowledge problem usually happens in groups with marked status differences. What this research shows is that lower-status group members tend to be ignored by their peers when compared against higher-status group members, even if the former have key data. Thus, lower-status group members tend to hold back rather than participate in the debate.[81] But considering that, in well-functioning democracies, judges have a high degree

75 2006: 142–4.
76 2012: 156–7, 169–72.
77 Along with taking an initial vote, in these kinds of juries, jurors take several votes throughout the decision process. Vidmar & Hans 2007: 143; Devine 2012: 156.
78 Devine 2012: 156.
79 Vidmar & Hans 2007: 143.
80 Ferejohn & Pasquino 2004: 1692–6; Pasquino 2015: 201–2, 207–8.
81 Sunstein 2006: 67–9, 86–8; Liu et al 2012. See also Stasser & Titus 1985.

of legal expertise—and indeed a presumably equal legal expertise—there are no formal status differences among them. True, in constitutional courts, there may be some informal status differences among judges, owing mainly to seniority (whether measured by age or appointment). Yet if this is so, many common knowledge problems that can occur among judges may be tackled by ensuring that less senior judges speak their mind without fear of social punishment by their peers. So, in principle, debating-voting shouldn't be discarded for mixing these practices in constitutional courts.

Voting-Debating-Voting

Regarding voting-debating-voting, in principle, this procedure seems quite good at boosting judges' accuracy. In this procedure, initial votes are merely indicative—not conclusive. Thus, under voting-debating-voting, group members may change their initial judgments at the debate state. Voting-debating-voting seems quite similar to the 'Delphi method' and the 'Nominal Group Technique:' two decision procedures currently used in business strategy and science and technology policy making, among other areas.[82]

The Delphi method is a decision procedure developed by the Rand Corporation in the 1950s for forecasting aims. Under this method, group members intervene anonymously and mediators oversee their interactions. The method works as follows. First, each group member states their opinion and the reasons behind it. Second, group members give written feedback on each others' opinions. Finally, group members' revised opinions are statistically aggregated. That is, the average opinion is taken as the group opinion. The process is usually repeated two or three times before making a final statistical opinion aggregation.[83] The Nominal Group Technique is akin to the Delphi method, the main difference being that, while in the Delphi method group members intervene anonymously, the Nominal Group Technique allows face to face interactions at the feedback stage.[84]

According to research in group decision making, when counting factual judgments[85]—such as estimating heights or weights—the Delphi method and the Nominal Group Technique tend to produce better results than informal or unstructured discussions among group members.[86] This is especially so when group members aren't only informed about their peers' judgments, but also about the reasons behind such judgments during the feedback stage.[87] Part of this research also suggests that the Delphi method and the Nominal

82 Rowe & Wright 2001; Sunstein 2006: 208–10; Mercier & Sperber 2017: 267–70.

83 Rowe & Wright 2001: 126–7; Sunstein 2006: 208–10; Mercier and Sperber 2017: 268–9.

84 Rowe & Wright 2001: 130; Sunstein 2006: 209.

85 For research suggesting that the Delphi method also works for aggregating value judgments, see Dalkey & Rourke 1971.

86 Gustafson et al 1973; Van de Ven & Delbecq 1974.

87 Rowe & Wright 2001: 129-30; Sunstein 2006: 209.

Group Technique work better than unstructured discussions for solving problems that are 'difficult ... have no solution that would be equally acceptable to all interest groups involved ... and evoke highly emotional and subjective responses.'[88] If the results of this research hold true—and considering the similarities between the Delphi method, the Nominal Group Technique, and voting-debating-voting—this research suggests that voting-debating-voting may be a good way of mixing these practices in constitutional courts.

But we seem to be facing a contradiction here. As previously mentioned, some research suggests that initial voting frames group members against changing their views. Yet research on the Delphi method and the Nominal Group Technique seems to suggest that this isn't so. Thus, it isn't clear whether groups should or shouldn't take an initial vote. This contradiction may be resolved by noting that, at the initial stages of the Delphi method and the Nominal Group Technique, though group members state their initial opinions (and the reasons behind them), they do so by filling questionnaires.[89] Thus, there's no actual initial voting stage: nobody appears with devices typically associated with voting (eg, paper ballots, boxes, etc.) and asks group members to vote. So, it could be that, unlike voting, filling questionnaires doesn't prematurely close up people's minds since they may not feel that they are really deciding anything.

In any case, when comparing psychological[90] and deliberative democracy research[91] with research on Delphi and the Nominal Group Technique,[92] what seems clear is that—to curb social influences, peer pressure, and the common knowledge problem—all group members must have equal chances of intervening in the debate rather than being silenced by their more assertive peers. This implies that all group members must be confident that they won't be socially punished for dissenting. To create such an inclusive atmosphere, the role of the mediator or facilitator guiding the debate is key. Thus, in constitutional courts, what seems to matter the most is that this atmosphere also exists among judges rather than initially voting. So, considering initial votes' possible anchoring effects on people's judgments—and their differences with filling questionnaires—I'm sceptical of using these votes to declare statutes unconstitutional.

Now, on creating inclusive atmospheres in constitutional courts, these atmospheres partially exist due to judges' equal legal expertise and their

88 Van de Ven & Delbecq concluded that the Nominal Group Technique works better than unstructured discussions in 'defining the job description of part-time student dormitory [counsellors].' Their assessment criteria were (i) quantity of ideas developed by the group, and (ii) the perceived satisfaction of the group with the decision process (1974: 608–19).

89 Van de Ven & Delbecq 1974: 606; Rowe & Wright 2001: 126.

90 Oskamp & Schultz 2005: 250; MacCoun 2006: 116–7.

91 Fishkin 2009; Mendelberg 2002; Delli Carpini et al 2004; Ryfe 2005; Steiner 2012; Neblo 2015; Fishkin 2018; Smith & Setälä 2018.

92 Rowe & Wright 2001; Sunstein 2006: 208–10; Mercier & Sperber 2017: 267–70.

possibility of publishing separate opinions. Yet, creating these atmospheres also depends on the behaviour of judges leading or mediating judicial debates, which is something quite context-dependent and that can't be fully considered in this book.

Iterative Voting-Debating-Voting

Last but not least, iterative voting-debating-voting is quite similar to voting-debating-voting; the main difference being that, while in voting-debating-voting each stage of the process happens once, iterative voting-debating-voting works in rounds, hence also being similar to the Delphi method and the Nominal Group Technique. Since iterative voting-debating-voting is almost analogous to voting-debating-voting, both procedures share similar traits. Indeed, some may claim that, by giving judges more chances to debate the case and reach a sincere agreement, iterative voting-debating-voting works better than voting-debating-voting.

Still, alongside initial votes' possible anchoring effects on people's judgments, the main problem with iterative voting-deliberation-voting is that, absent a round-limit, if judges don't reach the supermajority threshold, this procedure may mirror a Conclave; meaning, it may go on for a very long time.[93] This is challenging considering judges' limited time and resources. True, this problem may be tackled by using a round limit (eg, two or three rounds). But since there are no conclusive reasons for choosing a specific round limit beyond needing to 'get on with the job,' using this limit may produce a justification problem akin to that produced by supermajority rules' indeterminacy. Put differently, people opposing a constitutional court's decision could question that court's round limit, and there wouldn't be a strong enough logic to explain why that limit was used rather than another limit.

Thus, in the same cautious spirit underlying my claim that constitutional courts should use the supermajority rule that's closest to majority rule, debating-voting seems the best way of mixing these practices in constitutional review. Conversely, due to initial votes' possible anchoring effects on people's opinions—and in the case of iterative voting-debating-voting, due to the indeterminacy of round limits—the rest of the procedures seen in this chapter seem worse than debating-voting for solving constitutional cases.

Conclusion

In this chapter, I tackled some of the main challenges involved in applying supermajority rules in constitutional review. Specifically, I focused on choosing the supermajority rule, shaping the voting protocol, and mixing debating and voting. On choosing the supermajority rule, among judges present,

93 For examples of long conclaves, see Colomer & McLean 1998: 9–12; Lagerspetz 2010: 31–4.

constitutional courts should choose the rule closest to majority rule for two reasons: first, the need to give claimants a good chance of winning, along with minimising coercion against dissenters, false negatives, and decision costs; and second, the fact that supermajority rules' indeterminacy suggests caution. On shaping the supermajority protocol, secret-public voting seems the strongest protocol for constitutional courts. So, to curb coercion against dissenters and information cascades, judges' votes should be secret at the time of voting, but to keep accountability, they should be public at the time of counting the votes. Lastly, constitutional courts should use debating-voting. This procedure avoids initial votes' possible anchoring effects on people's opinions and the indeterminacy problem caused by the need to impose limits if the decision process has several rounds of voting and debating.

References

Barry BM, *How Judges Judge: Empirical Insights into Judicial Decision-Making* (Routledge 2021) https://doi.org/10.4324/9780429023422

Baum L, *The Supreme Court* (13th edn, CQ Press 2019)

Bentham J, *Political Tactics (first published 1843*, James M, Blamires C and Please-Watkin C edn, Oxford University Press 1999) https://doi.org/10.1093/actrade/9780198207726.book.1

Berlin I, 'Two Concepts of Liberty' in Hardy H (ed), *Liberty: Incorporating Four Essays on Liberty* (Oxford University Press 2002) https://doi.org/10.1093/019924989X.001.0001

Bohm RM, 'Death Penalty Opinions: A Classroom Experience and Public Commitment' (1990) 60 *Social Inquiry* 285 https://doi.org/10.1111/j.1475-682X.1990.tb00146.x

Brennan G & Pettit P, 'Unveiling the Vote' (1990) 20 *British Journal of Political Science* 311 https://doi.org/10.1017/S000712340000586X

Buchanan J & Tullock G, *The Calculus of Consent: Logical Foundations of Constitutional Democracy* (Liberty Fund 1999) http://oll.libertyfund.org/title/1063

Caplin A & Nalebuff B, 'On 64%-Majority Rule' (1988) 56 *Econometrica* 787 https://doi.org/10.2307/1912699

Carson L, *Deliberation* (Research and Development Note, newDemocracy Foundation, 22 March 2017) <https://www.newdemocracy.com.au/research-and-development-notes/> accessed 04 April 2021

——— & Schecter D, *The Role of Voting in Citizens' Juries* (Research and Development Note, newDemocracy Foundation, 08 March 2017) <https://www.newdemocracy.com.au/research-and-development-notes/> accessed 04 April 2021

Caviedes C, 'Chang's Parity: An Alternative Way to Challenge Balancing' (2017) 62(2) *American Journal of Jurisprudence* 165 https://doi.org/10.1093/ajj/aux018

Chang R, 'Introduction' in Chang R (ed), *Incommensurability, Incomparability and Practical Reason* (Ruth Chang edn, Harvard University Press 1997)

——— *Making Comparisons Count* (Routledge 2014)

Cohen-Eliya M & Porat I, *Proportionality and Constitutional Culture* (Cambridge University Press 2013) https://doi.org/10.1017/CBO9781139134996

Colomer J & McLean I, 'Electing Popes: Approval Balloting and Qualified-Majority Rule' (1998) 29 *Journal of Interdisciplinary History* 1 https://doi.org/10.1162/002219598551616
Dalkey NC & Rourke DL, *Experimental Assessment of Delphi Procedures with Group Valued Judgments* (Rand Corporation 1971) https://www.rand.org/pubs/reports/R0612.html
De Sousa RB, 'The Good and the True' (1974) 83 *Mind* 534
Delli Carpini MX, Lomax Cook F & Jacobs LR, 'Public Deliberation, Discursive Participation and Citizen Engagement: A Review of the Empirical Literature' (2004) 7 *Annual Review of Political Science* 315 https://doi.org/10.1146/annurev.polisci.7.121003.091630
Devine DJ, *Jury Decision Making: The State of the Science* (New York University Press 2012) https://doi.org/10.18574/9780814704981
do Vale AR, *La deliberación en los tribunales constitucionales [Deliberation in Constitutional Courts]* (Centro de Estudios Políticos y Constitucionales 2017)
Duxbury N, *Random Justice: On Lotteries and Legal Decision-Making* (Oxford University Press 1999) https://doi.org/10.1093/acprof:oso/9780198268253.001.0001
Edwards HT, 'The Effects of Collegiality on Judicial Decision Making' (2003) 151(5) *University of Pennsylvania Law Review 1639* https://doi.org/10.2307/3313001
Elster J, *Securities Against Misrule: Juries, Assemblies, Elections* (Cambridge University Press 2013) https://doi.org/10.1017/CBO9781139382762
——— (ed), *Secrecy and Publicity in Votes and Debates* (Cambridge University Press 2015) https://doi.org/10.1017/CBO9781316015360
Farnsworth W, *The Legal Analyst: A Toolkit for Thinking about the Law* (University of Chicago Press 2007)
Ferejohn J & Pasquino P, 'Constitutional Adjudication: Lessons from Europe' (2004) 82 *Texas Law Review 1671* https://heinonline.org/HOL/P?h=hein.journals/tlr82andi=1687
Fishkin JS, *When the People Speak: Deliberative Democracy and Public Consultation* (Oxford University Press 2009) https://doi.org/10.1093/acprof:osobl/9780199604432.001.0001
——— 'Deliberative Polling' in Bächtinger A, Dryzek JS, Mansbridge J, & Warren ME (eds), *The Oxford Handbook of Deliberative Democracy* (Oxford University Press 2018) https://doi.org/10.1093/oxfordhb/9780198747369.013.10
Gaudemet J, Dubois J, Duval A, & Champagne J, *Les Elections dans L'Eglise Latine des Origines au XVI Siècle [Elections in the Latin Church since its Origins to the XVI Century]* (Fernand Lanore 1979)
Gastil J, *Political Communication and Deliberation* (Sage 2008)
Griffin J, *Well-Being: its Meaning, Measurement and Moral Importance* (Oxford University Press 1988) https://doi.org/10.1093/0198248431.001.0001
Goodwin B, *Justice by Lottery* (2nd edn, Imprint Academic 2005)
Gustafson DH, Shukla RK, Delbecq A & Walster GW, 'A Comparative Study of Differences in Subjective Likelihood Estimates Made by Individuals, Interacting Groups, Delphi Groups, and Nominal Groups' (1973) 9 *Organizational Behavior and Human Performance* 280 https://doi.org/10.1016/0030-5073(73)90052-4
Jellison JM & Mills J, 'Effect of Public Commitment upon Opinions' (1969) 5 *Journal of Experimental Social Psychology* 340 https://doi.org/10.1016/0022-1031(69)90058-4

Kelemen K, *Judicial Dissent in European Constitutional Courts: A Comparative and Legal Perspective* (Routledge 2019) https://doi.org/10.4324/9781315590769

Kiesler CA & Munson PA, 'Attitudes and Opinions' (1975) 26 *Annual Review of Psychology* 415 https://doi.org/10.1146/annurev.ps.26.020175.002215

Laplace PS, *Essai philosophique sur les probabilités [Philosophical Essay on Probabilities] (first published 1825*, Cambridge University Press 2009)

Lagerspetz E, 'Wisdom and numbers' (2010) 49(1) *Social Science Information* 29 https://doi.org/10.1177/0539018409354475

——— *Social Choice and Democratic Values* (Springer 2016) https://doi.org/10.1007/978-3-319-23261-4

List C & Pettit P, *Group Agency: The Possibility, Design, and Status of Corporate Agents* (Cambridge University Press 2011) https://doi.org./10.1093/acprof:oso/9780199591565.001.0001

Liu L, Yuan C & McLeod PL, 'Twenty-Five Years of Hidden Profiles in Group Decision Making: A Meta-Analysis' (2012) 16(1) *Personality and Social Psychology Review* 54 https://doi.org./10.1177/1088868311417243

MacCoun RJ, 'Psychological Constraints of Transparency in Legal and Government Decision Making' (2006) 12(3) *Swiss Political Science Review* 112

Manin B, 'Why Open Voting in General Elections is Undesirable' in Elster J (ed), *Secrecy and Publicity in Votes and Debates* (Cambridge University Press 2015) https://doi.org/10.1017/CBO9781316015360

Mendelberg T, 'The Deliberative Citizen: Theory and Evidence' in Delli Carpini M, Huddy L and Shapiro RY (eds), *Research in Micropolitics*, vol 6 (Elsevier Press 2002)

Mercier H & Sperber D, *The Enigma of Reason* (Harvard University Press 2017)

Neblo MA, *Deliberative Democracy between Theory and Practice* (Cambridge University Press 2015) https://doi.org/10.1017/CBO9781139226592

Nitzan SI & Paroush J, 'Are Qualified Majority Rules Special?' (1984) 42 *Public Choice* 257 https://www.jstor.org/stable/30023741

Oskamp S & Schultz W, *Attitudes and Opinions* (3rd edn, Psychology Press 2005) https://doi.org/10.4324/9781410611963

Pallak MS, Cook DA & Sullivan JJ, 'Commitment and energy conservation' (1980) 1 *Applied Social Psychology Annual* 235

Pasquino P, 'E Pluribus Unum: Disclosed and Undisclosed Votes in Constitutional/Supreme Courts' in Elster J (ed), *Secrecy and Publicity in Votes and Debates* (Cambridge University Press 2015) https://doi.org/10.1017/CBO9781316015360

Paterson A, *Final Judgment: The Last Law Lords and the Supreme Court* (Hart 2013)

Posner EA & Vermeule A, 'The Votes of Other Judges' (2016) 105 *Georgetown Law Journal* 159

Raz J, *The Morality of Freedom* (Reprinted edn, Oxford University Press 2009) https://doi.org/10.1093/0198248075.001.0001

Rosenbaum ME & Zimmerman IM, 'The Effect of External Commitment on Response to an Attempt to Change Opinions' (1959) 23(2) *Public Opinion Quarterly* 247 https://doi.org/10.1086/266869

Rowe G & Wright G, 'Expert Opinions in Forecasting: The Role of the Delphi Technique' in J Scott Armstrong (ed), *Principles of Forecasting, vol 1: A Handbook for Researchers and Practicioners* (Springer 2001)

Ryfe DM, 'Does Deliberative Democracy Work?' (2005) 8 *Annual Review of Political Science* 49 https://doi.org/10.1146/annurev.polisci.8.032904.154633

Saks MJ, 'What Do Jury Expertiments Tell Us about How Juries (Should) Make Decisions' (1997) 6 *Southern California Interdisciplinary Law Journal* 1
Schwartzberg M, 'The arbitrariness of supermajority rules' (2010) 49(1) *Social Science Information* 61 https://doi.org/10.1177/0539018409354474
——— *Counting the Many.* The Origins and Limits of Supermajority Rule (Cambridge University Press 2013) https://doi.org/10.1017/CBO9781139013970
Seok Hong J, 'Signalling the Turn: The Supermajority Requirement and Judicial Power on the Constitutional Court of South Korea' (2019) 67 *American Journal of Comparative Law* 177 https://doi.org/10.1093/ajcl/avz008
Sinnott-Armstrong W, 'Moral Dilemmas and Incomparability' (1985) 22 *American Philosophical Quarterly* 321 https://www.jstor.org/stable/20014112
Songer DR, Johnson SW, Ostberg CL & Wetstein ME, *Law, Ideology and Collegiality: Judicial Behaviour in the Supreme Court of Canada* (McGill-Queen's University Press 2012)
Smith G & Setälä M, 'Mini-Publics and Deliberative Democracy' in Bächtinger A, Dryzek JS, Mansbridge J, & Warren ME (eds), *The Oxford Handbook of Deliberative Democracy* (Oxford University Press 2018) https://doi.org/10.1093/oxfordhb/9780198747369.013.27
Stasser G & Titus W, 'Pooling of unshared information in group decision making: Biased information sampling during discussion' (1985) 48(6) *Journal of Personality and Social Psychology 1467 https://doi.org/10.1037/0022-3514.48.6.1467*
Steiner J, *The Foundations of Deliberative Democracy: Empirical Research and Normative Implications* (Cambridge University Press 2012) https://doi.org/10.1017/CBO9781139057486
Stone P, *The Luck of the Draw: The Role of Lotteries in Decision Making* (Oxford University Press 2011a) https://doi.org/10.1093/acprof:oso/9780199756100.001.0001
——— (ed), *Lotteries in Public Life: A Reader* (Imprint Academic 2011b)
Stone Sweet A, 'Constitutional Courts' in Rosenfeld M and Sajó A (eds), *The Oxford Handbook of Comparative Constitutional Law* (Oxford University Press 2012) https://doi.org/10.1093/oxfordhb/9780199578610.013.0040
Sunstein CR, *Infotopia: How Many Minds Produce Knowledge* (Oxford University Press 2006)
Urfalino P, 'The Rule of Non-Opposition: Opening Up Decision-Making by Consensus' (2014) 22(3) *The Journal of Political Philosophy* 320 https://doi.org/10.1111/jopp.12037
——— & Costa P, 'Secret-Public Voting in FDA Advisory Committees' in Elster J (ed) *Secrecy and Publicity in Votes and Debates* (Cambridge University Press 2015) https://doi.org/10.1017/CBO9781316015360
Van de Ven AH & Delbecq AL, 'The Effectiveness of Nominal, Delphi, and Interacting Group Decision Making Processes' (1974) 17 *Academy of Management Journal* 605 https://www.jstor.org/stable/255641
Vermeule A, Open-Secret Voting' in Elster J (ed), *Secrecy and Publicity in Votes and Debates* (Cambridge University Press 2015) https://doi.org/10.1017/CBO9781316015360
Vidmar N & Hans VP, *American Juries: The Verdict* (Prometheus Books 2007)
Wilson B, 'Decision-Making in the Supreme Court' (1986) 36(3) *University of Toronto Law Journal* 227 https://heinonline.org/HOL/P?h=hein.journals/utlj36andi=231

Conclusion

A Call for Gradual Experimentation

In this book, I've tried to show that there are no definitive reasons for using majority rule in constitutional review, and that—considering supermajority rules' traits—there are strong reasons for replacing majority rule with these voting rules for declaring statutes unconstitutional.

Currently, few courts use supermajority rules for checking the constitutionality of legislation. As far as I am aware—and excluding courts with even numbers of judges in which the presiding judge doesn't have a casting vote (eg, the German constitutional court)[1]—the only courts that constitutionally adjudicate by supermajority rules are the Mexican court,[2] the Peruvian court,[3] and the courts mentioned in the appendix. And among these latter courts, the ones implementing supermajority rules that are closest to the ideal presented in this book are the Czech,[4] Nebraskan,[5] North Dakotan,[6] and South Korean[7] courts, since they apply the supermajority rule that's closest to majority rule. (Though they apply these voting rules among all judges—not among judges present.) Thus, I'm acutely aware that I'm arguing for an uncommon way of doing constitutional review.

Therefore, to test this book's claims, it's worth emphasising the need for more empirical research on supermajority rules' effects on constitutional review. True, due to reasonable disagreement, it may be impossible to directly probe these voting rules' effects on judges' accuracy. But one may at least assess their effects on judicial deliberation and on courts' reputation (both quantitatively and qualitatively),[8] and then use these results as indirect proxies

1 Kelemen 2019: 30–5

2 In Mexico, the supermajority rule is only used to void statutes—not to dis-apply them in specific cases. In dis-applications, the voting rule is majority rule. Ferrer Mac-Gregor & Herrera 2009: 335; Mex Jud Law, art 7 inc 1°.

3 See Carpio & Grandez 2009: 446–7; Per CC Law, art 5° inc 1°.

4 CzR CC Act, § 13.

5 Neb Const, art V-2.

6 ND Const, art VI, §§ 4–5.

7 Seok Hong 2019: 184–6, 200–4.

8 For examples of these studies in judicial decision making, see Barry 2021.

DOI: 10.4324/9781032723952-8

for accuracy. After all, though people may disagree on whether a judicial decision is accurate, one may at least reasonably claim that, all else equal, a court whose members deliberate—or that has a high degree of reputation among citizens—likely issues better decisions than a court that doesn't deliberate, or that isn't very reputable.[9]

Further, though I'm a generalist when making my claims, when applying supermajority rules in specific constitutional review systems, one should be context-sensitive, thus carefully tracking these voting rules' effects on other officials, particularly judges and legislators. And to avoid democratic erosion worries, it would be prudent to establish that any reform to constitutional courts' voting rules for checking the constitutionality of legislation should start working after the government, legislature, or constituent assembly that suggests it finishes its term.

Last but not least, this book is an invitation to reflect more on how institutional design affects constitutional courts' performance, and hence on how it affects their claims to authority. Compared to other topics in constitutional review debates, institutional design issues tend to be the typically ignored 'poor relative' or 'elephant in the room.'[10] So, if anything, I hope this book helps in reversing that trend. After all, if one doesn't examine the institutional design issues involved in shaping constitutional courts, one likely deprives oneself of the chance of unlocking constitutional review's full potential. Thus, insofar as this book boosts research on constitutional courts' institutional design, this book will add something (however little) for improving this practice.

References

Barry BM, *How Judges Judge: Empirical Insights into Judicial Decision-Making* (Routledge 2021) https://doi.org/10.4324/9780429023422

Bryman A, *Social Research Methods* (4th edn, Oxford University Press 2012)

Carpio Marcos E & Grandez Castro P, 'Tribunal Constitucional (Perú)'['Constitutional Court (Peru)'] in Ferrer Mac-Gregor E (coord) *Crónica de Tribunales*

9 Eg, on courts' reputation, Zink et al.'s experiment may be replicated (2009). And on judicial deliberation, judicial decisions may be statistically analysed to see if there are significant links between constitutional courts' voting rules and judges' levels of agreement. Epstein & Martin 2012: ch. 6–9. Also, judicial decisions may be analysed via qualitative comparative analysis to see if there are any necessary or sufficient links between constitutional courts' voting rules and judges' levels of agreement. (On qualitative comparative analysis, see Ragin 2014. For examples of judicial decision making studies using qualitative comparative analysis, see Cortés Salinas 2014.) Lastly, if a statistically significant link is detected between a constitutional court's voting rule and its judges' levels of agreement, interview studies or survey studies may be done in that court to examine any causal relations between these variables (Bryman 2012: ch 20; Barry 2021: 7–8).

10 Some salient exceptions are the works of Elhauge (1991), Komesar (1994), Vermeule (2006), Hübner Mendes (2015), and Yowell (2018).

Constitucionales en Iberoamérica [Chronicle of Constitutional Courts in Iberian America] (UNAM Marcial Pons 2009)

Cortés Salinas J, 'Análisis Cualitativo Comparado: las decisiones de la Suprema Corte contra el Ejecutivo en México' ['Qualitative Comparative Analysis: The Supreme Court Decisions Against the Executive in Mexico'] (2014) 73 *Revista Mexicana de Sociología* 413

Elhauge E, 'Does Interest Group Theory Justify More Intrusive Judicial Review?' (1991) 101 *Yale Law Journal* 31 https://doi.org/10.2307/796935

Epstein L & Martin AD, 'Is the Roberts Court Especially Activist? A Study of Invalidating (and Upholding) Federal, State, and Local Laws' (2012) 61 *Emory Law Journal* 737 https://scholarlycommons.law.emory.edu/elj/vol61/iss4/3

Ferrer Mac-Gregor & Herrera García A, 'Suprema Corte de Justicia de la Nación (México)' ['Supreme Court of the Nation (Mexico)'] in Ferrer Mac-Gregor E (coord), *Crónica de Tribunales Constitucionales en Iberoamérica [Chronicle of Constitutional Courts in Iberian America]* (UNAM Marcial Pons 2009)

Hübner Mendes C, *Constitutional Courts and Deliberative Democracy* (Oxford University Press 2015) https://doi.org/10.1093/acprof:oso/9780199670451.001.0001

Kelemen K, *Judicial Dissent in European Constitutional Courts:A Comparative and Legal Perspective* (Routledge 2019) https://doi.org/10.4324/9781315590769

Komesar NK, *Imperfect Alternatives: Choosing Institutions in Law, Economics, and Public Policy* (University of Chicago Press 1994)

Ragin CC, *The Comparative Method: Moving Beyond Qualitative and Quantitative Strategies* (University of California Press 2014)

Seok Hong J, 'Signalling the Turn: The Supermajority Requirement and Judicial Power on the Constitutional Court of South Korea' (2019) 67 *American Journal of Comparative Law* 177 https://doi.org/10.1093/ajcl/avz008

Vermeule A, *Judging Under Uncertainty: An Institutional Theory of Legal Interpretation* (Harvard University Press 2006)

Yowell P, *Constitutional Rights and Constitutional Design: Moral and Empirical Reasoning in Judicial Review* (Hart Publishing 2018) https://doi.org/10.5040/9781509913626

Zink JR, Spriggs II JF & Scott JT, 'The Influence of Decision Attributes on Individuals' Views of Court Opinions' (2009) 71(3) *Journal of Politics* 909 https://doi.org/10.1017/s0022381609090793

Appendix

Courts in Which the Core Cases Apply—A Preliminary View

In this appendix, I list some traits of the constitutional courts of polities that—at first sight—likely satisfy this book's assumptions. This appendix has two aims: first, it gives examples of the kind of polities and constitutional courts to which this book's claims mainly apply; and second, it's a small database of decision procedures in these courts, hence serving as a jumping-off point for further research. All the constitutional courts listed here belong to polities ranked as 'free' by Freedom House's 'Freedom in the World Report 2023,'[1] or to polities ranked as 'consolidated democracies' by Freedom House's 'Nations in Transit Report 2023.'[2] Also, I include the supreme courts of the US states of Nebraska and North Dakota since these courts use supermajority rules for declaring statutes unconstitutional.[3]

I exclude from this appendix: (i) polities that don't have constitutional review (eg, Switzerland, the Netherlands);[4] (ii) polities with weak-form constitutional review (eg, New Zealand, the UK);[5] (iii) polities in which the constitution doesn't have a bill of rights (eg, Australia);[6] (iv) polities in which judges can't publish separate opinions (eg, Austria, Belgium, France, Ireland, Italy, and Luxembourg)[7]; (v) polities in which judges' inner debates are public (eg, Brazil,[8] Mexico);[9] (vi) polities in which the Judicial Committee of the Privy

1 Freedom House 2023a
2 Freedom House 2023b.
3 Shugerman 2002: 954–62; Waldron 2016: 248, 265.
4 On Switzerland, see Swi Const, art 190; Lienhard et al 2017: 405, 416–9. On the Netherlands, see Ned Const, art 120; van der Schyff 2010.
5 Gardbaum 2013: ch 1. As mentioned in Chapter 2, I consider the Canadian system as a strong-form system. See Kahana 2001; Weinrib 2016: 163–4.
6 Foley 2007: 281–91.
7 Kelemen 2019: 82; European Parliament 2012: 17–23.
8 da Silva 2013: 567–9, 579–83; do Vale 2017: ch. 2.
9 Ferrer García 2009: 333–4; Mex Const, art 94 inc 2°; Mex Jud Law, art 6.

Council is the court of last resort (eg, Jamaica);[10] and (vii) polities with small populations, of two million people or less.[11]

This appendix has the following data. First, whether these polities' courts are Kelsenian or supreme courts.[12] Second, the number of judges in these courts. Third, whether the judges generally decide constitutional cases in plenary sessions or in panels. Fourth, the number of judges needed to get a quorum. Fifth, the voting rule for declaring statutes unconstitutional. Finally, whether the judges are just allowed to publish separate opinions, or whether they are obligated to do so if they have them.[13] I organise the information according to geographical areas. This appendix was mainly made by using legal texts, joined in some cases by secondary sources and by personal communications with legal scholars of the respective polities. It's worth remarking that this appendix is limited since it focuses on legal texts instead of actual practices.[14] Thus, I may be ignoring key data on how these polities' constitutional courts work. All errors in showing and interpreting this data are mine alone.

10 Judicial Committee of the Privy Council nd.

11 As mentioned in Chapter 2, I also don't include Israel due to the debates on whether Israel has a constitution. On this debate, see Weill 2012.

12 On this distinction, see Cappelletti 1971; Brewer-Carías 1989; Stone Sweet 2012.

13 When referring to judges' obligation to publish separate opinions, I'm not necessarily holding that they must issue such opinions seriatim. Even if a judge must publish concurrences or dissents if they have them, that judge may publish such opinions jointly with their peers.

14 Eg, this appendix doesn't focus on the fact that, in Japan and the Nordic countries (Denmark, Finland, Iceland, Norway, and Sweden), courts have been reticent to declare statutes unconstitutional. On the Japanese case, see Law 2011; Matsui 2011. On the Nordic case, see Husa 2000: 345; Hirschl 2011.

Table 1: Courts of Africa

	Kind of Court	*No. of Judges*	*Distribution*	*Quorum*	*Voting Rule*	*Separate Opinions*
Botswana[a]	Supreme court	Nine	Plenary	Five	Majority rule	Allowed
Ghana[b]	Supreme court	15	Panel of nine	All panel judges	Majority rule	Allowed
Namibia[c]	Supreme court	Four	Plenary	Three	Majority rule	Allowed
South Africa[d]	Kelsenian	11	Plenary	Eight	Majority rule	Allowed

[a] I'm grateful to Charles Manga Fombad for filling my gaps on the Botswanan court. Manga Fombad 2003: 91–4; Manga Fombad, email 3 September 2021; Bots Const, §§ 18(1), 105–6; Bots CA Act, §§ 9(2)–(3).

[b] The Ghanian Supreme Court needs a quorum of at least seven judges to review its previous decisions. I am grateful to Akongburo Raymond Atuguba and Maame Mensa-Bonsu for filling my gaps on the Ghanaian court. Atuguba, email 1 September 2021; Gh Const, arts 1(2), 2(1)–(5), 33, 128(1)–(2), 130, 133; The Republic of Ghana Judiciary nd.

[c] I'm grateful to John Baloro and Sebastiaan Kanunda for filling my gaps on the Namibian court. Nam Const, arts 78(1), 79(1)–(2); Nam SC Act, ss. 13(1)–(2); Namibia Superior Courts nd.

[d] I'm grateful to Nurina Ally, Heinz Klug, Theunis Roux, and Francois Venter for filling my gaps on the South African court. Roux, email 31 August 2021; Venice Commission nd-d; SA Const, §§ 8, 39, 166(a), 167, 172, 173.

Table 2: Courts of the Americas

	Kind of Court	*No. of Judges*	*Distribution*	*Quorum*	*Voting Rule*	*Separate Opinions*
Argentina[a]	Supreme court	Five	Plenary	Majority	Majority rule	Allowed
Canada[b]	Supreme court	Nine	Plenary	Five	Majority rule	Allowed
Chile[c]	Kelsenian	Ten	Plenary	Eight	4/5	Compulsory
Costa Rica[d]	Supreme court	22	Panel of seven	All panel judges	Majority rule	Compulsory
Panamá[e]	Supreme court	Nine	Plenary	All judges	Majority rule	Allowed
Uruguay[f]	Supreme court	Five	Plenary	All judges	Majority rule	Allowed
US[g]	Supreme court	Nine	Plenary	Six	Majority rule	Allowed

[a] I'm grateful to Roberto Gargarella and Pablo Manili for filling my gaps on the Argentine court. Gargarella,email 25 August 2021; Arg Jud Law, arts 6, 9.
[b] I'm grateful to Bill Flanagan for filling my gaps on the Canadian court. Flanagan, email 8 September 2019; Wilson 1986; Songer et al 2012: ch 4; Can Const, s 101; Can Cht, s 24(1); Can SC Act, ss 3, 4(1), 25, 28(2), 29.
[c] In Chile, the 4/5 rule is only used for voiding statutes—not for dis-applying them in specific cases. In dis-applications, the voting rule is majority rule. Bordalí Salamanca 2009: 112; Ch Const, arts 92 inc 1°, 92 inc 5°, 93 inc. 1° n° 1°, 93 inc. 1° n° 6°, 93 inc. 1° n° 7°; Ch CC Law, arts 4, 20 inc 1°; Ch Courts Code, art 81.
[d] In Costa Rica, only the Supreme Court's 'Constitutional Panel' (Sala Constitucional) can check the constitutionality of legislation. Jinesta Lobo 2009: 152, 159. CR Const, art 10; CR Jud Law, arts 4, 14.
[e] Sánchez González 2009: 402–3, 405–7; Pan Const, art 206 n° 1; Pan Jud Code, arts 113, 115.
[f] I'm grateful to Eduardo Esteva, Diego Gamarra, María Paula Garat, Walter Guerra, and Martín Risso for filling my gaps on the Uruguayan court. Esteva Gallichio 2009: 490, 495–6; Uru Const, arts 234, 256–9; Uru Jud Law, art 56(1); Uru Proc Code, arts 19.2, 201, 519.
[g] Baum 2019: 12–6; 114–20; US Const, art III, § 1; 28 USC § 1.

Table 3: Courts of Asia

	Kind of Court	*No. of Judges*	*Distribution*	*Quorum*	*Voting Rule*	*Separate Opinions*
Japan[a]	Supreme court	15	Plenary	Nine	Majority rule	Compulsory
Mongolia[b]	Kelsenian	Nine	Plenary	Seven	2/3	Allowed
South Korea[c]	Kelsenian	Nine	Plenary	Seven	Six-to-three	Compulsory
Taiwan[d]	Supreme court	15	Plenary	2/3	Majority rule	Allowed

[a] Jpn Const, art 81; Jpn Jud Act, arts 5(3), 9(2), 10, 11, 75, 76, 77(1). See also Matsui 2011.
[b] Initially, the Mongolian constitutional court (the 'Tsets') decides by majority rule. Yet for producing legal effects, those decisions must be approved by the legislature (the 'State Great Hural'). If the State Great Hural refuses its approval, the decision returns to the Tsets for reconsideration. The Tsets can only override the State Great Hural's refusal by a two-thirds rule. Ginsburg 2003: 165–73; Mong Const, arts 65(1), 66; Mong CC Proc Law, arts 3, 8(2) and 10.
[c] I'm grateful to Hyo-Won Lee for filling my gaps on South Korea. Seok Hong 2019: 184–6, 200–4; SK Const, arts 107(1), 111, 113(1); SK CC Act, arts 34(1), 36(3).
[d] In Taiwan, only the so-called 'Constitutional Court' can check the constitutionality of legislation. But I classify this institution as a supreme court since, along with constitutionally adjudicating, this Court unifies statutory interpretation. Until 2022, the voting rule for declaring statutes unconstitutional was 2/3 of all judges. Ginsburg 2003: 115–7, 120–4, 132; Lin 2022; Kuo & Chen 2022; Twn Const, arts 78 and 79; Twn CC Proc Act, arts 35 and 44; Twn C Int Proc Act, art 14(1).

Table 4: Courts of Central and Western Europe

	Kind of Court	*No. of Judges*	*Distribution*	*Quorum*	*Voting Rule*	*Separate Opinions*
Czechia[a]	Kelsenian	15	Plenary	Ten	Nine-to-six	Allowed
Germany[b]	Kelsenian	16	Panels of eight	Six	Majority rule	Allowed
Portugal[c]	Kelsenian	13	Plenary	Majority	Majority rule	Allowed
Slovakia[d]	Kelsenian	13	Plenary	Majority	Majority rule	Allowed
Slovenia[e]	Kelsenian	Nine	Plenary	Majority	Majority rule	Allowed
Spain[f]	Kelsenian	12	Plenary	2/3	Majority rule	Allowed

[a] Venice Commission nd-a; Kelemen 2019: 24, 82; CzR Const, Č 4 odst, 83 odst, 84 odst 1 pism, 87 odst 1 pism ahelp_outline; CzR CC Act, §§ 11 odst 1 pism, 13 odst, 14 odst, 53 odst 1 pism.

[b] In the German court, two-thirds of a panel's judges may exceptionally deprive someone of their basic rights. And the court must resolve an issue in a plenary session if a panel wants to deviate from the other panel's legal views. Kommers & Miller 2012: 18–20, 25–9; Kelemen 2019: 18–29, 24, 82; Ger Const, §§ 1 Abs 3, 18, 93 Abs 1, 94, 100; BVerfG Act, §§ 2 Abs 1–2, 15 Abs 2–4, 16 Abs 1, 17, 30 Abs 1–2.

[c] In Portugal, the court divides itself into panels to dis-apply statutes in specific cases. Yet to void statutes, the court decides in a plenary session. I'm grateful to Jõao Carlos Loureiro for filling my gaps on the Portuguese court. Nogueira de Brito 2009: 467, 469–73; Kelemen 2019: 26, 82; Port Const, arts 221, 222, 281(1), 281(3), 283; Port CC Law, arts 40, 42, 62(2).

[d] Kelemen 2019: 27, 82; Slk Const, arts 124, 125(1)(a), 131(1), 134(1); Slk CC Law, §§ 3, 6(1), 7(1)(a), 8 (4)–(5), 9, and 67.

[e] Kelemen 2019: 27, 82; Slv Const, arts 160, 161; 162(3), 163(1); Slv CC Act, arts 35(1), 40(1), 40(3), 41(1), 41(2); Slv Proc Rules, arts 53, 54, and 71.

[f] In Spain, the court may decide some constitutional issues divided into panels. Brage Camazano & Reviriego Picón 2009: 229, 234–5; Kelemen 2019: 28, 82; Spn Const, arts 9, 53, 159, 161; Spn CC Law, arts 5, 6, 7(1), 10(1), 11, 14, 80, 90; Spn Jud Law, art 233.

Table 5: Courts of Eastern Europe and Finland

	Kind of Court	*No. of Judges*	*Distribution*	*Quorum*	*Voting Rule*	*Separate Opinions*
Estonia[a]	Supreme Court	19	Panels of three, five, or nine	Three, five, or nine	Majority rule	Allowed
Finland[b]	1. Supreme Court ('SC') 2. Supreme Administrative Court ('SAC')	19 in SC, and 22 in SAC	Panels of five	Five	Majority rule	Allowed
Greece[c]	Supreme Court	13	Plenary	All	Majority rule	Compulsory
Latvia[d]	Kelsenian	Seven	Plenary	Five	Majority rule	Allowed
Lithuania[e]	Kelsenian	Nine	Plenary	2/3	Majority rule	Allowed

[a] In Estonia, the Supreme Court's 'Constitutional Chamber'—made of nine judges—usually checks the constitutionality of legislation, but the Chamber may refer the issue to the plenary. Venice Commission nd-b; Kelemen 2019: 82; Est Const, §§ 15, 149(3), 152; Est CC Proc Act, §§ 3, 57(2), 57(5).

[b] The SC may decide in a plenary session when significant principles are involved or the court wants to depart from its doctrine. And the SAC may decide in a plenary session when its cases are of 'special interest.' In these cases, SAC judges are joined by two non-legal experts. I'm grateful to Olli Mäenpää and Janne Salminen for filling my gaps on the Finnish court. European Parliament 2012, 28; Fin Const, 9 luku 98§, 10 luku 106§; Fin SC Act, 2§, 7§, 7a(1)§, 13§; Fin SAC Act, 1 luku 5§–7§, 3 luku 10(1)§–11§; Fin Proc Code, 1 luku 7§, 23 luku 6§, 24 luku 8§, 17§, 19§; Fin Crim Proc Act, 10 luku 2§.

[c] The Greek 'Special Highest Court' is an ad-hoc court that unifies constitutional interpretation. It's made of the presidents of other courts, and by randomly selected judges and law professors. I'm grateful to Akritas Kaidatzis for filling my gasps on the Greek court. Kaidatzis, email 13 July 2017; Kaidatzis, email 14 October 2019; Kelemen 2019: 82; Gk Const, Arthro 93(3), 100(1)–(2); GK CC Law, Ar 1 (1)–(2), 19, 51.

[d] Venice Commission nd-c; Kelemen 2019: 25, 82; Lat Const, §§ 85, 89; Lat CC Law, §§ 3, 25(1), 28(1), 30.

[e] Kelemen 2019: 25, 82; Lit Const, art 103; Lit CC Law, arts 18(7), 19, 53, 55(4).

Table 6: Courts of Scandinavia

	Kind of Court	*No. of judges*	*Distribution*	*Quorum*	*Voting Rule*	*Separate Opinions*
Denmark[a]	Supreme court	19	Panels of nine or 11	Five	Majority rule	Allowed
Iceland[b]	Supreme Court	Seven	Plenary	Five	Majority rule	Allowed
Norway[c]	Supreme court	20	Panel of 11	11	Majority rule	Compulsory
Sweden[d]	1. Supreme Court ('SC') 2. Supreme Administrative Court ('SAC')	16 in SC, and 18 in SAC	Panels of five	Five	Majority rule	Compulsory in SC and allowed in SAC

[a] I'm grateful to Jens Elo Rytter for filling my gaps on the Danish court. Rytter, email 12 July 2017; Zahle 2007; Dan Const§ 3; Dan Jud Act, § 2(1), 2a(1).
[b] In key cases, the Court's President can decide that all the judges shall constitute a quorum. I'm grateful to Pétur Dam Leifsson and Trausti Fannar Valson for filling my gaps on Iceland. Supreme Court of Iceland, nd; Ice Proc Law, art 189(1) and (2).
[c] In key cases, the issue may be resolved in a plenary session. Nor Const, § 89; Nor Jud Act, §§ 5(4), 6 (2)–(3); Nor Disp Act, §§ 19–3(4) and 19–6(3). See also Supreme Court of Norway nd: 11–2, 36–48, 65–6.
[d] In key cases—or when necessary for unifying statutory interpretation—the SC can decide the case in a plenary session or by a nine-judge panel. Swe Const, ch 11 pt 1 art 1(1), pt 8 art 14; Swe Proc Code, ch 3 ss 1, 4(1)–(3), 5, and 6, ch 4 s 11, ch 5 s 5(1), ch 6 s 3(8), ch 16 s 3, ch 17 s 9(6), ch 29 s 3; Swe AC Proc Act, ss 16, 31. See also ACA-Europe 2016: 8–13; Stockholm Institute for Scandinavian Law 2007: 629, 638–40.

Table 7: Courts of Nebraska and North Dakota

	Kind of Court	*No. of judges*	*Distribution*	*Quorum*	*Voting Rule*	*Separate Opinions*
Nebraska[a]	Supreme court	Seven	Plenary	Four	Five-to-two	Allowed
North Dakota[b]	Supreme court	Five	Plenary	Majority	Four-to-one	Allowed

[a] Shugerman 2002: 893, 954–62; Neb Const art V-2.
[b] I'm grateful to Penny Miller for filling my gaps on the North Dakotan court. Miller, email 20 September 2019; Shugerman 2002: 954–62; ND Const art VI, §§ 4–5.

References

ACA-Europe: Association of the Councils of State and Supreme Administrative Jurisdictions of the European Union, 'Administrative Justice in Europe: Report for Sweden' (ACA-Europe 2016) https://www.aca-europe.eu/index.php/en/115-annual-reports

Baum L, *The Supreme Court* (13th edition, CQ Press 2019)

Bordalí Salamanca A, 'Tribunal Constitucional (Chile)' [Constitutional Court (Chile)] in Ferrer Mac-Gregor E (coord), *Crónica de Tribunales Constitucionales en Iberoamérica [Chronicle of Constitutional Courts in Iberian America] (*UNAM Marcial Pons 2009)

Brage Camazano J & Reviriego Picón F, 'Tribunal Constitucional (España)' ['Constitutional Court (Spain)'] in Ferrer Mac-Gregor E (coord), *Crónica de Tribunales Constitucionales en Iberoamérica [Chronicle of Constitutional Courts in Iberian America] (*UNAM Marcial Pons 2009)

Brewer-Carías AR, *Judicial Review in Comparative Law* (Cambridge University Press 1989)

Cappelletti M, *Judicial Review in the Contemporary World* (Bobbs-Merrill 1971)

da Silva VA, 'Deciding Without Deliberating' (2013) 11(3) *International Journal of Constitutional Law* 557 https://doi.org/10.1093/icon/mot019

do Vale AR, *La deliberación en los tribunales constitucionales [Deliberation in Constitutional Courts]* (Centro de Estudios Políticos y Constitucionales 2017)

Email from Atuguba AK, Dean, University of Ghana School of Law to author (01 September 2021)

Email from Flanagan W, Professor of Corporate Law, Queen's University Faculty of Law to author (08 September 2019)

Email from Gargarella R, Professor of Constitutional Law, University of Buenos Aires Faculty of Law to author (25 August 2021)

Email from Kaidatzis A, Professor of Constitutional Law, University of Thessaloniki Faculty of Law to Author (13 July 2017)

——— (14 October 2019)

Email from Manga Fombad C, Professor of Constitutional Law, University of Pretoria Centre for Human Rights to author (03 September 2021)

Email from Miller P, Clerk of the Supreme Court of North Dakota to author (20 September 2019)

Email from Roux TR, Professor of Law, University of New South Wales to author (31 August 2021)

Email from Rytter JE, Professor of Constitutional Law, University of Copenhagen Faculty of Law to Author (12 July 2017)

Esteva Gallichio EG, 'Suprema Corte de Justicia (Uruguay)' [Supreme Court of Justice (Uruguay)] in Ferrer Mac-Gregor E (coord), *Crónica de Tribunales Constitucionales en Iberoamérica [Chronicle of Constitutional Courts in Iberian America] (*UNAM Marcial Pons 2009)

European Parliament, 'Dissenting Opinions in the Supreme Courts of the Member States' (PE 462.470, Directorate-General for Internal Policies. Policy Department C, Citizens' Rights and Constitutional Affairs, November 2012) <http://www.europarl.europa.eu/studies> accessed 30 September 2021

Ferrer Mac-Gregor E & Herrera García A, 'Suprema Corte de Justicia de la Nación (México)' ['Supreme Court of the Nation (Mexico)'] in Ferrer Mac-Gregor E (coord), *Crónica de Tribunales Constitucionales en Iberoamérica [Chronicle of Constitutional Courts in Iberian America]* (UNAM Marcial Pons 2009)

Freedom House, 'Marking 50 Years in the Struggle for Democracy' (Freedom House 2023a) <https://freedomhouse.org/report/freedom-world> accessed 16 November 2023

Foley KE, 'Australian Judicial Review' (2007) 6 *Washington University Global Studies Law Review* 281 https://openscholarship.wustl.edu/law_globalstudies/vol6/iss2/4

Gardbaum S, *The New Commonwealth Model of Constitutionalism: Theory and Practice* (Cambridge University Press 2013) https://doi.org/10.1017/CBO9780511920806

Ginsburg T, *Judicial Review in New Democracies: Constitutional Courts in Asian Cases* (Cambridge University Press 2003) https://doi.org/10.1017/CBO9780511511189

Hirschl R, 'The Nordic counternarrative: Democracy, human development, and judicial review' (2011) 9(2) *International Journal of Constitutional Law* 449 https://doi.org/10.1093/icon/mor034

Husa J, 'Guarding the Constitutionality of Laws in Nordic Countries: A Comparative Perspective' (2000) 48(3) *American Journal of Comparative Law* 345 https://doi.org/10.2307/840859

Jinesta Lobo, E. (2009), 'Sala Constitucional de la Corte Suprema de Costa Rica' ['The Constitutional Panel of the Supreme Court of Costa Rica'] in Ferrer Mac-Gregor E (coord), *Crónica de Tribunales Constitucionales en Iberoamérica [Chronicle of Constitutional Courts in Iberian America]* (UNAM Marcial Pons 2009)

Judicial Committee of the Privy Council, 'Role of the JCPC' (Judicial Committee of the Privy Council) <https://www.jcpc.uk/about/role-of-the-jcpc.html> accessed 22 June 2022

Kahana T, 'The Notwithstanding Mechanism and Public Discussion: Lessons from the Ignored Practice of Section 33 of the Charter' (2001) 44(3) *Canadian Public Administration/Administration Publique du Canada* 255 https://doi.org/10.1111/j.1754-7121.2001.tb00891.x

Kelemen K, *Judicial Dissent in European Constitutional Courts: A Comparative and Legal Perspective* (Routledge 2019) https://doi.org/10.4324/9781315590769

Kommers DP & Miller RA, *The Constitutional Jurisprudence of the Federal Republic of Germany* (3rd edn, Duke University Press 2012)

Kuo MS & Chen HW, 'Constitutional Review 3.0 in Taiwan: A Very Short Introduction of Taiwan's New Constitutional Court Procedure Act' International Journal of Constitutinal Law Blog (7 January 2022) http://www.iconnectblog.com/constitutional-review-3-0-in-taiwan-a-very-short-introduction-of-taiwans-new-constitutional-court-procedure-act/

Lin CC, 'The Pros and Cons of Taiwan's Constitutional Court Procedure Act' (2022) 2(17) *USALI Perspectives* 1 https://usali.org/usali-perspectives-blog/the-pros-and-cons-of-taiwans-constitutional-court-procedure-act

Manga Fombad C, 'Protecting constitutional values in Africa: a comparison of Botswana and Cameroon' (2003) 36(1) *The Comparative and International Law Journal of Southern Africa* 83 https://www.jstor.org/stable/23252225

Matsui S, 'Why Is the Japanese Supreme Court So Conservative?' (2011) 88 *Washington University Law Review 1375* http://openscholarship.wustl.edu/law_lawreview/vol88/iss6/2

Namibia Superior Courts, 'Supreme Court Judges' (Namibia Superior Courts 2021) <https://ejustice.jud.na/JUDICIARY/Judges/Pages/SupremeCourtJudges.aspx> accessed 30 September 2021

Nogueira de Brito M, 'Tribunal Constitucional (Portugal)' ['Constitutional Court (Portugal)'] in Ferrer Mac-Gregor E (coord), *Crónica de Tribunales Constitucionales en Iberoamérica [Chronicle of Constitutional Courts in Iberian America] (*UNAM Marcial Pons 2009)

Law DS, 'Why has Judicial Review Failed in Japan?' (2011) 88 *Washington University Law Review 1425* https://openscholarship.wustl.edu/law_lawreview/vol88/iss6/3

Lienhard A, Kettinger D, Bühler J, Mérillat L and Winkler D, 'The Federal Supreme Court of Switzerland: Judicial balancing of Federalism without Judicial Review' in Aroney N and Kincaid J (eds), *Courts in Federal Countries: Federalists or Unitarists?* (University of Toronto Press 2017) http://www.jstor.org/stable/10.3138/j.cttlwhm97c.17

Sánchez González S, 'Corte Suprema de Justicia (Panamá)' ['Supreme Court of Justice (Panama)'] in Ferrer Mac-Gregor E (coord), *Crónica de Tribunales Constitucionales en Iberoamérica [Chronicle of Constitutional Courts in Iberian America] (*UNAM Marcial Pons 2009)

Seok Hong J, 'Signalling the Turn: The Supermajority Requirement and Judicial Power on the Constitutional Court of South Korea' (2019) 67 *American Journal of Comparative Law* 177 https://doi.org/10.1093/ajcl/avz008

Shugerman JH, 'A Six-Three Rule: Reviving Consensus and Deference on the Supreme Court' (2002) 37 *Georgia Law Review 893 https://heinonline.org/HOL/P?h=hein.journals/geolr37andi=915*

Songer DR, Johnson SW, Ostberg CL & Wetstein ME, *Law, Ideology and Collegiality: Judicial Behaviour in the Supreme Court of Canada* (McGill-Queen's University Press 2012)

Stockholm Institute for Scandinavian Law, 'The Swedish National Courts Administration' (2007) 51 *Scandinavian Studies in Law* 629 https://www.scandinavianlaw.se/court-administrations/

Stone Sweet A, 'Constitutional Courts' in Rosenfeld M and Sajó A (eds), The Oxford Handbook of Comparative Constitutional Law (Oxford University Press 2012) https://doi.org/10.1093/oxfordhb/9780199578610.013.0040

Supreme Court of Norway, 'Supreme Court of Norway: Annual Report 2018' (Supreme Court of Norway 2018) <https://www.domstol.no/en/enkelt-domstol/supremecourt/annual-report/annual-report-2018/> accessed 04 October 2021

The Republic of Ghana Judiciary, 'The Law Courts. The Supreme Court' (The Republic of Ghana Judiciary) <https://judicial.gov.gh/index.php/the-supreme-court> accessed 30 September 2021

van der Schyff G, 'Constitutional Review by the Judiciary in the Netherlands: A Bridge Too Far?' (2010) 11 *German Law Journal* 275 https://doi.org/10.1017/S2071832200018526

——— (nd-a) 'CODICES Descriptions: Czech Republic Constitutional Court' <http://www.codices.coe.int/NXT/gateway.dll?f=templatesandfn=default.htm> accessed 30 September 2021

——— (nd-b) 'CODICES Descriptions: Estonia Supreme Court' <http://www.codices.coe.int/NXT/gateway.dll?f=templatesandfn=default.htm> accessed 04 October 2021

——— (nd-c) 'CODICES Descriptions: Latvia Constitutional Court' <http://www.codices.coe.int/NXT/gateway.dll?f=templatesandfn=default.htm> accessed 04 October 2021

——— (nd-d) 'CODICES Descriptions: South Africa Constitutional Court' (Venice Commission) <http://www.codices.coe.int/NXT/gateway.dll?f=templatesandfn=default.htm> accessed 30 September 2021

Waldron J, *Political Political Theory: Essays on Institutions* (Harvard University Press 2016) https://doi.org/10.4159/9780674970342

Weill R, 'Hybrid Constitutionalism: The Israeli Case for Judicial Review and Why We Should Care' (2012) 30 *Berkeley Journal of International Law* 349 https://doi.org/10.15779/Z384D36

Weinrib J, *Dimensions of Dignity: The Theory and Practice of Modern Constitutional Law* (Cambridge University Press 2016) https://doi.org/10.1017/CBO9781316026663

Wilson B, 'Decision-Making in the Supreme Court' (1986) 36(3) *University of Toronto Law Journal* 227 https://heinonline.org/HOL/P?h=hein.journals/utlj36andi=231

Zahle H, 'Judicial Opinion Writing in the Danish Supreme Court (Højesteret)' (2007) 51 *Scandinavian Studies in Law* 559 https://www.scandinavianlaw.se/pdf/51-26

Legal Sources Index

Cases

General Index

Page numbers in **bold have reference tables.

For Product Safety Concerns and Information please contact our EU representative GPSR@taylorandfrancis.com
Taylor & Francis Verlag GmbH, Kaufingerstraße 24, 80331 München, Germany

www.ingramcontent.com/pod-product-compliance
Ingram Content Group UK Ltd.
Pitfield, Milton Keynes, MK11 3LW, UK
UKHW020141200926
475702UK00005B/853
* 9 7 8 1 0 3 2 7 2 3 9 4 5 *